STAMPEDE!

STAMPEDE!

THE Rise of the West AND Canada's New Power Elite

GORDON PITTS

KEY PORTER BOOKS

Library and Archives Canada Cataloguing in Publication

Pitts, Gordon
　　Stampede!: the rise of the West and Canada's new power elite / Gordon Pitts.

ISBN 978-1-55470-120-9

　　1. Alberta—Economic conditions—1991–. 2. Corporate power—Alberta.
3. Businesspeople—Alberta—Biography. 4. Canada, Central—Economic
conditions—21st century. 5. Canada—Economic conditions—21st century.
I. Title.

HC112.5.A2P584 2008　　　　338.097123　　　　C2008-902420-6

The publisher gratefully acknowledges the support of the Canada Council for the Arts and the Ontario Arts Council for its publishing program. We acknowledge the support of the Government of Ontario through the Ontario Media Development Corporation's Ontario Book Initiative.

We acknowledge the financial support of the Government of Canada through the Book Publishing Industry Development Program (BPIDP) for our publishing activities.

Key Porter Books Limited
Six Adelaide Street East, Tenth Floor
Toronto, Ontario
Canada M5C 1H6

www.keyporter.com

Text design and Electronic formatting: Marijke Friesen

Printed and bound in Canada

08 09 10 11 12 5 4 3 2 1

To Doris and Scott,
always there for us

TABLE OF CONTENTS

INTRODUCTION
How the West has Won

CONSIDER CANADA IN THE YEAR 2020:

- The Calgary-Dominion Bank is holding its first annual meeting since the move from Toronto—and since the renaming of the institution that used to be known as the Toronto-Dominion Bank. It coincides with the demolition of the Toronto-Dominion Centre's bank tower in downtown Toronto—a victim of low occupancy and the shift of corporate head offices to the West.
- The wealthy Calgary Flames are celebrating their fourth straight Stanley Cup win, the product of the inspiring play of a terrific twosome—long-time Flames defensive anchor Dion Phaneuf and veteran superstar forward Sidney Crosby, who was acquired three years earlier in the fire-sale auction of players by the bankrupt Pittsburgh NHL franchise. Meanwhile, the Toronto Maple Leafs have marked more than a half-century of futility in their quest for the Cup.
- The Alberta Heritage Fund, now grown to $100 billion, six times its level in 2008, is offering an interest-free loan to Ontario for emergency repair work on a crumbling Highway 401.
- The University of Alberta has attracted its third Nobel Prize scientist in a year, using the blank cheque for medical and science spending provided by the Heritage Fund.

- Canada's last auto parts plant has closed, signalling the end of the North American car economy of the second half of the twentieth century. All cars sold in Canada are produced in China or India, and they all are priced under $10,000.
- Canada has finished negotiating a common market agreement with the nation of Newfoundland and Labrador, which acquired independence under Danny Williams, still premier after all these years.

Preposterous? Yet this could be the future of a Canada where Alberta and Saskatchewan are the kingpins, Ontario is on the ropes, Quebec is almost irrelevant, and Newfoundland is wealthy enough to chart its separate course. At one time, all these scenarios would have been considered ludicrous, but they are now within the realm of possibility as corporate clout, political influence, and population shift dramatically from East to West—and, to some extent, back East again to Newfoundland and Labrador.

This westward push of power has been the story of Canada over the past one hundred years, as first Halifax, then Montreal, and finally Toronto assumed commercial dominance. But now the westward movement is as earth-shaking as trucks rumbling across the muskeg in Fort McMurray. Now it is the time for Calgary and Edmonton, and, perhaps, Vancouver and Saskatoon to take command of the financial and corporate landscape. The age of Ontario is over. Toronto's utter dominance is history.

When the word West is used, there is a tendency to think only of Alberta—and let's face it, Alberta's economic clout, its business leadership, and its political tenacity make it the leader of the region between the Great Lakes and the Rockies. But it is easy to lapse into the lazy assumption that the West equals Alberta. The gap between western provinces will close in the next decade as Saskatchewan and, to a degree, Manitoba feel their oats from a resurgent grain economy and the shift of resource exploration and extraction to new locales. In this Age of the Commodity, those provinces that are commodity exporters will thrive over the long term. Those that are commodity importers, such as Ontario, will falter. And then there is complex, shape-shifting British Columbia, which will emerge from hosting the Winter Olympics in 2010, and assert its natural role as the laboratory of the New Economy, built on ideas, access to Asia, and Alberta money.

The result is a changing of the Canadian guard in corporate, political, and social leadership, powered by the hard-charging entrepreneurs who are creating the New West. Central and eastern Canadians: it is time to meet your new bosses—the engineers and financiers of Calgary and Edmonton. There will be winners and losers across the country—from the wannabe Albertans in Newfoundland to Bay Street bankers and industrialists, who are facing unprecedented challenges to their supremacy.

The West has been in this position before, seemingly poised on the edge of greatness in the 1970s, only to see it snatched away by plunging oil prices and an overreaching federal government dominated by eastern and central Canadian interests. Alberta, in particular, is keenly sensitive to this possibility. It is practically a canon of faith for Albertans to quote that famous bumper sticker, "Please Lord, give us another oil boom and we promise we won't piss it away this time." This time, they may not piss it away so easily, but how will they build on it?

And how does Canada adapt to an economy based predominantly on natural resources? We have a long history of capitalizing on commodities like fish, fur, lumber, and minerals, only to see those markets capriciously dip and dive. We worked hard to diversify into manufacturing, technology, and financial services. But once again, alas, we've struck it rich with oil, which is both our great gift and our great burden. Can Canada ever make the transition from a country that extracts its wealth from its land and sea to one that exports ideas from the brains of its people? Are the black tar sands and the BlackBerry compatible?

In its economic and social ramifications, this westward shift is the most important economic phenomenon in Canada's 140-year plus life—more important than the building of a transcontinental railway, the Great Depression, and the economic boom of the post–Second World War era.

The fallout from this shift is the stuff to fill many books, but here are seven things you need to remember:

- Already blessed with great conventional energy resources—and now bolstered by the oil sands—Canada is fourth in world energy production and will soon be second, behind Saudi Arabia.

- If development proceeds as planned, by some estimates the oil sands will have added more than $1 trillion to the country's wealth—its gross domestic product—over the two decades leading up to 2020. That's equivalent to adding the entire economy of Russia from the power of bitumen alone. And more than 70 per cent of that growth will be captured in Alberta.

- During that period, the oil sands will have generated more than $120 billion in government revenue, of which the federal government will reap more than 40 per cent of the take.

- At one point in this decade, Albertans were, on average, 60 per cent wealthier than their counterparts in the rest of Canada, as calculated on the basis of the province's per capita GDP.

- Regina and Saskatoon, the major cities in Saskatchewan, were the country's hottest real estate markets in early 2008, with house prices having soared an average of 50 per cent from the previous year.

- Alberta is home to just 10 per cent of Canada's population but is responsible for more than 30 per cent of its greenhouse gas emissions—a gap attributable to the deleterious effects of oil and gas extraction. On a per capita basis, Alberta and Saskatchewan emit more than three times as much as the rest of the country.

- It takes up to 1,500 cubic feet of "clean" natural gas to produce one barrel of "dirty" bitumen from Fort McMurray's oil sands—and it also takes two to four barrels of fresh river water (which, admittedly, can be recycled a number of times). The oil sands process produces two to three times the carbon emissions of a conventional oil well.

Those numbers illustrate the strains and the costs in environmental degradation and economic imbalance from this great wealth. As Alberta's economy outpaces much of the country, it is also attracting more people—as many as 80,000 in net inflow a year, mostly from other provinces. Even Saskatchewan, long a net loser of people, is experiencing a positive net migration from other provinces. But the West's population numbers still do not reflect its new economic clout and, therefore, it feels politically frustrated. That is the most dangerous tension in Canada right now, particularly as a strengthening sentiment in all of Canada, including Alberta, seeks to harness greenhouse gas emissions, and thus slow down the rate of global climate change. This tension is further exacerbated by the sheer economic imbalance, as one region, small in population, becomes ultra-rich, and another, large in population, becomes poorer than before. The signal that the tide has turned was a Toronto-Dominion Bank economics report in early 2008 announcing that Ontario, the great funder of Confederation, home to 40 percent of the country's population, would likely receive equalization payments by 2010–2011 to prop up its fading economy.

As the West is surging, it is hampered by its own grievances and excessive attachment to mythology. Its politicians too often play to regional hurts, rather than national vision, thus limiting their effectiveness. Alberta in particular is convinced that this is its time and it does not need the East. However, the East terribly needs the West, thus turning the tables on the old Confederation deal.

Alberta is poised for a cultural and intellectual break-through—in architecture, opera, ballet, theatre, and intellectual firepower to reflect its economic clout. This is a tough transition, as it must shed some of the cherished anti-intellectual cowboy myths, but there are signs everywhere of a flowering of a new thought leadership.

The West is also more united than ever before. British Columbia and Alberta are in economic cahoots, linked by a new labour and capital mobility deal, and Saskatchewan is more closely integrated than ever with Alberta, and is likely to join the Alberta–B.C. accord. Manitoba is not officially in, but it benefits directly from the integration.

The West will set the agenda. Even when the commodity bubble deflates—which will inevitably happen—Canada will remain a vital source of globally scarce commodities, not just oil and gas, but uranium, potash, canola, and wheat. A global recession could shake those markets but not alter the long-term reality. Whatever the short-term price gyrations, who has these commodities, who controls them, and how they are taxed and regulated will be the issues that subsume all others on the Canadian and global agendas. They are frightfully central to the debate over the future of Canada. It is the end of the supremacy of the old Ontario–Quebec accord, the comfortable nod and wink that have run this country since 1867. While the West still does not have the population, it has everything else—food, energy, science, education, and entrepreneurial drive. And its future is inextricably tied to the destiny of the emerging superpower, China, which needs the West's grain, its oil and its resources. But if the West is on top, where exactly is Canada?

PART ONE

NEW LANDSCAPES

CHAPTER 1

SANDSTORM

The making of the mega-projects

IT'S A GLORIOUSLY SUNNY DAY over the oil sands near Fort Mc-Murray, as the tiny Cessna glides above the massive Suncor and Syncrude mining operations. It is an awe-inspiring sight that should be viewed by anyone interested in the future of Alberta and of Canada. We are 900 metres up and can take in the vast tailing ponds, the smokestacks, the immense ziggurats of yellow sulphur, and the mining fields adorned with what look from here like tiny Tonka toys, but are actually 400-tonne trucks.

Right over the smokestacks at the Syncrude complex, we suddenly run into a thick cloud with a burst of turbulence. The Cessna is tossed around like a model airplane in a sandstorm. There is no visibility for what seems like a minute but I'm sure is much shorter. I'm panicking but Vic, my young pilot, is cool. He's seen it all before. "They create their own weather systems here," he explains calmly as we fly back into the sunlight.

The rocky ride is my rude introduction to the sheer immensity and the ecological footprint of the oil sands. It's reflected in the blasts of hot vapour that rise above the Syncrude plant, meeting the cold air of the early Alberta winter to create a microclimate of its own. Later, I ask a Syncrude official about the turbulence, and he shrugs it off as nothing special. He also dismisses my concerns when, during a tour of the plant, I point out the snow falling around the plant on an otherwise sunny day. Just a natural occurrence, he says.

This is Canada's Three Gorges, its Egyptian pyramids, its Pittsburgh, its Love Canal—all in one vast, messy, glorious tribute to engineering prowess. The Syncrude people say they are working hard on the environmental side, on cutting emissions, and reclaiming land—that buffalo roam where shovels once scraped off soil and rock and that the water used in the extraction and upgrading is recycled eighteen times. And that they are truly sorry when 500 ducks die on the toxic tailing ponds, an incident in early 2008 that delivers an irreparable black eye to the oil sands' international environmental image.

But the enormity, the scale, of the devastation is what hits you, not only at Syncrude but also at Suncor's massive complex, at the Shell/Albian Sands project, and at all the ones yet to come—Canadian Natural Resources' Horizon, PetroCan's Fort Hills, Nexen's Long Lake, and on and on. The imprint is not only at Fort Mac, but also in the fume-spewing upgrader alley to the northeast of Edmonton, and in Calgary, where the dire labour shortage closes fast food restaurants by 8 p.m. on busy Macleod Trail.

Up in the air, there is a crazy beauty to the place on this November morning, when you take in the sun, the forests, the tailings now covered in snow like a typical northern lake—but a toxic kind of lake—and where seismic paths cut through the bush as exploration crews seek more and more bitumen to feed the thirsty U.S. beast. And there is the view of Fort McMurray, so neatly nestled at the confluence of the Clearwater and Athabasca Rivers. Whereas the reality on the ground is traffic chaos, housing shortages, and drug addiction.

It is a place where the ecological reality is diminished by the language: the industrial areas are expressed in euphemisms—sands, pools, and ponds—that sound like the language of a Hawaiian vacation. But the earth, rock, and forest that are scraped away are called overburden. In this place where Big Oil rules, where government has ceded many of its ownership rights, nature is a burden, an engineering problem that has to be overcome.

The oil sands contain deposits of bitumen, a molasses-like viscous oil that will not flow unless heated or diluted with lighter hydrocarbons—but this gooey mess is also the largest supply of oil in the world outside Saudi Arabia. The bitumen is contained in three major areas beneath 140,000 square kilometres of northern Alberta—an expanse almost as large as Florida, twice the size of New Brunswick, more than four times the size of Vancouver Island, and twenty-six times larger than Prince Edward Island. The most extensive oil sands deposits are in the area around Fort McMurray in the sprawling regional municipality known as Wood Buffalo. Fort McMurray is an island of human hyperactivity in a vast boreal forest, five hours and 435 kilometres northeast of Edmonton, connected to the rest of Alberta by dangerous Highway 63, where exhausted oil sands workers drive at breakneck speed to get home to the family—or to Edmonton for some riotous R and R.

To make oil out of bitumen, it must be surface-mined or forced out of deeper ground using water and steam. Then the real work begins. It goes through an extensive upgrading process that makes it fluid enough to ship to refineries and turn into usable crude. The combination of extraction and upgrading has turned Fort McMurray into a $100-billion money pit, and an industrial landscape that will surely make Sudbury's huge nickel mines and tailing ponds look like a school kid's diorama model.

They say if Fort McMurray had been plopped onto Highway 2 between Edmonton and Calgary, it would have been an outrage—Albertans wouldn't have stood for it. But it was conveniently out of sight, out of mind for decades—until two things happened. Peter Lougheed, the former premier of Alberta, the man who created the modern Alberta, the man who helped keep the oil sands afloat in the difficult 1970s and 1980s, took a trip by helicopter to Fort McMurray in early 2006 and was appalled by the uncontrolled development. Then the CBS television program *60 Minutes* aired a report that exposed Fort McMurray to the world as poster child for growth run amok but also the answer to America's post–9/11 paranoia about secure energy supplies.

And here I am as part of the media pilgrimage. After my Cessna ride, I hit the ground in Fort McMurray, and head back to my hotel where I wander into a Liberal party delegate meeting—for it is just a few weeks ahead of the Liberal leadership convention of 2006. A politician named Stéphane Dion is standing in the middle of the room wearing a suit and snow boots, looking a little lost, a little awkward and totally overwhelmed by what he had just seen—for he had taken the same Cessna ride a few hours earlier. We chat about the runaway train of development and it is an epiphany of sorts for Dion. He would ultimately win the Liberal leadership on an environmental plank, pledging, among other things, to solve the nightmares of carbon emission, forest depletion, and water-sucking excess, of which the oil sands present the most critical challenge. As of this writing, those are still faint hopes. It is one thing to visit the oil sands and another to control them.

I had been in Fort McMurray before—in fall of 1979 when the deposits were called tar sands not the more euphemistic oil sands. (Indeed, whether you use oil sands or tar sands depends on your ideological stance. The CBC uses tar sands; the energy industry prefers oil sands.) The story I wrote for the *Ottawa Citizen* seems almost quaint now. It talked of the town bracing for the influx of 5,000 more workers to build the next new project. Yet almost three decades later, at the time of my second visit in 2006, there were 10,000 people working on the Canadian

Natural Resources' Horizon site alone. In 1979, there were 26,000 people in Fort McMurray; today, there are 65,000 and that figure is climbing fast. Twenty-nine years earlier, there were two projects in operation, Suncor and Syncrude. As you read this book, these two are much expanded, two more are in operation, fifty more are being contemplated, although many will not be built because of the pressure on costs, labour, and the environment—even at $100 to $140 U.S. for a barrel of oil.

In 1979, the price of oil was $24.50 a barrel; now economist Jeff Rubin of CIBC World Markets is predicting $200-a-barrel by 2012. In 1979, they were projecting a trillion barrels of oil in place, of which 26 billion were recoverable with the technology of the time. Today, the technology is better and there are estimated to be 1.7 trillion barrels, of which 175 billion are recoverable.

But some things remain the same. The mayor in 1979, a feisty ex-Mountie named Ted Mason, told me the biggest pressure came from mega-project growth pushing on overwhelmed social services. "In Fort McMurray they are unprepared for the population growth and accompanying human problems," I wrote. The article quoted Mason's concern that in the future, there would need to be more agreement with the province to finance services for a fast-growing population. "The spread between the population and the tax base is too damn far and too hard to handle," he said.

Twenty-eight years later, Ted Mason's warnings seem tragically prophetic. His words suggest there was no reason to be caught unprepared when Fort McMurray exploded with unplanned growth in the first decade of the twenty-first century. This was a disaster that could have been anticipated—it had been forecast decades earlier—but the province was asleep at the switch.

When I was writing in 1979, the mining technology was crude, consisting of massive contraptions called drag lines, not the super-efficient truck and shovel methods of today. But the social problems were the same: I started my 1979 story with a scene of a woman in a tight dress making the rounds of tables at a local watering hole. After an hour she leaves the lounge and "seconds later a hard-hatted young man follows her to a chorus of taunts and laughter from his friends." Later, I got angry letters from Fort McMurray's town fathers for emphasizing the Wild West atmosphere. Yet when I returned in late 2006, prostitution was, if anything, an even larger industry, and Fort McMurray was now being crushed under an avalanche of additional burdens—insufficient health services, infrastructure gaps, native illness, crystal meth labs, inadequate housing. And in 1979 I did not even mention the ecological footprint of the oil sands mines. That was not on the radar. I was just scratching the surface. Today the sands are an ecological disaster zone, but also an economic juggernaut that is turning Canada into a resource-driven economy.

It seems like Fort McMurray crept up on us even though the bitumen has been here for a million years, the product of prehistoric plankton that was pushed to the surface by the erupting Rocky Mountains. It was exploited first by aboriginal peoples who boiled the bitumen into tar, which they slapped on damaged birchbark canoes. The first Europeans in the area were fur traders in the employ of the Hudson's Bay Company. Alexander Mackenzie, the great explorer, landed at the junction of the Athabasca and Clearwater rivers, and marvelled at fountains of sulphurous bitumen in which you could stick a pole and see it sink in as deep as seven metres.

The twentieth century saw increasing interest in the vast tar sands, but there was total ignorance about how to extract the bitumen economically from the sand and turn it into crude oil.

The age of the automobile and the internal combustion engine fired up the motivation of a new wave of scientists. Among them was an Ontario-born colloidal chemist named Karl Clark who had been lured to the infant University of Alberta by its first president and builder, Henry Marshall Tory. Clark developed the process for separating the oil from sand, a major step in the oil sands' commercialization. Karl Clark realized his life dream when the first truly commercial oil sands mine, Great Canadian Oil Sands, began operating in 1967. But it was a mixed triumph, says his daughter, Mary Clark Shepherd, whose apartment over-looking the river valley in Edmonton still serves as a kind of shrine for her brilliant but conflicted father.

When Clark attended the turning of the sod at GCOS—which would later become Suncor—he was devastated when the bull-dozers began ripping down all the trees along the Athabasca River, his daughter recalls. Later, he visited Mary at her home in England and told her, "I don't want to go back to see the dev-astation." She is troubled by the memory: "Poor guy, he was sad. I'm glad he's not around to see what's happening now."

Karl Clark's angst reflects a thoroughly Albertan condition, indeed a Canadian condition. Canada is a nation whose history is a continuous process of bending nature to the human will—from the cod fisheries, or the forests of Northern Ontario and Quebec, to the vast tailing ponds of Sudbury's smelters. The oil sands are part of that long train of history, except that the scale of development there is so grand, the state of the planet is so perilous, and environmental sensitivity is so heightened. Alber-tans, from Karl Clark to Peter Lougheed, have grappled with that balance of development and preservation, and that battle is entering its most critical stage.

The fate of the planet was not on the minds of the oil sands' two early developers in the 1960s and 1970s, Great Canadian and Syncrude, which is a consortium of oil companies headed by Imperial Oil, the Canadian subsidiary of giant Exxon. They soldiered on in the oil sands, despite high costs, equipment breakdowns, and extreme risks. It was venture capital, but with a difference: everyone knew the oil was there—it was a matter of efficiently extracting and upgrading it. When I arrived for the first time in 1979, Fort McMurray was bracing for a boom of mining and oil sands plants. But those dreams all came to a crashing halt in the early 1980s when the air went out of the energy balloon, prices plunged, and the industry was paralyzed by the ill-timed National Energy Program (NEP).

There had been grand plans for a burst of new oil sands projects north of the Great Canadian site, including Shell's big Alsands site. A bridge was even built on the Athabasca River at a then staggering cost of $27 million. But the project was shelved and it became known as the Bridge to Nowhere—a structure that connected Fort McMurray to nothing more than a bunch of trappers' cabins. It was the end of the road, literally, for the paved highway and for the oil sands boom.

And so it sat there until the mid-1990s, when the spark was ignited that finally kick-started the oil sands boom. It was not a new deposit, a new technology, or any brilliant entrepreneurial moxie, but a bureaucratic solution—a planning solution. Eric Newell, a savvy Imperial Oil executive who was running Syncrude, was part of that solution. He had come to Fort McMurray after spearheading a management reorganization of Imperial Oil. When he got his next assignment, he remembers calling his wife and asking what would be the worst place to go in Canada. She suggested Norman Wells, an isolated refinery site in the Northwest Territories. Well, it's not Norman Wells, he told her. "Fort McMurray?" she asked and he said "you got it." But she followed her husband north, for their fifteenth move in twenty years of married life—and they made a good life there.

As a senior executive and ultimately president of Syncrude, Newell knew the bad times and the good times. One night in 1995, he and three other oil sands people were kicking around the paradox of this huge safe energy deposit sitting untapped in Northern Alberta at a time of unstable Mideast politics that put the world's oil reserves in peril. Someone suggested: Why not assemble a task force to study the sands and come up with a game plan? They got it on the political agenda, and a new era was born.

It is hard to think of something as prosaic as a task force setting off a new gold rush—and it seems bitterly ironic in light of the total absence of planning that followed it. But the oil sands task force presented a vision of how the sands could be kicked into high gear. A key component was a generic royalty structure that would cut through the maze of special taxes and fees. The breakthrough came when the province agreed to take only 1 per cent of a project's net profits until the capital costs were recovered, when rates of 25 per cent of net revenues would kick in. It was a massive giveaway, the kind of thing Alberta's free marketers abhor, but it got the job done.

The task force concluded that the oil sands could triple production over twenty-five years at a cost of $21 to $25 billion in new projects. "People looked at us as if we were smoking something funny," Newell recalls. In fact, production was much more rapid and much more expensive. The tripling of production took not twenty-five years but only eight years, and at a cost of $32 billion "with no end in sight." On the task force's projections: "We blew it so badly I broke out in a cold sweat," Newell cheerfully admits today.

A mix of technology, timing, and politics made the oil sands. Shovels replaced drag lines, and conveyer belts and pipelines moved the bitumen briskly from mining sites to the upgraders. The other development was even more profound. The pioneering Suncor and Syncrude sites operated as mining projects, but only 20 per cent of the available bitumen could be recovered from surface mining. The vast majority of future bitumen production would have to be extracted in situ—from forcing the goo up from deep wells. The technology became known as SAGD—steam-assisted gravity drainage, in which steam was pumped into the ground, pushing out the bitumen.

This process did not scar the surface like the massive mines. In fact, there is something eerily beautiful about the networks of pipes through the poplars. At PetroCan's SAGD project at Mackay River, north of Fort McMurray, deer wander peacefully through the woods and around the pipes. But the SAGD process also leads to issues of energy use, greenhouse gas, and, particularly, the massive appetite for water and steam. And as the boreal forest is stripped away for pipes, it creates forest freeways over which wolves can speedily travel to attack caribou and deer. Nothing happens in the oil sands that does not touch nature.

With the new royalty structure and new technology in place, projects that were on the shelf were dusted off again. The most striking move was the decision in 1997 by a Colorado-born engineer, Rick George, the president of Suncor, to bring a proposed $2.2 billion expansion project, called Millennium, to his board for approval. It was a gutsy move, George recalls. "We made the decision when crude oil was at $12 U.S. a barrel. And that was within a month of when the *Economist* put out a front-page story saying crude oil was going to $5 a barrel."

George admits now that, even though the lessons of history suggested oil prices would eventually turn higher again, he had to operate largely on his own intuition and hope that his board would share his gut feelings. "I bless the board at that time for having enough nerve to go with it. It would have been an easy thing to turn down."

The board gave its approval and, by September 2001, the Millennium expansion was close to completion, but costs were running 60 per cent above budget—a harbinger of overruns to come as construction and materials shortages began to take their bite. Rick George invited a group of journalists to Fort McMurray on September 11 to see the project as it approached completion. When the reporters landed in Fort McMurray, they learned the news from a continent away—that morning terrorists had flown passenger jets into New York's World Trade Center and Washington's Pentagon. The Fort McMurray airport was immediately closed, and some journalists scrambled to get home right away by the few available cars. For those who stayed, it was a strange feeling, touring the vast, barren oil sands mines, wondering if this scene of desolation was the fate of the entire world.

The *Globe and Mail*'s Dave Parkinson used the lack of air travel as a chance to stay on a couple of days and report more fully on the implications for the oil sands. "The tragedy not only knocked Millennium's media unveiling off most news pages," he wrote, "but, more importantly, the attack also threw the oil market and the larger global economy into limbo, just as Suncor's big expansion gears up for production." He then quoted Rick George as saying: "We'll have to wait and see how this plays out."

It played out very well, in fact. The isolation of Fort McMurray from the events of 9/11 only underlined the appeal of the oil sands. They were far away and they were safe. The terrorist attacks, followed by military action in Afghanistan and Iraq, ignited concerns about energy security, particularly in the U.S. It was also the age of the peak oil cultists, a group of consultants and academics who were convinced that the supply of recoverable hydrocarbons had peaked and now the world would settle into long net production declines. The radical projections of this group gradually sifted into the mainstream and today we are all peak-oilers. (In fact, a much more appropriate name for the local hockey team would be the Edmonton Peak-Oilers.)

Suddenly, the mucky mounds around Fort McMurray constituted the most valuable piece of ground on earth. The oil sands expansion caught the wave of price increases, as West Texas Intermediate Crude went to $60, then to $90, and more than $100 a barrel—and it dragged along the soupier, cheaper bitumen. Instead of a total investment of $35 billion or more, the planned capital outlay around Fort McMurray had climbed to $100 billion over twenty years. It was clear that the oil sands were changing Northern Alberta, the province, the country, and increasingly the world was taking notice. The oil sands were supplying close to half of Canada's hydrocarbon needs, but more than that, they were changing the lives of a host of people caught up in the biggest boom in Canadian history.

One man in the centre of the sandstorm was Jim Boucher, who had passed through the whole gamut of emotions and opinions on the oil sands. As a young native man in Fort MacKay, a Cree and Dene reserve north of Fort McMurray, he was a fire-brand who had protested the sweep of oil sands development. He was loyal to the old ways of a society that still lived by hunting and trapping, and could feel proud about salvaging a degree of independence from the white man's world. "Our people were hunters and trappers and gatherers," he says. "The land was a food basket, and so was the river. We trapped and people made a good living. Some of our trappers made $100,000 a year."

Brigitte Bardot changed all that. The global boycott against fur trapping, spearheaded by the French sex kitten, devastated the natives' livelihood and, by 1986, left the band in an economic crisis. "We had some pretty bleak choices in terms of making a living," says Boucher, a lean fifty-year-old with a thinning hairline. What it meant was discarding big parts of the traditional lifestyle and embracing the oil sands. "We had to change the way we did things, and the oil sands were there on our doorstep. We decided to take advantage of the opportunities."

Twenty years later, Boucher, as the hard-charging chief of the Fort Mackay band, stands atop a business pyramid that encompasses 350 employees and $80 million in annual revenues from businesses that span janitorial services, tree planting and environmental services, busing, heavy equipment, and real estate. The Fort Mackay band has committed itself to a 24/7 provision of services to the oil sands operators. Besides the band's mini-conglomerate of businesses, it had spawned fifteen private entrepreneurs, some of whom had cut their teeth in Jim Boucher's organization. Fort Mackay is now a neat, bungalow community of 400 people, with a new community office building, whose final cost had ballooned to $8 million, twice its original estimate, in the crazy oil sands–induced run-up in construction expenses.

Yet all this is a mixed blessing and Boucher has warned of the oil sands projects' heavy toll on water in the Athabasca River, particularly during the winter months when the flow is much reduced. Other Fort MacKay natives have expressed alarm over health hazards in the air and water. Farther downriver, in more isolated Fort Chipewyan, the protests were more vociferous because people have been dying of unexplainable cancers.

Like many Canadians, Jim Boucher had made his peace with the oil sands devil. There was no going back to a pristine era of purely hunting and trapping. Boucher talks of using the oil sands wealth to create the best-educated community in Alberta, of sending graduates from Fort Mackay to Stanford, Oxford, and Harvard. It is a remarkable vision for a man who quit school partway through Grade 12 because a job opened up at Syncrude.

Jim Boucher feels he has a substantial ace up his sleeve. A land claim settlement has given the Fort Mackay band control of a piece of land that, in Jim's opinion, holds enough bitumen to generate hundreds of millions of barrels of oil. He could see Fort Mackay becoming the first native oil sands operator—although a decade-long negotiation with Shell Canada to develop the deposit had stalled by early 2008.

I had no doubt Boucher would continue to press his case.

"We will be in the oil business one way or the other eventually," he vowed to me, adding that "patience is required in respect to what we do." After all, his people had lived in that region for hundreds of years. They had been with Alexander Mackenzie as he dipped his oar in the sulphurous bitumen. They had watched Karl Clark and his pioneers try to separate the sand from the oil. They had seen Rick George ride the Millennium project to reality. They had marvelled at the spectacular rise in the price of crude. They could wait a while longer.

CHAPTER 2

PROPHETS AND BOSSES

The people of the sands

The Prophet

It is rare to find a corporate executive, a man who has never been a CEO, who has utterly changed an industry and a country. But as soon as you meet Neil Camarta, you know why he is Mr. Oil Sands. You are drawn by his flashing eyes, his sense of mission, his charisma. He believes in the oil sands to his very core. Spend a half-hour with Neil Camarta and you come away convinced that the oil sands are the greatest thing in Canada's industrial history. He is the prophet of the oil sands and everything he has predicted is coming to pass.

He has even created a vocabulary that, if you travel around the industry, has crept into the argot of every project manager, every supervisor. The famous Camartaisms include "pots and pans," his shorthand for the upgrading and refining plants; "good dirt and bad dirt," referring to the quality of the bitumen; and "dirty dirt," the most intractably mucky bitumen of all.

He has no illusions about the environmental havoc these dirty sands can play, but he believes it can be overcome. For him, all problems are engineering challenges. I first talked with him when he was a vice-president of Shell Canada, and it was the early days of angst over the labour shortages. I was impressed by his eloquent and forceful argument for the need to import more foreign labour to the oil sands. It has remained one of his

obsessions, and he is convinced there will have to be a huge influx of non-Canadian workers over the next decade and longer.
There is no choice.

Later, I met him at a restaurant in downtown Toronto, after
he had switched employers and gone over to Petro-Canada. His
job was the same—to bring oil sands projects to reality. Again,
I was drawn into his boyish engineer's optimism, the kind of
thinking that makes Alberta great, but that also, at times, limits
its vision—that the environmental problems are meaningful but
they can be solved in a technological fix. The pressure on water
supply actually worried him more than greenhouse gases. "But
at the end of the day, there is more good than bad," he insisted.

He told me the age of the energy explorer—the old Jed
Clampett types who strike oil or, more often, hit dry holes—is
over. The old industry consisted of a bunch of guys, going out
and finding oil through the magic of seismic surveys and drill
bits. "You had to explore your brains out," he says. But this is
the age of the chemical engineer, people like himself. With the oil
sands, everyone knows the stuff is there—it's been there a million years. It's a question of making crude profitably out of the
dirty sands. "This stuff is easy to find and hard to produce." It's
a manufacturing process, not an exploration process.

It requires vast injections of labour, capital, and engineering
know-how to run the mines, the SAGD wells, and the upgraders,
which are "the space shuttle side of the refinery," Neil says. His
vision for Alberta is that, within a generation, it would be the
major manufacturing zone of Canada. In his view, the province
was moving from hewer of wood and drawer of water to proces-
sor of bitumen, and it would never be the same. He calls it diversification that is not outside energy but within it—in the
chemistry, upgrading, pipelines, cracking, mining—with a supply chain that runs all the way back to the steel companies.

"We make oil," he says. "We don't just dig it out of the
ground."

Camarta is the son of an Italian-Canadian farmer from Edson, west of Edmonton. His grandfather emigrated from Italy to the tumultuous entry point of Ellis Island, New York, and then pushed inland to Minnesota where he was an iron miner on the rich Mesabi Range. One day some Canadian officials came to town promoting Alberta as a place to homestead, and the group of Italian buddies and their families moved to Edson. They constituted, Neil says with a chuckle, the largest Italian ranching community in Canada, a locale inhabited by extremely short cowpunchers.

"I always wanted to work in the oil sands. I grew up in their shadow," Neil says, referring to his birthplace west of Edmonton. He graduated in engineering from the University of Alberta, and joined Syncrude, the oil sands pioneer. There he became immersed in the sands. He eventually went over to Shell Canada and became their oil sands guru, driving the construction of the $5 billion Athabasca project, operated by Shell and a company called Albian Sands.

But in the Shell order of things, it was time to move on. He was offered a job at the parent company's headquarters in The Hague, the Netherlands, and he didn't want to move. He had a family in Calgary, a lawyer wife and three daughters. One of the children has type 1 diabetes and he had become a strong advocate for and donor to the cause. He also had a ninety-four-year-old father, John Camarta, whom he was moving off the farm and into a detached house in Edson, where Neil paid for round-the-clock care.

When I caught up to him, he was at Petro-Can being touted as a contender for the top job when CEO Ron Brenneman retires. He would be a natural candidate, but life was not that simple. In addition to his daughter's illness, Camarta himself was diagnosed with muscular dystrophy, a debilitating and hereditary condition that had also afflicted his mother. It affects his face and upper arms, and forces him to sleep with his eyes open.

It's hard for him to lift even a suitcase. "It just pisses you off," he says, in a rare moment of frustration.

But typical of Neil, at fifty-five, he is looking ahead to his next big oil sands project, Petro-Can's massive Fort Hills venture. "I'd like to get one more of these suckers going," Neil says, those eyes flashing once more.

The Elder

I went to Fort McMurray because Peter Lougheed told me to. Lougheed had visited the area and the sight from the helicopter had both overwhelmed and appalled him. So when I called him for an interview, he urged me to fly over the site, as he had done. It had all come home for him at that point, and he felt it would do the same for me.

It is hard to turn down Peter Lougheed, Alberta's legendary leader who became the province's Conservative premier in 1971 after thirty-six years of Social Credit rule. A lawyer, Harvard Business School graduate, and a former pro football player, he ushered in a new wave of professional management in the provincial government. The son of a patrician Alberta family, he walked the thin line between provincial rights and a strong federalism that was severely tested when the Trudeau government dropped the odious National Energy Program on him.

He left a province that was much richer, much better managed, and he succeeded in embedding the constitutional right to own its natural resources. Although he left as Alberta was entering a slowdown that somewhat blurred his regime's legacy— and particularly that of his successor, Don Getty—he also left behind a long-term ace in the hole, the secure control of the vast treasure that lay beneath the soil.

Since then, he has been a lawyer with Bennett Jones, one of Calgary's elite firms; a corporate director; a rainmaker; and an elder statesman, highly respected in his party and the province. But he is mistrusted by some people in his own party and in the oil industry because he is at heart a pragmatic interventionist, a "progressive conservative" who is willing to use state power for public goals.

As he approached eighty, his face was deeply lined, but the eyes were still penetrating. He was very thoughtful on public issues, and he had gently taken to the role of a kind of village elder. Yet he was careful about making pronouncements on government policy, speaking only when he felt he had no choice but to help inform and guide public opinion. He never wanted to second-guess his successors, but the trip to Fort McMurray changed that. "This was when I saw all the operations in one day, and it was just the magnitude," he recalled. "I knew what I was going to see but it makes a huge difference to see it, to visualize it."

First, there was the scene on clogged Highway 63 around Fort Mac. "You fly over the highway and it looks like you are going into Times Square in New York. It's just incredible, when you realize where you are, and it just gets you that it is all going on at the same time and recognizing the cost factor."

He came back to Calgary and he started writing and talking about the pace of oil sands development. He started chiding the Klein government for letting development get out of control. And Ralph Klein, the boisterous premier who had presided over the oil sands boom years, acknowledged the validity of Lougheed's criticism when he admitted to reporters on the eve of his own departure from office: "They were right about not having a plan."

Of course, Lougheed felt some responsibility. As a premier, he had developed a royalty system based on net profits that allowed Syncrude to develop its project. But, more than that, there was his role as the province's—the country's—elder statesman: "I do things because I enjoy it and my mind gets stimulated and I care so much for my country."

For Lougheed, it was all about owning the resources, as it had always been since he was premier. The people of Alberta were the proprietors and had the right to set the pace of development—to slow it down, if necessary, to build the infrastructure, the roads, the hospitals, the schools, the highways, including a twinned Highway 63. He was angry that the ownership principle that he had fought so hard to maintain, against the incursions of Ottawa and the oil companies, had been squandered. Ownership rights had been handed over to the oil companies to do what they wanted. He did not blame the oil companies that were just pursuing their self-interest—he blamed his own successors. "The main thing is making sure you recognize this resource belongs to the people and you have to manage it as an owner," he told me. He was encouraged that the new Conservative premier Ed Stelmach seemed to recognize that more clearly.

Having alerted the world to Fort McMurray, he was on to a raft of other issues—particularly, the looming battle over water, which he worries will become a huge bilateral issue as the Americans go after Canada's water supply. Water is a crucial issue for Fort McMurray but also in the parched and heavily irrigated agricultural areas of the south of the province.

Then he made one of his periodic sorties into the energy debate by predicting a potential constitutional clash over the environment between the provincial government, which is the steward of the resources, and the feds, who have ultimate jurisdiction over the environment. "I'm troubled in my own mind in the conflict between the environment and the economy and nothing focuses it more than the Alberta oil sands," he said.

I reminded him that my *Globe and Mail* colleague David Ebner had recently described Lougheed in an article as a "left-leaning premier." And indeed in the context of today's polarized politics, he probably was. "Did you notice that phrase?" he said, breaking into loud laughter. "I got a big kick out of that. There are a fair number of people in the city who'd say, 'See, I always said that.' Down at the Petroleum Club, they sure agreed with that."

The Warrior

I am chasing Murray Edwards. It is in the waning moments of the 2007 annual meeting of Canadian Natural Resources Ltd., the oil sands giant that Murray had built and now controls, and the wealthy financier has escaped my grasp. I am at the meeting partly to capture the news on CNRL's massive Horizon project, the latest in a series of blockbuster oil sands projects that are changing the face of Northern Alberta—and Canada. It is an undertaking that ranks with the pyramids in magnitude—10,000 people, $9 billion in investment, large camps of workers imported from Shanghai and Corner Brook. You almost expect the ghost of Charlton Heston to appear at the microphone to explain how he was planning to part the Athabasca River.

Most of all I am there to see Edwards, the burly elusive butterfly of the oil patch, to arrange an interview with the man who is surely the most important figure in the modern Alberta economy. What Lougheed was to the 1970s, Edwards is to the 2000s—the man who makes Alberta work. A son of a middle-class Regina family, he is a lawyer and financier who in twenty-five years has parlayed a $100,000 investment in CNRL into a fortune of more than $2 billion, according to the calculations of my *Globe and Mail* colleague Brent Jang.

Famously reclusive, Edwards has chosen a seat at the front of the meeting. He has no executive role at CNRL but he is on the board. The meeting is a strange affair—a dark cavern of a room, with a huge hushed crowd of analysts, shareholders, and CNRL executives. There are lots of numbers and slides but no mention of two Chinese workers who died just a week earlier in a workplace accident—although I am told that the incident was discussed during a conference call with analysts. It's a jarring reminder of how human lives and livelihoods are being tossed aside as cannon fodder for engineering dreams in the soil of the Athabasca.

I wait for the proceedings to wind up so I can engage Edwards, but before the meeting ends, he suddenly bolts from his chair and strides out of the room ahead of the pack of journalists. I leap out of my own seat to follow but he moves very well for a big man, more like a pulling guard than a defensive tackle. He is up the stairs and onto the network of pedestrian walkways that connect downtown Calgary. All I can see were the soles of his large shoes. He has too much of a head start, which in a way, sums up the Murray Edwards advantage: He is always just a little bit ahead of the pack.

Eight months later, after periodic emails and phone calls, we finally meet and he apologizes for being so hard to get. He doesn't know half the story. I meet him on another important day for CNRL: it has raised its projections of costs for Horizon's first phase by 28 per cent to almost $9 billion. But what it is really amazing is how little attention the market pays to the soaring costs. In fact CNRL stock (widely known as CNQ for its trading symbol) rises slightly on the day. In the overheated economy, this is a drop in the bucket, when almost every project is coming on-stream far beyond cost estimates.

Edwards is not particularly happy about the overruns, but it is not unheard of with a project as complex as Horizon. There are 10,000 people still on the site as CNRL pushes ahead to a fall 2008 launch. "When you are managing this big a project, with that many people, there are challenges," he says. The months of January and February were extremely cold and it damaged the project's productivity. "We had sixteen hundred guys who were not able to do any productive work on site." That is typical of life in the oil sands.

"Gordon," he says—Edwards likes to address you by your first name—"there is no lack of focus on keeping the costs managed because any cost you pay comes right out of your pocket. But in these big projects, you have sometimes these challenges and it is about finding the balance." He worries that people think the big oil sands projects are a sure thing—they are the geese that are laying Alberta's golden egg. In Edwards' view, they are massive, challenging, complex beasts that have to be managed very closely, or they will fly out of control.

Edwards is the Alberta phenomenon of the twenty-first century, a financier whose reach extends across industries, to resorts in the Rockies, manufacturing in Ontario, and the Calgary Flames Hockey Club. He is sometimes lauded as the Warren Buffett of Canada because of his nose for value, his eerily prescient moves, his patience, his golden touch in most of his endeavours. His core business is oil and gas, and his crown jewel is Canadian Natural Resources, an energy juggernaut that the stock market has valued at $35 billion. And most of that value is based on the Horizon project. Edwards says he has visited the Horizon site, but you get the impression he does not spend a lot of time wading through the muck of Fort McMurray.

That is why he has executives. "Our operating management team has done an outstanding job in building a complex project," Edwards says. He describes the effort to build a decent quality of life, under difficult conditions, for the thousands of people engaged in the construction project. In the camps, every employee has his or her own bedroom. "The camps are clean; they've got amenities from a Tim Hortons doughnuts to workout rooms. It's a good environment."

CNRL has attracted some attention, and controversy, for importing labour from China, but Edwards says it was always the plan to build the project with Albertan and Canadian workers first—"because everyone is worried about all the migration of foreign workers." He insists that the project has relied on foreign labour for only 3 to 4 per cent of its workforce.

He is particularly proud of how the company has flown people to the site from their homes in Newfoundland, Nova Scotia, New Brunswick, or Ontario. There is no wasted time in Fort McMurray or in Edmonton—workers fly directly to the isolated

Horizon site for two or three weeks and fly back home for one week. "They go right to the site, they finish their shift and within five hours they are home," he boasts. "They can keep their family, earn a good income, they don't give up their home where they want to stay. Ultimately some people may end up moving to Fort McMurray or some may just do it for a period of time to earn some money."

This mobile labour force is part of what local people call the shadow workforce: outsiders who come and go, who use the roads, go to hospitals and doctors, but never put down roots or pay taxes in the community. It is a sore spot for local officials, but for Edwards, the way his company has hired, housed, and looked after its shadow people is one of the triumphs of the oil sands. "For me it's been a success story for Canada in the mobility of labour."

The Alchemist

Thomas Friedman, the *New York Times* columnist and author of the bestselling book *The World Is Flat*, says natural resource economies are dumb economies. They don't need to innovate—they live off nature's bounty and they get stupid as a result. But Friedman hasn't met Columba Yeung, the sorcerer of the oil sands, who promises to turn black ooze into Athabasca gold.

It's people like Yeung who hold the promise that the oil sands could spawn a technological revolution. The modern oil patch is different from the old image of energy extraction, which was to stick a drill in the ground and hope that something happened. The new oil patch is technology-intensive, whether it is upgrading, refining, pipelines, or the still elusive promise of carbon sequestration. Yeung is working on an oil sands technology that can change the way the game is played. And he is doing it on his own, without big company backing, using private equity investment from Hong Kong and Canada.

Sit down with Columba Yeung, a small sprite of a man, and

brace yourself for an hour of nonstop lecture in colloidal chemistry and the tortuous refining of bitumen into light crude. He can tell you the composition of bitumen as the thick oil works its way from the ground through intensive upgrading, only to be pumped long distances while mixed with a cheap crude oil called diluant.

To put it simply, he has found a way—through a process very similar to creating a sugar solution in water—to remove a low-value component of bitumen, called asphaltine, and turn it into something commercial. Then by ultra-fast chemical cracking of the oil, he figures he can efficiently remove the additional residue. The result, he says, is a fluid that is pumpable and refinery-ready—and at a much lower cost than all the alternative technologies. What's more—and this is an important kicker—it is more environmentally friendly because the technology eliminates much of the intensive processing to remove impurities in the bitumen, thus cutting the scale of emissions.

This is the kind of thing that sets hearts pumping in the oil sands. If it works, Yeung will be very, very wealthy. If it doesn't, he will join the legions of visionaries whose dreams have crashed on the Athabasca muskeg. But he is a bit different from the penniless dreamers. His company, called Value Creation, is building an upgrader northeast of Edmonton that should start turning out the product in spring 2009. His real ace in the hole is a huge holding of land north of Fort McMurray, which he sees as the cornerstone of a future $3 billion oil sands project. He claims the land holds 38 billion barrels of bitumen that could, on refining, be converted into 6 to 12 billion barrels of oil. That would give him an independence that other freelancers in the oil sands would lack.

He acquired the land in stealth over a two-year period, using four different companies. To be successful in the oil sands, he explains, "You just have to have a lot of dirt." And Value Creation has a lot of dirt, although the jury is still out on how valuable it all is.

Yeung aims to be a serious player, on his own or in league with a multinational giant, and people take him very seriously. Yeung's primary backers in the early days were a number of friends in Hong Kong and Calgary, who supported him when he was working as a consultant while pouring his weekends into his dream. I first heard about Yeung through Hartley Richardson, scion of the wealthy Winnipeg investment family, who was explaining that the investment strategy of his family and its managed private equity funds is to look for technological innovation in the oil patch. Yeung is one of those innovators Richardson is betting on.

An intense man in his fifties—he won't disclose his age—Yeung was born in Hong Kong, the son of a surgeon. He grew up in a Catholic family and his English name is that of an Irish saint. He defied his father's dreams of a medical career by striking out on his own in chemical engineering. He ended up at the University of Toronto doing his PhD, and he joined Shell Canada after graduation. He became a legend at Shell for pioneering oil sands work on its Scotford upgrader at Edmonton. He also developed a massive petrochemical project for Shell in China's Guangdong province. Why he left Shell is a bit fuzzy. He said he could not pursue his dream in a large corporation, and he clearly felt unappreciated at Shell.

When he set out on his own, "There was a more than even chance I wouldn't make it. But I was able to live on hot dogs. You are in that place in life when you can try your best and if you can't make it, life goes on."

Yeung is not a facile communicator. It is not only the accent, but also the scientist's obsessiveness. So he has brought in an experienced communicator and savvy oilman named Ray Cej, another Shell expatriate, to be his front man. "I am much more a builder," Yeung says. "Sometimes the complexity intimidates people, but I don't mind the complexity because nothing goes exactly the way you want."

He confides that the company has many suitors and a large international oil company has already courted his investors, but they have held steady so far. He suspects they might yield to offers in the future. Asked if Value Creation is going to be a giant in its field, he says simply: "We are not going to be Exxon Mobil but if you talk about Suncor as a giant, well then, I'm pretty sure we will get there."

The Healer

Earl's restaurant in Fort McMurray is one of the classy eateries in town, but that doesn't stop the waitress from totally blowing an order. It's like that in Fort Mac where service people lack training, experience, and, often, the rudiments of service mentality. Surly is a kind word for many front-line workers. But a little lapse like a missed order doesn't stop the conversation from running loud and enthusiastic among the MBA class of the University of Alberta, Wood Buffalo branch.

These are the Fort McMurrayites you never hear about—smart, ambitious, and absolutely dedicated to the town. They are young engineers on the fast track, and they are doing important work far more quickly than if they were in, say, Edmonton or Calgary. They are buying houses, taking night courses, and a young Indo-Canadian couple have joined the local curling club. Aparna Verma, a bright Syncrude engineer from Calgary, says she is determined to create a life and a career in this benighted little city. After all, she says, "Melissa" brought her to Fort Mac, and at that point, more people chime in: Yes, Melissa Blake, the mayor of Wood Buffalo municipality, recruited them to Syncrude too.

This is the Army of Melissa, those who share her view that Fort Mac can be a civilized and humane place, despite the gaping void of infrastructure, the traffic jams, and the shadowy young men with too much money, too much time, and too little hold on their sexual appetites.

Blake was a recruiter for Syncrude when she discovered people were rejecting her pitches because they didn't want to live there. She took it personally because she is that rare person who was actually raised from a young age in Fort Mac. Her family is from Montreal and her parents came to Northern Alberta when her father got a job at Syncrude. On graduation from university, Melissa joined Syncrude too and became a company recruiter.

When she tried to attract candidates, she would hear the same concerns about isolation and quality of life. When people came to Fort Mac, they often liked its outdoor life, but there were problems: Can I get ice time for my kids? Can I get a doctor? "Whenever I had declines, I took it quite personally," she says. "People had reasons for not wanting to come to my region, and I decided to push for positive change—for people not to have reasons for not coming."

She became a councillor but was frustrated by the lack of planning for a future that was going to mean many more people and many more challenges. The council was living in a dream world. "I'd love to tell you running for mayor was a tough decision but it wasn't," she says. "I had a level of dissatisfaction with representation I was working under."

She knows the problems of the shadow people but she also realizes that in a tight, expensive housing market, it is not easy to persuade people to make permanent homes in the city. "My job becomes creating the kind of community that's going to convert some of these commuters to permanent residents. We believe that sort of thing will happen over time, but capacity constraints mean I can't help but understand those concerns . . ."

One of the challenges is a doctor-patient ratio, which, she says, is "off the charts." There are too few doctors, too many people, although medical workers have become very efficient in moving people along. "There is no funding allocation for shadow people in the population base," she explains. "You can't create the hospital infrastructure if you don't have the population base for it."

Blake did not blame former premier Ralph Klein by name, but the province had left her high and dry. It is a sad statement on the ineptitude of the Klein government, which was willing to pay $400 to every Albertan in a massive giveaway, but unwilling or unable to respond to the needs of its fast-growing, most critical community—the source of so much of its present and future wealth. In fact, people associated with the oil sands said they urged the Klein cabinet to step up infrastructure spending, but there was little or late response. The government retreated into inaction on all fronts. After it had tamed Alberta's deficit and debt, it was simply bereft of any ideas.

Yet Melissa Blake is optimistic. She believes that in a decade, her city will have overcome many of its financial challenges, pinning her hopes on gaining more control over property taxes and the rising value of assessments. She is talking of 140,000 to 150,000 people in ten years, depending on levels of oil sands investment.

She ran again for mayor in 2007 and won handily, but, at thirty-seven, with a young child, she insists she won't do it forever. The one thing that still appalls her is the one-dimensional reporting on the city she loves. I talked to her just after *Chatelaine* magazine had done a number on the city in a story called "Down and Dirty in Fort McMurray." It was yet another drive-by treatise on the prostitution, escort services, and the sleazy life in the oil sands. Of course, I can't feel too smug, because I had written the same kind of story thirty years earlier.

There is something about Fort McMurray that invites this portrayal. All the ugly stuff is in full view along the highway— the bars, the strip malls, the casino, the traffic, and the banal Peter Pond Shopping Centre, named incongruously after the first white explorer to visit the region in 1778. You have to drive up onto a plateau, to a hidden suburb called Timberlea, to find the

Fort Mac of families, nice detached homes (at $600,000), and ordinary people trying to make a life.

But on a morning after the *Chatelaine* article appeared, Blake cannot be consoled: "The article is dominated by dark images of escorts and greedy women and we all take offence to that because this community is so much bigger and more inclusive.

"I'm sure elements of that exist anyplace. But you are not tripping over it here. So an article like that discounts all the positive things. I've probably got ten women who would be excellent material from the community accomplishment side." And that list would start with Melissa Blake.

Children of the Oil Sands

I meet Kristin and Oliver in a funky Whyte Avenue diner called Dadeo, which makes the best Cajun food in Edmonton. They are immensely likeable engineers, both in their late twenties, who met at the University of Alberta, got married and managed to buy a house in the supercharged Alberta real estate market. Increasingly, the house is the biggest thing they share, because they stand on the gaping cultural divide that is today's Alberta.

Oliver, the dark and serious son of a Ukrainian family, works for an engineering firm, and he is a veteran of the oil sands, having worked for months on one of the big projects. It has given him insight. "Those jobs are so big they are unmanageable," he says. "There isn't a company yet that has hit its target."

He doesn't like everything he sees in the oil sands, particularly the degradation of the environment and the potential for continuing climate change. But he is skeptical that anything much can change. "I believe there is a problem but I'm powerless, while she believes she can make a difference," he says, referring to Kristin, whom he clearly admires and loves.

She is a small vivacious woman who, Oliver says, has to do work that she believes in. Oliver calls her "an authenticity seeker" who believes she can change the world, but he admits "that is not part of my makeup."

Kristin has taken an entirely different career path. She got out of university just before the energy boom, and was hard-pressed to find work. She hooked up with a firm making heating and ventilation systems but the work bored her. She then got involved in a government project to make houses more energy efficient, where she got to know the Pembina Institute and went to work for it.

The institute is an environmental think tank that is leading the charge to educate Albertans on the huge environmental crisis in the Athabasca region. This virtual organization, with members scattered around Canada, has published some of the most searing indictments of the oil sands projects, their scarring of the land, and their massive impact on the water supplies in parched Alberta. Yet the Pembina does not say the oil sands projects should be stopped—just that they can be managed in an ecologically sustainable way. In fact, Pembina provides consulting services around that idea.

It is a view that has resonance among the Alberta population, which is sharply divided between a laissez-faire business philosophy and a deep respect for the beautiful land. It is Albertans' most profound crisis of conscience: how to reconcile their love of nature with their economic ambitions in Fort Mc-Murray and other bastions of energy production. Pembina has a reputation for standing up for ordinary, often rural-based landowners in the face of the oil industry's surge. Its origins lie in a classic standoff between Big Oil and individual residents in Drayton Valley, Alberta. In 1982, an explosion from a sour gas well killed two people and emitted poisonous gas into the atmosphere for sixty-seven days, creating nausea and other health problems. It motivated a group of teachers to launch a movement to try to enhance safety and prevention standards. The "Lodgepole incident" was a catalyst for a citizens' movement and was the beginning of the Pembina Institute. Kristin became attracted to its mission.

There clearly are tensions in the couple's lives. They own a couple of small cars and she has opposed his idea of buying an SUV. Now the two are teasingly at odds over Oliver's desire to have a light truck to haul his stuff around. There are also money issues, which are common in the high-income atmosphere of the oil sands. Highly sought-after welders are making much more than university-trained Oliver—and Oliver is making twice as much money as Kristin's annual salary of about $40,000. It was a struggle to buy a house—1,200 square feet for $300,000—the good part was it had appreciated 50 per cent in a year.

And then there is a basic difference in temperament. "I tend to like to do what everyone else isn't doing," Kristin says. But Oliver has no such world-changing goals. He wants a meaningful career, not a cause.

When I left the restaurant, I was hoping they would resolve their tensions. I didn't hear from Kristin and Oliver for more than eight months. Then I emailed Kristin and she responded that they had decided to separate. I was saddened but not totally surprised. In that conversation at Dadeo, I could see the differences forming in their relationship. Perhaps they are incompatible, like the growing divisions across Alberta and the clashing visions of where the oil sands will take the province and the country. It is the eternal Canadian tension, writ large in the oil sands—to subdue the land and make it profitable, or protect it and allow it to survive.

CHAPTER 3

TERRY AND THE PYRITES

How resources are trumping tech

SIR TERRY MATTHEWS is Canada's entrepreneurial machine, the creator of billions of dollars' of value for himself and other investors. As a young immigrant engineer from Wales in the 1970s, he co-founded Mitel, a maker of telephone office switches that became our first high-tech growth stock. Since getting out of Mitel in the early 1980s, he has helped create eighty companies, many of them in his adopted hometown of Ottawa. Only two of his "ecosystem" of companies have bitten the dust, he maintains, as he has merged and morphed his start-ups into ever-bigger enterprises.

In 2000, he sold his telecommunications manufacturing company Newbridge to the French company Alcatel for $7 billion, then turned around and founded dozens of new companies, usually by backing bright kids recruited on college campuses. He bought back the remains of Mitel, now one of his core holdings in a sprawling complex of companies that spans wireless gear, golf courses, and Internet start-ups. At sixty-five, he is one of Canada's richest people, with a fortune estimated at $1.5 billion but is also the wealthiest man in his native Wales, where he maintains homes and companies.

So, by rights, Sir Terry should be extolling the virtues of the high-tech life, and how great wealth can be generated from computer chips, fibre optics, and human ingenuity. But no. Sir Terry, who speaks in equal bursts of profanity and profundity, is absolutely awed by the power of western Canadian dirt, heavily laden with oil, to generate huge instant margins. "The biggest value add in the world is when you stick a shovel in the ground," he marvels in a tone that is both contemptuous and admiring. It is not labour and technology that are adding the most eye-popping value these days, he says, but the ability to take an inhospitable piece of ground and with one scoop of a shovel turn it into a billion-dollar windfall.

This technology titan is an unlikely worshipper at the altar of the oil sands. He believes passionately in Canada's technology future but he knows technology has met his match in the forests of Northern Alberta and Saskatchewan. He sees a crowding-out effect, in investment, labour, and government policy attention. Whereas the oil sands have attracted $100 billion of new investment, in his view the Canadian tech industry is wallowing in the doldrums. "It's affecting the balance of everything we do," says the goateed, hyperactive Sir Terry, "and in manufacturing— Man! is that a problem! We have a problem in this country for industry. We have been falling below critical mass, and how do we catch up?"

Sir Terry is expressing the odd paradox of Canada in the early twenty-first century. This was supposed to be the age of high technology and of human capital that would be the underpinnings of the vaunted knowledge economy of the future. This was supposed to be the time of a war for talent—a war for computer scientists and software engineers; not for pipefitters, welders, and labourers, the people who command huge incomes in the oil sands, In fact, Canada's base of technological enterprise is declining, as promising companies are bought by foreign players, research and development slip away to China and India, and our best engineers are gobbled up by Google and Microsoft. Sir Terry has nothing against foreign investors—he sold his own company to a French firm—but for every Canadian company sold, there should be one, two, or three potential new champions being created and built. And still, there is a dreadful paucity of such firms. He blames it on a series of things, including the drought in venture capital, the difficulty of dealing with government funding bodies, the damaged tax system, and a Canadian dollar that has been supercharged by the energy wealth of Alberta and Saskatchewan. And, to some extent, he blames it on the exasperating, overpowering oil sands, which have tilted the entire Canadian economy towards feeding their voracious appetite for labour, capital, and public policy attention.

Wherever I go in Canada, I meet people who share Sir Terry's frustration. They say the tech malaise is symptomatic of a broader crisis in manufacturing, although technology is, of course, not limited to manufacturing. Manufacturing is dying in its major centres, mainly in central Canada—except for the occasional bright light, such as Waterloo, Ontario's Research in Motion with its iconic BlackBerry. Instead, resources are on top, poor dumb resources, particularly energy, but also potash, nickel, canola, wheat, and uranium. Most of those resources are in the West, and thus the economic momentum is shifting that way. In the view of many technology people, it represents a triumph of the shovel over the human mind.

We have thus entered a new phase in Canada's historical tension between resources on the one side and manufacturing and processing on the other. In the early days, the country's growth was built on staple resources, led by cod, beaver, forests, and wheat. But in the nineteenth century, manufacturing based in urban central Canada developed strongly, partly as a response to the U.S. market being closed to Canadian exports of raw materials. Sir John A. Macdonald's National Policy of the late nineteenth century was designed to force-feed the settlement of the West, thus making it both a source of raw materials and of markets to serve eastern manufacturers. Migrants *to* the West and resources *from* the West would travel on a network of railways built by Sir John A.'s friends and supporters, who got rich in the process. Hence, the origins of the old Western resentment of being treated as a servant and colony of the industrialized centre of the country.

But now in an age of free trade, the major commercial routes run north-south. Today, the Canadian Pacific and Canadian National railways have a continental vision, as do those new railways, the pipelines that carry oil and gas south to the United States, or west to the Pacific and the markets of Asia. The other north-south pipelines are the movement of autos and auto parts—the product of free trade in automotive products that has existed since the mid-1960s. These are the trains and transports that convey vehicles and parts from Ontario to the U.S. Northeast and beyond. But those pipelines are narrowing with the decline of the auto industry's Big Three, combined with the rise of the dollar and the competitive tsunami of a surging China. Manufacturing in central Canada is in retreat, at a time when western resources are on the rise, as the world clamours for more oil, more gas, and, increasingly, more wheat.

This is actually a good thing to some extent, because it underlines the strength of having a portfolio of industries, some of which may be declining at any moment, while others are flourishing. Where would we be if we had only a collapsed auto trade and lacked a strong energy industry or a rebounding wheat economy? Indeed, what will pick up the slack when oil and gas go into cyclical declines—and there is no manufacturing left? For many Canadians, this imbalance flies in the face of our 150-year effort to escape the resources trap. Despite our rich heritage in energy, mining, and forestry, there has been an ingrained contempt towards resources as an industrial base, particularly in the intellectual circles of Toronto, Montreal, and Ottawa. Resources are seen as temporary boom-and-bust phenomena—they inevitably run out—while manufacturing and technology are viewed as sustainable sources of wealth. Resources are considered low in added value, while technology adds huge value—a point that Sir Terry would probably dispute these days. And profiting from resources is based on plain luck, while secondary industry is supported by innovation and the intellectual wealth of a country. And, in Canada, manufacturing has simply employed more people, often in secure, highly paid unionized jobs that usually stay at least for decades in the communities where the factories are based.

There is some truth in this indictment of resource extraction, but it is not all bleak. In fact, resource wealth is increasingly very smart in its application of technology. Yet Canada, particularly central Canada, has fostered a mentality that manufacturing and processing are good and resource extraction is if not entirely bad, at least badly flawed. Now, the worst possible thing has happened: the bad stuff is our best bet for the future and our good stuff is going down the drain.

And people who lose their jobs in manufacturing in the East cannot shift easily to extracting resources in the West. If only it were so simple. In fact, manufacturing job loss is more likely to be balanced by a gain in service employment. Some are highly paid services but many of these positions are just McJobs. In 2007, Canada experienced an historical tipping point that underlines the utter collapse of manufacturing. Statistics Canada reports that for the first time, just as many people were employed selling stuff in retail stores as were making stuff in factories in Canada. Retail job numbers hit 1.8 million people, up 4 per cent. Many of those new retail jobs are in the West, where the energy boom is creating a bubble in consumer spending. Meanwhile, employment in manufacturing, once the engine of the economy, declined 3 per cent to about the same number— about 1.8 million people.

Should we mourn the loss of these manufacturing jobs, particularly since Canada's overall unemployment rate has remained quite low? The problem is the quality of the jobs. These people are not going to work at Research in Motion (RIM) or even in Alberta's oil sands, but they are instead going to welfare, Tim Hortons, and the checkout counter at the Bay. The new jobs are simply not as well paid as the ones lost. The average retail worker made $14.87 an hour in 2007, compared with $21.66 in manufacturing, Statistics Canada says. Think of this shift in employment as a big hit on Canadians' standard of living—and it is not over.

The ex-manufacturing workers are a lost generation, and nobody, save their unions, seems to be fighting for them. Many lack marketable skills because they joined the manufacturing sector in the great auto-trade boom of the 1970s to 1990s when there was really no need to get your tradesman's papers. How about heading to Alberta? One Kitchener unemployed worker, who had worked as an uncertified welder in the auto parts industry, said he could find work framing houses in Calgary, but at fifty-five, how long could he physically perform that work? Besides, there were kids and grandkids home in Kitchener.

Of course, the losses in traditional mass manufacturing would be palatable if we were offsetting these declines with a surge in high-value-added technology. If the new service jobs were in computer services, not retail employment, we would feel better. But there are problems in the tech industry, too, symbolized by the malaise in Sir Terry's hometown. There has been a decline in the vitality of the Ottawa technology cluster, which in the 1980s and 1990s earned the label Silicon Valley North. It enjoys such status no more. Still a prosperous civil service town, Ottawa has simply failed to create homegrown high-tech champions of the kind fostered in other hubs such as California's Silicon Valley or Bangalore, India. Mitel is the rare Ottawa-based company that approaches an annual revenue of a billion dollars, the absolute minimum required to be a global player, Sir Terry believes.

So much of what happens in Ottawa depends on the ebb and

flow of Nortel Networks, the telecommunications equipment giant that is based in Toronto but maintains its research and development hub in Canada's capital city. R&D is valuable because it fosters an innovative culture and employs very smart people. R&D offers the promise of sustainable wealth. For the past century, Nortel has been Canada's R&D darling and its alarming decline in recent years has been both materially and psychologically damaging.

Nortel hit a wall in 2000–2002, the victim of an imploding tech bubble, strategic miscues, and the greed of its own executives. Today, a much shrunken Nortel is led by a U.S. executive who is bravely trying to craft a turnaround, but that revival is no longer built on Ottawa's brainpower. Ottawa must share its status as Nortel's R&D headquarters with Beijing, and believe me, it is the Beijing part that will grow as a result of the steady supply of low-cost technical talent out of China's engineering schools. These may not be the best engineers in the world but there is strength in sheer numbers.

Research in Motion has opened an Ottawa R&D facility mainly, it says, to take advantage of the availability of engineers in the wake of Nortel's shrinking industrial imprint. This is good news because RIM is a great company with a great product. I underline "product" not "products." As I go around Canada, people point to RIM as evidence of Canada's continuing manufacturing and technology viability. But this amounts to a form of denial. Even with its decline, Nortel is by far the largest R&D spender in Canada, and it is shifting a lot of that R&D abroad. Meanwhile, RIM is a glorious comet of a company built on a brilliant wireless device, but it is not an industry. The glorification of RIM is no substitute for a real industrial policy that balances resource strength with technology sustainability.

There may still be a reprieve for manufacturing if China becomes more costly as a manufacturing centre and transportation gets massively expensive because of the rise of energy prices. Jeff

Rubin, chief economist with CIBC World Markets, projects the potential reversal of globalization as the rising cost of moving goods threatens to force the shift of some manufacturing back to North America from China, India, and other low-cost centres. The longer it takes goods to get to market, the more uneconomic such transportation becomes. Rising oil prices act as a de facto import tariff on goods transported over extended distances.

What if our manufacturing capability has already been destroyed? What if all our best technology people are already in the United States? Don't we have some obligation to keep our manufacturing going? Not to prop up uncompetitive players but at least to prepare for the inevitable swing in the global economy as China becomes a high-cost location and long-distance transportation becomes uneconomic.

In fact, it is credible to predict that the 2020s will be the age of anti-logistics, when economics will be attuned to local production for local markets. To be profitably sold, goods might have to travel a few hundred kilometres from factory to shop, not a few thousand. But what if there were no local manufacturing infrastructure, no local skills, no local training left? What if Canadian manufacturing is irretrievably broken? A sustainable economy to keep its options open, simply needs a balance of manufacturing, resources, services, and technology. We may be missing out on the next big economic boom fashioned from the potential revival of North American manufacturing.

Canadians have never done a very good job at guiding our economy onto the next big thing. We are content to let geography determine our future. We leave more to chance than any major economy in the world, and we have always had geography to bail us out—whether it has been forests, nickel, oil and gas, wheat and potash; or the proximity of the U.S. market and our access to Asia. In a sense, we have had it too easy, and we have never needed to scramble and think in order to gain economic advantage. Canada has not been tiny and resource challenged, like Hong Kong or Singapore. We have never had to recover from the devastation of war and invasion, like Finland or France. Prosperity has been handed to us by bountiful geography; we never had to work for it. For now, this complacent non-strategy is working again, because Alberta, Saskatchewan, British Columbia, and Newfoundland are bailing out the rest of the country. Can we assume we can rely on geography, not brains, to keep us alive and well in the age of China and India? I don't think so.

CHAPTER 4

···

MAÎTRES CHEZ NEWF

Can Danny bring his people home?

MURRAY EDWARDS WOULDN'T seem to have much in common with Brandon Cheeseman. Edwards, at forty-eight, is one of Canada's richest men with a net worth of billions. He owns mountain resorts, oil companies, and part of an NHL hockey team. Brandon, a twenty-year-old Newfoundlander, makes $18 an hour as an apprentice tradesman. His major possessions are a Ski-Doo and a small truck. But the oil sands have linked their dreams and destinies in a dramatic way. Brandon is one of Murray's militia, the battalions of tradesmen working on the $9 billion Horizon oil sands project being built by Canadian Natural Resources, controlled by Edwards, on an isolated site north of Fort McMurray.

One day every month, Brandon gets up in the morning to leave his parents' home in Rushoon, a quiet harbour village on the bleakly beautiful Burin Peninsula, three hours west of St. John's. He catches an airport bus into St. John's where he gets on a flight that, save a stop or two, takes him straight to a camp near the Horizon site. There, he labours ten-hour days for an engineering firm that is a contractor to the project. And twenty days later, he catches a flight back the other way—at no cost to him.

He is a shadow worker, part of the ghost-like Fort McMurray workforce who are not residents, not even captured on the Alberta census, but living in the camps. These are the people who ruin Melissa Blake's municipal planning projections, but they are money in the bank for Edwards and his oil sands colleagues who are desperate for labour and have already plundered the human resources of small-town Alberta. "You are a skilled worker in the oil sands if you have a pulse," one economist told me.

At the Horizon site, Brandon works from early morning until far into the evenings, and then retires to his three-by-three-metre dorm room. He might watch a bit of TV and work out at the gym, but he never goes into Fort McMurray, which means he spends little money, and never gets enticed by drugs, drink, or those fast women of the kind depicted in the typical magazine portrayals of Fort McMurray. He is living this soulless existence to collect apprentice hours so he can earn the big bucks—like his welder buddy from down the road at Palmer's Cove, Newfoundland, who, at twenty-four, makes $80 an hour, which is low-hanging fruit in the sands of Fort McMurray.

After all, Brandon wants to buy a new truck back home in Newfoundland. Fort McMurray holds no interest to him except as a base camp. "It's just a working town," Brandon says. "I just work there—I'm not there to joyride around." And Brandon says he would come home in an instant if he had a chance. "As soon as they hire pipefitters in Newfoundland, I'm coming home," he says.

⁂

Brandon Cheeseman is one of the unsung heroes of the Canadian economy of the early twenty-first century, one of the legions of Newfoundlanders who pack their bags and become continental commuters—to Toronto, to Sudbury, to Oshawa, and now to Fort McMurray. There are 10,000 people working on the Horizon site, and many of them are Newfoundlanders. Fort McMurray is estimated to have about 20,000 temporarily or permanently transplanted Newfoundlanders in a population of close to 70,000 people. The economists say labour mobility is the key to an efficient economy. When the terms of trade change to favour one region over another, those who are disadvantaged should ideally hit the road and find work where it exists. The terms of trade have certainly shifted against Newfoundland's fishery—the plants are overstaffed, the seas are overfished, and there is not much new employment in the Burin Peninsula, except the Wal-Mart, the grocery stores, and some car dealers.

In a resource economy, the terms of trade change in an instant and now Danny Williams, Newfoundland's pugnacious premier, wants to bring his people home, to give them real jobs on the Rock. His dream is built, like Fort McMurray, on more energy and more resources and why not? In Canada, resource jobs are the best game in town. And Danny has a plan—a cascade of energy and resource projects to be strung out over the next twenty years.

He rhymes off the names: the Hibernia, Terra Nova, and White Rose fields are now producing and he's just done the royalty deal on the Hebron oil field, winning a tough game of chicken with the big companies. In short order, there should be a new liquefied natural gas terminal; a new refinery at Come by Chance; the Voisey's Bay nickel processing facility; and the prospective Lower Churchill power project. He can plot the mega-projects as they come on-stream, not quite in lockstep, all the way out to 2041. That's the year when the Upper Churchill project, the huge hydroelectric power project whose major benefits were negotiated away to Quebec in the 1960s, will come back to Newfoundland's control, and Danny's people will finally be *Maîtres chez Neuf*.

So that is why Danny feels he can promise to bring the workers back, like Winston Churchill pledging to bring home the armies stranded on the beaches from Dunkirk. With 10,000 or more working away—people who want good jobs, not stop-gap jobs—can you really reverse that trend?

"Yes, we can," Danny asserts with his typical confidence that has made him Newfoundland's poster boy for defiance, the guy who stared down former prime minister Paul Martin, who has gone the limit against the big oil companies to get a sweet deal on Hebron, and is now sticking it to Stephen Harper— "Steve," as Danny mockingly calls the PM, who allegedly broke a promise to him on the split of resource revenues.

"Our problem here has been the peaks and valleys, the boom-or-bust situations," Danny tells me. "We get a construction project, and everybody goes like mad and makes a lot of money in three years. Then if it's an oil project, it goes out to the production stage, and 5,000 workers are no longer on the project. I am trying to levelize employment and also income over a long period so it's sustainable without wild fluctuations."

In January 2007, Danny went to Fort McMurray with a tour of Atlantic premiers. "I said to those people: 'When I bring you home, you're going to be home to stay, with long-term employment so that you're not just going to uproot your family and come back for two years.'

"I'm trying to put in place sustained employment. I'll never get it so the projects just start in sequence—there will always be some overlap—but the goal is to get them home. Newfoundlanders and Labradorians love home. They'll come if the work is here and we owe it to them to pay them a comparable wage."

Until he does, we will witness one of the most amazing income transfers in the history of Canada, an indication of how Canada really can work as a country despite the odds of climate, distance, and economies that seem to be going all different ways at the same time. This is, of course, nothing new for Newfoundland, which was originally explored by Europeans whose lives were very much like Brandon Cheeseman's—Basques, Portuguese, West Englanders, Frenchmen, who would spend weeks and months away from home working in the fishery, then head back home for time with their loved ones.

When the island was finally settled by Europeans—driving a large segment of the native population into extinction—Newfoundlanders plied the waters of the North Atlantic as fishermen and traders, carrying salt cod and herring to the Caribbean in exchange for rum, which came back as that inimitable Newfoundland libation called screech. In the sixty years of Confederation, Newfoundlanders have been Canada's equivalent of the Turks in Europe and the Indians in Abu Dhabi—hard-working people who get things done. The bonus is they speak English and they are Canadian citizens with no problems of illegal immigration. According to some Newfoundlanders, they are now simply Mexicans with sweaters.

Newfoundland is the colony of itinerant dreams, so poignantly and raucously expressed in David French's evocative *Leaving Home*, the tumultuous tale of the Mercer family transplanted to 1950s working-class Toronto. They have figured Canada out much better than folks who joined Confederation much earlier. Their motto is: Follow the resources, follow the coal and iron and fish and oil and gold and diamonds, and wait till it all comes back—because in a resource economy, wealth is not self-sustaining. It keeps coming around and around as one oil field is capped and another takes its place. Yesterday, it was Sudbury, today it is Fort McMurray, tomorrow it is Voisey's Bay or Come by Chance, we hope, so keep your bags packed. It means a large floating population that doesn't really have an anchor.

Newfoundland is the province that understands Alberta, is tied to Alberta, is a second Alberta in the making. It shares a feisty combative tone, as if to say, "We're not going to take it any more." Danny's mega-projects in the making may pale beside the oil sands but they could see the province become one of the powerhouses of Confederation. Newfoundland could also tell Alberta a thing or two about the illusion of wealth, and how prosperity can turn to dust, sending a province on the move hunting for income. There is a need to be adaptable in an age when markets shift. That has been the Newfoundlanders' great achievement, to survive when they really shouldn't. And now they might just pull it off again.

Danny will have to move quickly to tie down his roaming workforce, argues Jim McNiven, a savvy public policy professor at Dalhousie University in Halifax who predicts the country is on the verge of a demographic crisis that will decide once and for all who are the winners and losers.

He watches the draining of small-town Alberta, where young people have departed to chase the oil sands dream. That, he says, is just the beginning. By 2016, Canada's aging population and smaller families will ensure that we will have severe shortages of labour. A lot of regions will not have the money that is available in Alberta to lure young workers. Says McNiven: "Alberta is the canary in the coal mine"—or, more accurately, the bitumen mine. "It is Canada seven years out. But Alberta has the money so they can buy their way through it."

There are ways to address the demographic crisis, but they require time and smart strategic policy. You can increase the participation rate of adults, and people will work to an older age than they do now. Even higher percentages of women will join the workforce. You can wring more productivity out of the same people, which Canada seems unable to do so far with much skill or imagination—although there is some hope from the high dollar and its boost to foreign equipment purchases. And you can have immigration, much more of it, much less restrictive, and at all skill levels.

McNiven says the whole question of regional development gets tossed on its head. "Why attract companies if you don't have labour?" he wonders. In fact, he often tells U.S. audiences that if they catch any illegal aliens in their part of the world, just put them on a bus and send them to Halifax, Montreal, or Toronto. What Canada needs now is not just lawyers and doctors, but the kind of people who make your bed in hotels or clean your houses.

He worries about Nova Scotia, a province seemingly stuck in its self-image as a pretty-postcard kind of place that attracts retirees from central Canada, but not engineers from Delhi or Hong Kong. In a post-manufacturing Canada, where resources are king, Nova Scotia, and its major city, Halifax, have some attractions—the Deep Panuke gas well, for example—but not enough. They will also be competing with other Maritime centres for scarce human capital. Indeed, perhaps its biggest looming rival is the hardscrabble, poverty-ridden port town of Saint John, New Brunswick, which seems poised to become a flourishing energy hub, as the vision of its dominant business family, the Irvings, begins to take shape. New Brunswick has little upstream oil and gas but it does have location, close to the U.S. Northeast, and it does have deep, all-season harbours.

So the Irvings, who already own the largest refinery in Canada, hope to vastly expand that Saint John facility and are adding a terminal to bring liquefied natural gas from the Middle East and South America. Now, the city planners in Saint John are worrying not so much about chronic unemployment, but about severe labour shortages and a boom-town economy that might resemble Fort McMurray over the next decade. Who would have thought that the industrial meccas of the twenty-first century might be two up-and-down East Coast cities that are often confused for each other by non-Atlantic Canadians—Saint John and St. John's?

No one understands the shifting fortunes of Atlantic Canada better than Frank McKenna, the former premier of New Brunswick who is now deputy-chairman of the Toronto-Dominion Bank. "The centre of gravity is shifting to western Canada," he warned a gathering of young Atlantic Canadians who were living and working in Toronto. The West was amassing huge wealth, while Ontario was on the verge of falling into the status of an equalization-grant recipient. The implication, he said, was that Atlantic Canada, which has traditionally benefited from equalization, did not have a lot of friends when it came to re-distributing wealth in Canada. "We are on our own," he said, "which means we have to get out to earn things for ourselves."

In this shifting tide of fortunes, Danny Williams looks to be in pretty good shape—he has money, or at least the potential of money. But his situation is urgent because his workforce is not in Marystown or Stephenville, but in Fort McMurray and Grande Prairie—and someday it could be in Saint John, New Brunswick. That means Brandon Cheeseman, as a factor of pro-duction, is much more valuable than the black earth he is help-ing extract from the ground.

In the village of Rushoon, a couple of young men are loading an all-terrain vehicle on a truck parked in a driveway. They are the only people around on this bright November day in this village with its deep harbour, rocky shores, and collection of neat white houses. The two guys explain they are offshore oil workers who have come home for the season and are getting in a little R and R. Most other men in town are "away," in Alberta or Ontario or offshore, they explain, and so are many of the women.

It is what a wartime British village must have felt like when all the men and many of the women of a certain age were in France fighting a war. Except the cause of this exodus is to sus-tain a standard of living at a time when Newfoundland is reel-ing from a depleted fishery and forest business, and the far-off battlefields are in Fort McMurray, Grande Prairie, and Edmon-ton. "It's so quiet here," says Rushoon mayor Jill Mulrooney, selling stamps in the little post office where she doubles as the postmistress. Then, she adds quickly with a laugh, "It's not so quiet when a few of the boys are home on a turnaround."

Head down Rushoon's main drag—really, its only drag—and you will find one of those boys home on a turnaround: Brandon, who is roaring around his yard on his own ATV. The vehicle is the product of doting parents and his job as apprentice pipe-fitter on the Horizon project.

Inside the house, his mom, Bev, a substantial woman with a gift of the gab, explains that this is nothing new for the Cheeseman household: her husband, Gord, has been away every summer for the past twenty years, working for Canadian Pacific in Ontario, and Bev herself, at forty-seven, spent five months working in Fort McMurray cleaning offices. It's the new trend, she explains, to have female Newfoundlanders heading off on their own to Fort McMurray—and why not?

Bev likes to talk, to socialize in her comfy living room with her big picture of Elvis and her smaller but much more prolific shots of her son, Brandon, who is clearly her pride and joy. "He's my boy," she says lovingly. There are also photos of Brandon's daughter, who lives in St. John's with her mother—and is another reason he is adamant to keep coming home.

The entire Cheeseman household worked away in 2007, as did all of Bev's four brothers and much of Rushoon and nearby Parker's Cove. On the Burin Peninsula, an area racked by fish-plant closings and an uncertain future for its shipbuilding yard, this is the new way of life. Sam Synard, mayor of Marystown, the Burin Peninsula's biggest town, estimates more than 1,000 workers out of Marystown's catchment area of 15,000 people are working away. The itinerant workers are like ghosts wandering through the villages. On one Sunday night, Bev saw a fleet of cars and a bus stream through Rushoon and Parker's Cove, pick up twenty-nine people, and carry them away to the St. John's airport for the long trip to Fort McMurray.

That monthly exodus brings so much cash to the peninsula that a lot of people are driving nice cars or new pickups. The ATV dealers on the Burin are among the busiest in the country.

But there is a cost. Alberta is ripping the soul out of rural New-foundland, as it is ripping the soul out of areas of Cape Breton Island, the Miramichi, and rural Manitoba. It is still a bit of an adventure to Brandon, but some of the older ones can no longer sustain the commuting. They put down roots in Alberta, they buy homes—although fewer and fewer can afford them—and their children become Albertans.

Bev also has the adventuring spirit. With Brandon, her only child, gainfully employed, it was time for her to get out of the house after twenty-five years of being "a stay-at-home mam." She could have gone to a local Sobeys or Dominion for $10 an hour or she could fly across the country to pull down $17 an hour cleaning offices. Her brother had lived there for several years, and bought a house and could charge her a decent rent, so she got on the Internet and before long she was cleaning offices at Nexen Inc.'s Long Lake site outside Fort Mac.

"At one time I did everything for my husband and my son," she says. "When Brandon could look after himself, I said I think it's time for ma. Now when he came home yesterday, he said, 'I'm glad you're home.' But I told him I'm not here to stay. I need a life."

In fact, she loves the life away much more than Brandon does—the close-knit feeling of the Newfoundland community in Fort McMurray and the chance to be her own woman. She would leave her brother's house in Fort Mac at 3:30 each after-noon and travel about two hours by bus to the remote Long Lake site. She would get back to her brother's house at 3 in the morning

After five months, she came back home with $8,000, enough to pay some bills and get the family back on a financially even keel. "Oh yes, I'm going back to Fort Mick," she pledges. Now she's in the network of Newfoundland employment, she knows people, and she can upgrade her job and make a bit more money, maybe moving up to $20 an hour or more.

Fort McMurray means fun and adventure compared with her depressed hometown—although she feels the Newfoundland Club in Fort Mac could use a little sprucing up. While St. John's is booming from Hibernia, tourism, and construction, "the Burin Peninsula is gone; we might as well be honest; it's gone. All the men are gone and even the women are going. You don't have a choice."

While the Cheesemans are bravely moving out in the world, their culture still carries a high degree of traditional dependence. Bev and Gord both claimed employment insurance over the winter months. They built it into their budgeting, just as Gord has done for the past twenty-five years. In Rushoon, in the wintertime, a two-income family still means having two UI cheques.

A few miles down the road Sam Synard ruefully agrees with Bev that the Burin is suffering from a lack of homegrown employment. There is hope for the former fish plant, which has new owners, and for the shipyard, which is angling for a federal supply-boat contract. Meanwhile, a hole in the ground 6,600 kilometres away in Alberta has become the biggest source of wealth generation in this community.

In a sense, he says, the good jobs that once existed at the fishery and the shipyard have contributed to the large number of people who have left the Burin Peninsula. They have ensured that Marystown has an unusually strong complement of skilled trades. The college in town has churned out pipefitters (like Brandon), electricians, and welders. For a while these people kept busy building the big rig for Hibernia, but those jobs evaporated once the rig was shipped out to sea. It means the skill set of the welders and pipefitters is among the best in the country, but those people are now in the West.

And not just in Fort McMurray. Sam's own brother works in the diamond mine in the Northwest Territories, along with forty other Newfoundlanders. By working thirty-five weeks a year on rotational basis, they can all make $100,000, says Sam, himself a high-school guidance teacher who dabbles in local real estate. Also, about 300 fishery workers have been retrained and have headed for Alberta. And they aren't going to come back, because the take-home pay at the fish plant was only $400 a week and they are now making $1,200 a week. It's just too good to give up.

Synard figures that Danny may bring them home as long as the employment is meaningful. Meanwhile, he wonders how long they will buy into this itinerant lifestyle of three weeks on and less than two weeks off. "Right now they buy in because it's an anomaly, but at some point will the wage earner say, 'let's move the family to Alberta?' When that happens, they might not come back so fast."

In Danny Williams' office in St. John's, there is a big blue painting over the comfy couch showing a ship being tossed about on a North Atlantic gale. "That's the way I feel at times," cracks Williams as he walks by. Indeed, it often seems the captain of the Good Ship Newfoundland actually looks forward to the gales more than the calm. In Danny's world, there is actually such a thing as the perfect storm. He has won a second term in office on the pledge that he is no pushover. He has drawn the line in the sand on resource giveaways, and Newfoundlanders love it.

In Williams' view, this is Newfoundland's second chance, or maybe its third or fourth, and he is not about to blow it. Like Alberta, Newfoundland has a dark and simmering grievance. In Calgary, the dirty words are the National Energy Program. In St. John's, Marystown, and Corner Brook, "the Upper Churchill" is spoken like it is an obscenity. Danny figures the province has lost more than a billion dollars for each year that it has not controlled royalties from the big Labrador power project. That's a backlog of $38 billion, Newfoundland's rueful contribution to Confederation.

Danny is a classic Newfoundland motormouth with a quick wit and a spectacularly controlled coiffure that, in its absolute immobility, resembles the veneered coif of former Pakistan strongman Pervez Musharaff. But Danny faces much less opposition on his home turf than Musharraf died in his strife-ridden country. There are some who feel Danny is killing this golden chance by playing the part of an unbending, uncompromising zealot in his negotiations with Ottawa and the oil companies. He responds that his approach, even when he was a lawyer in St. John's, was to start off with certain principles, and bend his strategy—without deviation—to those principles. He insists confrontation is not necessarily part of that plan. "I'm dealing with the public treasury here, with the people's resources, but once I establish the principle, I'm prepared to stand live or die on that.

"We decided there would be no more giveaways in the province. We decided we should get a fair share on our resources. We decided we would be the principal beneficiaries of our offshore oil and gas, and based on those principles, then, I will try to strike a fair deal for both sides.

"I think the mistakes some others have made is to think I'll just back off and give ground ... I will compromise to get a deal done but I won't move off those basic principles and prepare to sacrifice those."

The test was the brinkmanship over the Hebron project with the consortium of oil companies. When he insisted on an ownership stake, the energy titans walked away from the table in 2006. But they came back in 2007 and Williams got what he wanted—a better royalty deal and a 4.9 per cent stake in the project at a cost of $110 million. He clearly relishes the image of taking on the big guys and winning. "To me it is a David and Goliath thing. It's a matter of okay, fine, we'll just dig in here, and take out the slingshot and see if we can't take you down."

The business magazine of my newspaper ran a cover picture of Danny in the manner of a famous Che Guevara poster, beret and all, and portrayed as the Hugo Chavez of the North, a Canadian version of the somewhat crazed leftist Venezuelan president who nationalizes oil companies and wields authoritarian power. It reflects a common characterization of Danny as a Hugo clone. Williams figures the whole caricature came out of Ottawa and the Office of the Prime Minister. "Anytime we get into a dispute, he tries to portray me through their public relations mechanism of just being a loud-mouthed guy, a hothead down in Newfoundland and Labrador. So no, I took it with a grain of salt."

Yet Williams says there are some parallels with Chavez in his determination to draw a line in the sand with multinationals. In fact, Williams and Chavez are part of the growing trend of state ownership and powerful government companies that seek to assert local control over rich energy ventures. The state oil companies in Norway, China, Russia, and Venezuela are becoming significant players in their own right.

Still, Danny insists he is offended by the authoritarian implication. Besides, in seeking ownership of resources, he is just drawing on his own experiences as a lawyer. He didn't want to rent his office building but to own it. "I believe in equity building. I believe that in a good society and in a progressive society, your value should increase. So if I bought an office building downtown fifteen years ago, it should be worth more today.

"From the oil perspective, it is a scarce commodity, it is a valuable commodity, it is a nonrenewable resource and they are not making any more of it, and therefore the value will do nothing, I think, than go up. And if I get it at a reasonable price, and we did, I get the benefit of the growth."

The other advantage to a stake in the ownership is that it puts Newfoundland at the table with Chevron, Exxon, PetroCan, and Norsk Hydro—the companies in the Hebron consortium.

"So I get the benefit of expertise. I'm inside the tent and I know exactly what is going on with the field and projects that we own and you can't put a price on that either."

Newfoundlanders feel they should have a piece of the action, he says. They feel hard done by from the typical pattern of resource extraction. The resources get explored, commercialized, and developed, and "they go out in big boats and nothing happens on the ground here."

Asked how he gets misunderstood by the rest of Canada, Danny bristles a bit. "I'm not a person who just seeks a fight for the sake of seeking a fight. Nothing is further from the truth. I lay out fairly for the person I am dealing with what the ground rules are and what we consider reasonable terms."

He points out that he had a successful outcome with Paul Martin, and an unsuccessful one with Stephen Harper. "Yes I am a fighter and I fight till I drop to stand by a principle and that's how I am. But I'd much prefer to have a good relationship with the government of Canada."

He says you have to look at history, at how it all started with Upper Churchill, with Hiberna, and the verbal commitments on the division of the resources' royalties. "That's why we're standing on principle and why we're taking these prime ministers on when they completely, blatantly, pull back and renege on something that was clear and unequivocal. I don't mind taking them on. The difference with me is I won't back away. I don't mind getting into the fray."

Danny Williams grew up in St. John's, in a family that emigrated from Wales in the ninteeenth century. His father was a lawyer in St. John's, and the family was Conservative. Danny says they probably opposed Liberal premier Joey Smallwood's dream of Confederation with Canada, although they were not strong anti-Confederationists. Williams has always shied away from any personal criticism of Smallwood, who remains an icon despite his sad record on resource giveaways, particularly the loathsome Upper Churchill deal.

"Joey governed Newfoundland at a tough time; he got a lot of infrastructure in place, good roads, that's enough for me. I try not to criticize those who have gone before because they are not here to answer and I'll do my thing and someone will judge me and I hope fairly."

Danny got his BA at Memorial University and was a Rhodes Scholar at Oxford University in Britain—and a tough captain for the university hockey team—before heading back to get his law degree at Dalhousie University in Halifax. He settled into a career as a highly successful St. John's lawyer, taking a bunch of high-profile cases, including representing some of the sexual abuse victims during the Mount Cashel orphanage scandal.

That is where he honed his tough negotiating style that has worked so well in politics. For years, although pursued by the provincial Tories, he concentrated on his young family, his law practice, and a cable TV licence that he obtained, with partners, when he was fresh out of school. He eventually bought out the other owners in what had become Cable Atlantic, the major cable provider on the Rock.

Cable systems are often described as a licence to print money, especially during the 1970s and 1980s, before the onslaught of satellite TV, the Internet, and broadband, when they were a monopoly on mass TV access. Danny admits that's the impression, but he insists he had to be gutsy. His first investment of $2,500 was borrowed money—and he ended up sharing his ownership interest with his father. "He paid $2,500 and I had to pay $200,000 to get it back. Every time I took a shareholder out, I paid the top price in the country."

In the early 1990s, Cable Atlantic came to the crossroads

where cable was no longer the sure thing it once was. The telephone companies were invading this market, satellite was emerging, and the technology was shifting from co-axial to wireless and fibre optics. "We had to upgrade or die," Williams says.

At that point Danny had to shoulder the cost of new fibre technology, which was about $90 million in a company that was valued at the same amount. But he beat back the business challengers and, at the end of the 1990s, he owned a nice state-of-the-art cable system.

That got Toronto cable tycoon Ted Rogers very interested in the business, just at the time when Williams was reconsidering his future. He had done law, he had done business, the cable company was now in a mature market, and he was very well off. Politics was now an option.

Selling Cable Atlantic to Rogers was a big payday for Danny, who reaped a total of $260 million. With the demise of helicopter titan Craig Dobbin in 2006, he may now be the richest man in the province. With the independence of private wealth, he has been able to give away his premier's salary.

He does not mind all the pressure of expectations. "I'm driven and if I don't have lofty goals, I'm not motivated. So I always set my goals through the roof, and if you underachieve with lofty goals, you've still done a lot. As long as I am motivated in this job, and feel I can continue to improve, I will stay here. As soon as the point of diminishing returns comes, I am out of here, whether it takes eight years or four years."

Meanwhile, he knows a constant cash flow from resources is nice, but it is not a recipe for sustained growth. He is bound to be wary of any mad dash into diversification—Newfoundland has been home to many hare-brained schemes, including hydroponic cucumbers, cattle farming, and rubber-boot manufacturing. But he sees its ship coming in as the province turns from a have-not to a have jurisdiction.

Before there can be any thoughts about diversifying the economy, Williams would devote funds to narrowing a huge infrastructure gap and a giant debt burden, including massive unfunded pension liabilities to teachers, nurses, and public servants. The future, he says, is a debt-free, "have" province, but with a fascinating vision—to build a bridge from Newfoundland to Labrador. Williams sees the distance across the narrow passage in the Gulf of St. Lawrence as the same span, give or take a kilometre, as the causeway from New Brunswick to Prince Edward Island. "There is an opportunity to link Newfoundland to Labrador and to the rest of Canada." That won't happen during his next four years in office, or maybe during his lifetime, but even hard-nosed Danny Williams has to be allowed one out-of-the-box dream.

It is hard to find many critics of Danny in the province—after all, this is a guy who landed 70 per cent of the vote in the provincial election. But there are some who wonder about the wisdom of stoking so much discontent over the Upper Churchill grievance. There is no question that Newfoundland was screwed, but it is time to move on, says Rob Crosbie, a member of one of Newfoundland's most distinguished merchant and political families, the nephew of Lieutenant-Governor John Crosbie, and an important businessman in his own right.

Rob's late father, Andrew—John Crosbie's brother—went bankrupt in the 1980s, a casualty of ambitious expansion and crushing interest rates. It was a devastating blow to a proud family. But Rob and his three siblings have rebuilt the business in a smaller scale, working on property development, oil field services, and, in his case, making a big push in Alberta. He is the North American president—and a minority shareholder—in ASCO, a British company that is bringing its supply chain management capabilities, honed in the North Sea, to the oil sands.

He is an example of another strain of Newfoundland's human exports—some of the expertise going to Alberta is strategic and corporate, rather than blue collar.

"We need to find a way to take the pill and get over Upper Churchill," Crosbie says. "It has been a scar on the psyche of Newfoundland since the 1970s and it has interfered with the public's confidence that we are smart enough and bright enough to manage our own business ever since."

He adds that "maybe it requires muzzling the politicians. It's always there and if you can do something about it, great. But if the battle cry for every politician is no more giveaways, then the opposite side is that people automatically believe we are always giving it away."

He argues that to really analyze Upper Churchill, you would have to go back and look at the deals signed in other parts of the world, by other countries, during the same period. It's a hopeless task. Meanwhile, the revenge for the Upper Churchill deal is a political battle cry that has outlived its usefulness.

"I feel strongly it's a bad deal and unconscionable but I can't do anything about it. The deal was signed, you had to be there at the time, you had to be at the table and there is no one around who was.

"You can't change it so I don't know what value there is in rehashing it. It just drags you down all the time. You're just bringing people back into that mentality."

But after all, history is important in Newfoundland—it's celebrated in songs and stories, the kind of thing you might hear in the Ship Tavern in St. John's on a cold winter's night, when a fiddler or a storyteller starts to hold forth on the outports, the fish, the sea. Most of it revolves around the fishery, the industry that built the Rock, the industry of wooden ships and iron men. But that old industry in its present form is dying as plants close and consolidation rears its head. It is more a staple of folklore than of the real provincial economy.

To some extent, that transition is welcome news for Bill Barry, perhaps the most important fish-plant owner in the island, the master of Humber Arm near Corner Brook on the beautiful west coast of the island. In the case of the traditional fishery—the overstaffed, overmanaged, and overly controversial industry—"the most important thing that could happen is for everyone to be brutally honest with each other, give each other a great big hug, and say it's over," he says.

Like Rob Crosbie, he argues that the island has to move on, and Alberta is one of the prime catalysts of change. When he sees people like Brandon Cheeseman head off to Fort McMurray, he is saddened but somewhat encouraged too. The oil sands will be the saviour of the Newfoundland fishery, he figures, because it has triggered a mass exodus of striving young New-foundlanders to far-off places like the energy fields of northern Alberta and Saskatchewan. That drain of human capital, in pursuit of higher incomes and more satisfying work, will accelerate the end of the old fishery, and herald an era with fewer, better jobs, he says.

The salvation of the fishery is not more fish—they are actually in good supply, he argues—but a more productive fishery with many fewer people. "We will have a fish business in New-foundland but one that is capital intensive instead of labour intensive," he contends. "It will be technology based—producing the same amount of fish with many, many fewer vessels and many fewer plants."

Those words are typical of Bill Barry, a diamond in the rough who tilts at unions, governments, and even Danny Williams, whom he respects, but it is clear there is not enough room in the province for the two of them. They are like two Newfoundland bull moose meeting on a barren highway, both stubborn and eloquent, and not inclined to make room for the other.

"Any time anyone has asked me a question, I've totally told them whatever I believed. I haven't lived a lifetime of bullshit," says the trim fifty-five-year-old Barry, a man of many, and often conflicted, opinions. He is a libertarian who home-schools most of his nine children, yet he endorses government clout to help manufacturers and processors who are being driven out of business by the high currency rates. He is a fitness fanatic whose lean face and taut athletic frame remind you of Fred Astaire in his dancing prime. He cross-country skis hundreds of miles a year along the island's West Coast, and competes in Ironman triathlons around the world.

Barry is also one of the province's most successful entrepreneurs, a hardy survivor from an old fishing family whose Newfoundland roots date back to their immigration from Ireland in the 1830s. They were fishermen first, and ended up with fish plants on the Bay of Islands, into which Humber Arm flows as an estuary. From his base in Corner Brook, he runs an empire of ships and processing plants. He has operations in Iceland, he sends processing to China, and he employs 5,000 people in a range of activities.

Like the modern-day Newfoundlanders in the oil patch, the Barrys were once itinerant tradespeople—sailors and fishermen who plied the North Atlantic. For a time, his grandfather had moved his family, including eleven kids, to Massachusetts where he felt they would get a better education than in outport Newfoundland. Bill's father grew up in Gloucester, Massachusetts, and, when the Second World War came, he was a dual citizen and fought in the U.S. Navy before coming home to Newfoundland to stay. So like many Newfoundlanders, the Barrys looked more to their Atlantic ties than to the large country, Canada, to the west.

Barry believes the whole character of the province was undermined when the province joined Confederation in 1949. "My father used to say in 1949 that you couldn't starve or freeze a Newfoundlander. We were the most self-reliant group of people probably on the face of the earth. It was a place that was hard to settle and hard to live and only the resilient could stay or survive here. Successive years of being looked after by Ottawa have not served us well.

"We were a culture that was independent and self-reliant and we became ultimately convinced there was such a thing as a free lunch. We were convinced by politicians that UI was an okay thing, that to work for [employment insurance] stamps was a legitimate process. That was a process that would have completely nauseated any of our ancestors."

The other sad outcome, he believes, has been bad policy in the fishery, where an entire industry has been used as an instrument of social policy, and not as a real business with established property rights. The result is overcapacity with too many workers and too many plants. And that has made the fishery an uninviting industry for young Newfoundlanders to seek employment. And so they are leaving in droves.

"We are tremendous people, but we haven't built a stable enough environment so that people can earn a living and stay here. And we're a great thing for Alberta, a great thing for Fort McMurray, we export lots of really good civilized people; we may talk a little bit strange but we won't steal from you—or shoot you."

For all the controversy, Bill Barry says he loves the fishery and the people connected with it. His fish plant on the Humber Arm has been in continuous operation for 106 years, and there is a tradition of long service in the Barrys' employ by local families. He now hopes that his children can carry on, and he already has two sons, both in their twenties, working in the company.

All of his plants have huge overcapacity problems, but that will get fixed—just because there will not be enough people to go around. While it might create a more productive fishing industry, he does feel saddened by the depopulation of rural Newfoundland. "There is a demand for everyone with a heartbeat from the island of Newfoundland to go anywhere in Canada or anywhere in the world, really. And get good money and good pay.

"Because we have failed that economic test of viability, people are voting with their feet. Anybody who has any skill at all—and Newfoundlanders have lots of skills—they just leave."

Like Mayor Sam Synard in Marystown, he worries that someday, they will not come back. It may be a more productive fishery but not a vibrant place to live, he concedes. If Danny Williams can't pull it off, his young workers, like Brandon Cheeseman, could be anywhere—in Lloydminster, Boston, Shanghai, Dubai—anywhere except on the Rock.

CHAPTER 5

THE MOOSE IN THE MEADOW
Hard times in the industrial heartland

IT IS A CLEAR, BITTER EDMONTON DAY—the kind they have in mind in Alberta when they talk about a dry cold—and a delegation of Ontario manufacturers is trying to find some warmth in the industrial fields near the international airport south of the city. They are taking a bus tour of the Nisku Business Park, which is much like any industrial park you've ever seen—except it's on steroids. It is massive; it's muscular; it's frenetic in its activity—2,833 hectares, the equivalent of about 3,500 football fields—the Canadian ones with the deep end zones. It is home to more than 500 companies and 14,000 workers, who stream each day into Nisku to weld, rivet, fit, and assemble stuff for the oil sands—pipes, compressors, generators, wire, chain, and on and on. This is the key marshalling area in the supply chain for Fort McMurray, which is on up Highway 63 five hours north of Edmonton.

Yet, amidst this industrial cacophony, one of the Ontario manufacturers catches sight of a lone dark figure rumbling across the white snow in a field just outside the factory perimeter. It's a bewildered moose that has found its way into the midst of this Babel of modern industry. For the guys from Ontario, it is a startling revelation. They would never see a moose on the loose in an industrial park in Windsor or Cambridge or Markham. It's clear that this is still a wild place, very close to nature. There is a freshness and newness to the Alberta economic miracle that is lacking in the tired old manufacturing bastions of urban Ontario.

Perhaps the manufacturers empathize a bit with the moose, which, like them, represents an old way of life that is being trampled in the push to develop the oil sands. Like the moose, their livelihood is being threatened by forces over which they have very little control—by China, by a surging dollar, by globalization. In a sense, they too have stumbled into a bewildering new world, where the old realities, the old comforts, no longer hold sway. And like the moose, they are forced to scramble to survive. This is truly the new world, where moose, pipes, and billion-dollar projects come together in one crazy field, and the Ontario guys are part of the old world that is slipping away.

The moose is an exotic intruder, but the names in the business park are very familiar to all the guys on the bus. Everybody is here who counts in the oil sands supply business—from PCL and Ledcor, the construction giants; to the oil field services titans Precision Drilling and Ensign Energy Services—that's one of Murray Edwards' investments—and, of course, Halliburton, the company that brought you the Iraq invasion. A few weeks earlier, Ritchie Brothers, the big industrial auction house, had sold $35 million worth of equipment, trucks, and trailers—2,300 items in all—at a two-day auction at its rambling Nisku site.

And, appropriately enough, it is all happening a few kilometres away from the site of the Leduc gusher, the discovery by Imperial Oil that kicked the modern Alberta economy into overdrive in the late 1940s. There are no gushers for the Ontario manufacturers these days. They have a different, sadder story to tell: after decades of prosperity, many machine and fabrication shops are suffering from excess capacity, lost jobs, and money-losing operations. In the worst cases, they are part of a declining North American auto industry, sparked by the erosion of market share experienced by the Big Three carmakers. These are the companies that had propelled Ontario, and Canada, to huge economic growth in the 1970s, '80s and '90s, but were now stalling and sputtering. The machine operators come from around the city of Windsor, where auto-based machine shops are going under every day, from Cambridge and Kitchener-Waterloo, St. Catharines, and Hamilton—familiar names in the annals of manufacturing.

Mike Ouellette has come from Windsor where he runs a small shop called EK Machine and Tool, a company that was started by his father-in-law, taken over by Mike and whose business consists largely of engine machining for the big North American car companies. It's been a good living through the ups and downs of thirty years, Mike says, but this cycle is "different." It is the worst in its depth and seriousness. He is astonished that some departments of the big car companies just don't seem to have cash on hand to pay him promptly, and are relying more on credit terms than ever before.

People like Mike are looking for business in Alberta, and they are mightily impressed by the industrial complex that has grown up in the farmers' fields beside Highway 2 in Nisku. In fact they were overwhelmed; many of them never knew such a place existed, which tells me that our manufacturing companies just aren't getting around the country enough. But why would they? Until now their livelihood was handed to them by the Big Three automakers, and other large customers in the U.S. northeast and Ontario. Now, those benefactors are struggling themselves, and it's every manufacturer for himself.

The bus tour is given by the local development authority in Nisku, and the guide takes us through a mind-numbingly dense web of roads and factories. Peter Alden, a British-born tradesman who owns a machine shop in Kitchener, Ontario, had worked in Nisku more than fifteen years earlier when there were only a couple of roads and a handful of shops. "It's all juiced up now," he says, with a touch of wonderment. One machine shop manager from eastern Ontario puts it best: "It's like the damn Klondike gold rush out there."

Indeed it is. Alberta is in the middle of a gold rush—black gold as they called it on the camp TV sitcom *The Beverley Hillbillies*. Gold at $100 to $150 a barrel—oil for an insatiable United States, which now realizes that the safest big deposit in the world is right on their doorstep. It means that in Canada, economic power is shifting westward. And if the economic corridor from Calgary to Edmonton were a country, it would be the second-richest nation in the Organisation for Economic Cooperation and Development, the OECD, just behind Luxembourg in per capita GDP, but ahead of the United States and far ahead of Canada as a whole. Even prosperous Vancouver would be left in the dust. Toronto-Dominion Bank economists have a label for the 400-kilometre corridor from Calgary to Edmonton—they call it Canada's "economic tiger," and it has a roar heard not just along the route of Highway 2 but right across the province.

Indeed, across the country, for it is clear that the Calgary-Edmonton corridor, combined with its extension along Highway 63 to Fort McMurray, has supplanted another high-traffic corridor—Highway 401 from the Ontario-Quebec border to Windsor—as the major engine of Canada's economy. That has devastating implications for Ontario, where there are symptoms of serious decline in the manufacturing industry that led Canada's prosperity in the post–Second World War period. The death of manufacturing threatens to pull Ontario into have-not status, thus turning the tables of Confederation.

Another major victim is the Greater Toronto Area, whose strength as a commercial centre has fed partly off its status as a manufacturing hub. Manufacturing has largely departed the downtown area, including the area on King Street West, which was once the domain of farm equipment, furniture, and textile factories. Nowadays, that area is all about building condos for young people working in financial services or media. Toronto's manufacturing strength has fled to the suburbs, to the industrial sprawl of Mississauga, Markham, Brampton, Vaughan, and Pickering. But make no mistake, if manufacturing dies in the suburbs the centre is also in trouble. In fact, Toronto is turning into a one-industry town, just like Calgary or Edmonton. Only Toronto's one industry is financial services, which are now driving the entire Ontario economy.

Decline is not an issue in the Calgary-Edmonton corridor. Toronto-Dominion Bank economists argue that in the early years of the twenty-first century, the Corridor was the only Canadian region offering "a U.S.–style standard of living along with a Canadian-style quality of life." And it kept getting stronger, as high oil prices and Fort McMurray drove prosperity to ever higher heights. What's more, it was good for all of Canada, the bank insisted. "We estimate that for each one dollar increase in real GDP in Alberta, twenty cents in increased GDP flow to other provinces through higher demand for goods and services."

And Nisku is the motor that powers a lot of that 20-cent dividend. On the train that is now the Alberta economy, you could look at Fort McMurray as the fuel tank, Calgary as the grease, and Edmonton-Nisku as the engine. It is a machinist's wet dream, from which there is little sign of waking. Even as the conventional oil and gas industry in Alberta began to weaken in 2007–2008, the oil sands were just getting pumped up with investment. All that lies ahead are new projects in Fort McMurray and new upgraders around Edmonton—a local investment outlay that, by itself, will add up to more than $40 billion.

So on a cold day in November, here are Ontario manufacturers coming, cap in hand, to seek the crumbs falling from the overflowing bounty of companies based in the oil sands supply chain. And they get a rousing welcome at a breakfast meeting with Alberta companies that can't keep up with their orders because of dire labour shortages and cost run-ups. It hadn't always been like this, some members of the bus tour confide. In the old days, when you came to Edmonton for work, you couldn't get the time of day. Now with labour shortages at a dangerous level, there is a more open-handed greeting.

Many of these Ontario companies are in a life-and-death struggle, trying to drum up business where they can. There are a lot of factors in the plight of Ontario manufacturing, in addition to the auto woes and the worsening condition of the U.S. economy. There is the competitive threat from China, which has become the factory floor for the world, with its cut-rate labour, lax regulation of the environment, and acquiescent legal system. Every industrial country is losing jobs to China and India, and, as Toronto-Dominion Bank says, "the decline of the manufacturing sector is in no way unique to Canada."

In fact, Canadian manufacturing had held up fairly well compared with counterparts in the United States and Europe. It helped that, for more than two decades, it was propped up by a weak dollar that gave Canadian products an automatic cost break in the global market. But now Alberta's oil wealth was putting a charge under the loonie, with the Canadian currency soaring from its low of 61.79 cents U.S. in early 2002, to levels near or at parity—a fast, dramatic cost increase of 60 per cent for exporters and a killer for profit margins.

The weakness of the U.S. economy, and mismanagement by the Bush administration, no doubt have contributed to the ascent of the Canadian currency. Alberta's good fortune and, increasingly Saskatchewan's and B.C.'s, play a role, as well. The rise in the value of energy exports—from both conventional sources and the oil sands—set the already overheated loonie on fire.

For Canada it seemed to be a return to the status of "hewers of wood and drawers of water," to a nineteenth-century world when Canadians exported mainly primary resources, while all the value-added functions were performed offshore and, increasingly, that work was being done in Asia. In fact, it was more subtle than that. The wood industry was in fact in terrible shape, and the water industries, such as fisheries, were scrambling. It was the stuff under the ground, the oil, gas, potash, and nickel that everyone wanted now. "Rather than being 'hewers of wood and drawers of water,' it is more accurate (if less catchy) to say Canadians are 'conveyers of crude and moilers of metals,'" wrote Phillip Cross, the country's chief statistician.

Whatever the causes, the dollar was turbocharged—and yet the world had seen all this before. Call it the resource curse. The view of many economists is that great oil and gas endowments actually impede, rather than foster, economic growth and development. They may create great temporary wealth, but not self-sustaining, long-term growth. Natural resource countries get a bad rap—they are considered unprogressive, flabby, uncreative. They aren't driven to innovate, to get better, while many countries with no resources, such as Hong Kong, Singapore, and South Korea, were forced to undertake creative and smart initiatives to survive and prosper. Try to find a country in the underdeveloped world that has ridden its resource wealth to a high standard of living for all its citizens.

The nasty bug that spreads this affliction is something called "the Dutch disease," named after the condition suffered by the Netherlands in the 1970s when, with the discovery of natural gas in the North Sea, the Dutch manufacturing sector started to fall apart. The reason was a sudden rise in the value of natural gas exports, which in turn generated a massive increase in the currency's value.

That triggered an automatic cost increase that made it much more difficult to export non-resource commodities and made it almost impossible to compete with imports in domestic markets, economists say. Any surpluses of foreign exchange that came from commodities tended to be used to purchase internationally made goods at the expense of domestic manufacturers.

Another problem is that natural resource wealth does not have to be produced—it can simply be extracted. It operates independently of all other processes in the economy. Resources often function as a splendid enclave that do not stimulate other industrial functions. The work being done at Nisku is often very creative, but it is very focused on energy and specifically oil sands production. There is innovation at Nisku—a better pipe alloy, a better compressor—but it is confined largely to the energy industry. It is diversification inside energy, not outside, which limits its economic spillover effect.

Meanwhile, domestic factors of production, such as labour and materials, are shifted to the natural resource sector, creating shortages in other areas. Look at how the oil sands have been sucking up mobile labour in Alberta, indeed all of Canada, and still they can't get enough. Consequently the price of this labour rises on the domestic market, thus increasing the cost to other producers in other sectors.

If you think it is hard to be a manufacturer in Ontario—think about what it is like to be a manufacturer in Alberta. "We are not present in the oil sands, but we pay all of the costs," says Bernie Lesage, a Calgary manufacturer of geothermal power systems, who exports 80 per cent of his production—and a lot of it goes to China and India. His company, Global Geothermal, has seen its margins battered by high Alberta costs, the skilled labour shortage, and the soaring loonie, but it has been able to cope because it is a recognizable global brand name in its narrow niche field. In Calgary's manufacturing sector—which makes up about 7 per cent of total employment—there is a kind of gallows humour: we shouldn't really be alive but here we are. Lesage, in fact, is trying to diversify the company out of gas wells and pipelines into providing remote power for the oil business, including the oil sands. The theory is if you can't beat 'em, join 'em.

Indeed, according to economists, the massive extraction of natural resources usually benefits only two domestic sectors in a country—the natural resource sector itself and the non-tradable service sector, such as construction. These two thrive at the expense of more traditional export sectors. In the Dutch case, the victim was manufacturing—and that is the case for Canada as well.

The Dutch disease fosters a massive redistribution and inequity of wealth in a country. Those that have the resources capture massive windfall profits, and those that don't suffer. This polarization is most pronounced in underdeveloped countries that lack the democratic institutions to keep the poor from falling further into a pit of despair. The sheiks prosper more and the peons suffer more. Some democratic countries, such as oil-rich Norway, have done smart things to combat the Dutch disease, including the establishment of large funds to hold and invest all the government's revenue take, thus tamping down the potentially overheated domestic economy—and slowing the rise of the currency—and spreading economic wealth over generations.

Peter Lougheed created such a fund in the 1970s, calling it the Alberta Heritage Fund, but his successors have allowed the fund to languish, by promiscuously tapping it to pay down provincial deficits. Even inside Canada, the Heritage Fund has not kept pace with other public funds. In 2008, the Heritage Fund had grown to about $16 billion, small stuff beside Quebec's giant Caisse de dépôt pension fund, which is ten times as big. Not that Alberta's heritage savings don't do some good work, particularly in the field of medical research, but they are not the instruments of industrial policy and intergenerational transfer that Lougheed imagined. Any hope of developing a Canada-wide investment fund based on oil sands wealth is, of course, undermined by Canada's federal system. After all, Alberta owns the resources in its ground, and at this book's press time, the provincial government was studying the options for its various endowment funds, which total about $35 billion.

The call for a more robust Heritage Fund won a major advocate when the OECD strongly urged Alberta to devote all its oil revenues to a foreign asset fund, such as Norway does. The benefits would not only negate Dutch disease but would also allow Canada to pre-fund the costs of an aging population and share resource wealth with future generations. It also called for a dismantling of many of the preferential tax and royalty incentives accorded the energy industry, which, after all, hardly needs such props anymore.

The OECD endorsed a larger Heritage Fund as part of a raft of initiatives to deal with an historic dislocation in Canada in the relative competitive position of regions and industries. "The structural shift provoked in part by the terms-of-trade shock may be one of unparalleled magnitude in Canada's modern history," it warned in unusually stark terms. The danger would be that economically exposed sectors, such as manufacturing and forestry, would be excessively "crowded out"—that is, deprived of investment capital, labour, and other critical factors of production, while oil and gas and the public sector would benefit from rising energy price windfalls. The challenge for Canada would be managing these shocks in a sustainable way.

Yet many Albertans worry that if their savings get too big, and attract too much attention, they will become the target of envy from the rest of Canada and a repeat of the noxious money grab perpetrated by the National Energy Program, perpetuating the destructive mistrust among Canadians.

Besides, there is no tradition of methodical industrial strategy in Canada as you find in Norway, beyond the highly contested device of equalization payments. There is something Canadian about revelling in the boom-and-bust syndrome; it is almost a badge of honour to survive a resource bubble and the inevitable bursting of that bubble. Rags-to-riches-to-rags is as Canadian a phenomenon as strong beer and the Stanley Cup. However, Canada has had little experience with something as cataclysmic as the potential death of manufacturing—death by Dutch disease.

The manufacturing industry in Ontario and Quebec had already been reeling from Chinese competition, and was now being brutalized by the soaring loonie. You can talk all you want about who was to blame—some say our manufacturers were unaggressive in tackling their productivity gap with U.S. counterparts. Critics bemoan the appalling lack in investment in technology that has contributed to the productivity lag. Equally damaging has been a tax system that has inexplicably penalized capital investments, and contributed to underinvestment in equipment and technology. When all is said and done, a sector that is a source of great growth and innovation, of human development, and of pride, is being wiped off the map.

And just look at the human cost alone of this dislocation: a TD report in early 2008 said that since 2002 about 180,000 manufacturing jobs had been lost in Ontario—one in six of the total jobs in the sector—and 140,000 (one in five) in Quebec, Most of those were in the Toronto and Montreal areas and "the sector's fortunes are almost certain to deteriorate further."

Yet the picture need not be entirely negative. The oil sands require huge capital investment because this is oil that you make—you do not find it, as Neil Camarta loves to explain. Because of the intense upgrading and refining process, this oil is essentially manufactured from bitumen. The massive investment in the oil sands means more stability of business cycles—once a $10 billion investment has been made, the production tap cannot easily be turned off or on, although that doesn't mean it won't be turned down. So, surely there were opportunities for Ontario manufacturers to supply stuff for this $100 billion expansion that is occurring in the Athabasca region over the first two decades of the twenty-first century.

With the end of the auto industry as we know it, can Fort McMurray now take its place as a source of contracts and jobs? The oil sands operators need so many things—generators, pipe, chains, control valves, sheet metal, tools. To some extent this does seem to be happening. Although hard numbers are not readily available, it seems about 20 per cent of the oil sands' supply chain needs are going to be met in the rest of Canada. I know of Newfoundland engineering firms that are building gear in St. John's harbour to feed the oil sands' hunger for equipment.

A study performed for the Canadian Association of Petroleum Producers shows that of the 6.6 million person years in employment from 2000 to 2020 to be generated from the oil sands, about 56 per cent would be allocated to Alberta and another 17 per cent to workers outside Canada. That means 27 per cent of the work would be in the rest of Canada, including 16 percent in Ontario.

This same analysis projects the oil sands could add at least a trillion dollars to Canada's GDP over the 2000 to 2020 period. Alberta would reap a whopping 72 per cent of that, as opposed to 11 per cent outside Canada, and 17 per cent in the rest of Canada, including 11 per cent in Ontario. (It is astonishing that only 1 per cent of the oil sands value added is projected for Quebec.) The Ontario manufacturers I met in Alberta were hungry to be part of that action, and there was anecdotal evidence that some of them were making key contacts, but it was no bonanza. This would not be an overnight success and there would be return visits over the years. It was all about relationship building and there had not been enough of these delegations in the past.

And there were absolutely no guarantees. A group of Nova Scotia manufacturers also made the trek to Edmonton, in the fall of 2006, in search of new contracts. I visited a trade fair they held in the West Edmonton Mall's hotel, and it was a forlorn affair. A handful of people were walking through the fair, picking up business cards, but many of the Maritime company executives seemed happy to see me just to have someone to talk to. They explained that they needed work to fill idle capacity, just so that they could prevent their workers from slipping off to

Alberta, where the money was better and there was more job security.

I chatted with the general manager of Trenton Works, of Trenton, Nova Scotia, a railway car manufacturer that had been afflicted by sagging business, bitter labour disputes, and a perilous future. At one time the largest metal fabrication shop on Canada's East Coast, the company, now owned by Greenbriar, a U.S. manufacturer, was desperate to drum up some business to fill capacity. "We really need this work," the general manager, Bob Hickey, told me in an almost pleading voice. At its peak 1,300 people had worked at Trenton Works; now it was down to a few hundred and the future of this old and distinguished manufacturing tradition lay in the balance. As it turned out, the Alberta business did not come through. By the following summer, the plant was closed, the business was bankrupt, and key managers were transferred to Greenbriar's operations in the southern United States.

Soon Canada's manufacturing crisis had turned into a constant drumbeat of plant closings, company sales, and threatened shutdowns:

The forty-four-year-old Hershey chocolate plant in Smiths Falls, Ontario—much beloved of school and tourist visits—closed in early 2007, leaving more than 500 employees without jobs.

The Gibbard furniture plant in Napanee, Ontario, the oldest furniture factory in Canada, dating back to the 1830s, announced it was up for sale. Owner Bruce McPherson Sr., eighty-five, says he and his family lacked the health and energy to combat a barrage of competitive challenges, topped by the dollar's surge.

The Wood refrigerator and freezer business, based in Guelph for seventy-seven years, was sold to Japan's Mitsubishi as the Wood family exited the industry, citing uncompetitive tax policies.

Western Glove Works, the eighty-six-year-old firm that had won the coveted Victoria Beckham jeans contract for its Winnipeg plant, announced it was shifting this production to Asia, signalling the end of all garment making in its local factory. The line of $250 jeans, created by the woman also known as Posh Spice, had added a temporary measure of star power to Winnipeg's declining needle trade.

And the unkindest cut of all was the announced closing of a General Motors truck plant in Oshawa, with a projected loss of 2,600 jobs by the end of 2009. The announcement, in early June 2008, came just two weeks after the automaker had signed a three-year agreement with its union pledging to keep the plant open through the life of the contract.

Canadian manufacturers had been living in a dream world when the currency was 61.79 cents, but now they were living in a nightmare. Most had failed to prepare for a world in which the dollar might approach parity. Blame is easy to throw around in a crisis. What was remarkable was the lack of any concerted policy response by governments to the decline of a Canadian industry. It seemed the only joint federal–provincial action, particularly among the Ontario, Quebec, and federal governments, was to blame the other level of government. Politics was trumping policy, and a great Canadian manufacturing industry that had been built on fine craftsmanship and entrepreneurial moxie, might simply fade away.

They came to central Canada from wartorn Europe in the years after the Second World War. They were armed with tradesmen's papers and a zest for blueprints, and they were prepared to work very hard. Postwar Canada was suffering from a desperately short supply of skilled trades, and these men filled a huge void. They got good jobs and, when they got restless, they set out by themselves to create their own companies in the cities and towns of Canada's manufacturing heartland. While other generations of settlers built sod huts on the prairies, this generation built workshops in downtown Toronto, Kitchener, Guelph, and Windsor. When the Canada–U.S. auto pact and other free trade deals opened the borders, they jumped on the opportunity, creating empires of auto parts, plastics, machining, and tooling.

They fashioned the modern Ontario out of their ingenuity and risk-taking. They were people like Frank Stronach of auto parts giant Magna, Mike Schmidt of ABC Auto Parts, Vic de Zen of Royal Plastics, and Robert Schad of Husky Injection Moulding. Then the world changed. Some of them ran afoul of the new corporate governance climate and became the targets of securities regulators and investor advocates. Others were hampered by the shortage of skilled labour, driven by Alberta's voracious appetite for people. Their empires are under attack from low-cost China, India, Russia, Brazil, and other parts of the developing world. They tried to adapt to a new world order by building plants and, like Stronach, making deals with some of the new titans in the former Soviet Union and Asia. And what's more, they got older and their children were usually less enamoured with the world of manufacturing. They wanted to be lawyers, politicians or doctors, not tradespeople like the old man. The generation of the immigrant tradesman began to fade from view. Yet, there was little to replace them. And now came the hammer of the high dollar—and the spreading affliction from the Dutch disease and the reshaping of Canada's economy arising from a surging New West.

One of the survivors is Frank Hasenfratz who as a young man in Hungary was being trained as a technical officer in the army when the Soviets roared in and crushed the Hungarian uprising in 1956. He was on the losing side, and so he had to leave the country. That set off an improbable odyssey that saw the young soldier flee to Austria and then to Italy. He used his facility in German and Hungarian to work as a translator in refugee camps. Eager for adventure, he moved on to the French port city of Le Havre, where he met some Italian sailors toiling on a Greek freighter. They said he could obtain passage to North America if he was willing to work.

The young tradesman quickly found out how desperately Canada wanted people like him. The freighter docked in Quebec City, where a Canadian immigration officer boarded the boat and asked Hasenfratz to identify himself. "I told him that I was a Hungarian refugee. It took him five or ten minutes and he gave me immigration status including $5 to spend. I filled out the paper, he said 'sign here' and 'welcome to the country.'"

Young Frank ended up working on a farm near Guelph, where his friendly employer would drive him into town each day so he could look for a job in his tool-and-die-maker profession. Within weeks, he landed a job with a company that made components for the Avro Arrow aviation project, a landmark industrial venture that was later cancelled by the Conservative government of John Diefenbaker. Soon Frank was working for a firm whose products included fuel pumps for Ford Motor Co. The pumps were experiencing a 23 per cent failure rate, which frustrated Hasenfratz, who laboured in the machine shop. He decided to quit the company and negotiated the contract to supply the fuel pumps himself. It was a bold move. He was married, with two small children. Then the Canada–U.S. Auto Pact came into effect, providing free trade in autos, and he started getting more contracts from Detroit, Oshawa, and Windsor. His auto parts business took off, and became one of the success stories of the powerhouse Ontario economy of the 1970s to 1990s.

He built a company called Linamar (a combination of the names of his daughters Linda and Nancy and his wife Margaret). Linamar has been one of the beacons of Canadian manufacturing as a multinational producer of power train technology with annual revenues of more than $2.3 billion. It also has a huge wingspan in the Canadian economy as a source of jobs and careers. Frank Hasenfratz figures about a dozen of its former tradesmen have gone off and founded their own companies, often as suppliers to Linamar. And the company estimates that for every job it creates in its own walls, another six are created in other companies.

Linamar is also a rare instance where a father has successfully transferred management control to a child who shares his passion for the business. After university, daughter Linda worked at a pharmaceutical company for a while but, suddenly, she experienced an epiphany: she told her father she was ready to join the family company and she was ready to start at the bottom. Eighteen years after her fateful decision, the forty-two-year-old is Linamar's president and CEO, while Frank has settled into his role as chairman. This father-and-daughter partnership works as well as any family transfer I have seen. The top drawer in Linda's office desk contains a valuable document: a piece of paper that outlines the job responsibilities of her father, now that he has relinquished his CEO duties. Father and daughter worked out the arrangement when she took over. The paper says Frank will do four things: drive the company's cost-cutting initiative; work on its paper audit trails; help negotiate the purchase of capital equipment; and serve as board chairman. In case he steps over these boundaries, Linda says, the paper is "right there, under lock and key."

Linamar also aims to survive in a Canadian manufacturing industry that is dramatically shrinking in the face of global competitive pressures and the reshaping of the Canadian economy in favour of resources. When I talked to Linda, she admitted she was not familiar with the term "Dutch disease" but when I described it to her, she knew the condition all too well. She lives it, she battles it, and, to a large extent, she is beating it. How does she do it? It sounds a bit clichéd but it is about the things that always make you competitive—innovation and efficiency, not only in equipment and technology but also in the process of working—in the smart ways you organize your people.

Linda is a fanatic on taxation, arguing that it is hard for a manufacturer to compete globally unless it has a combined federal and provincial tax rate of 20 per cent or less. And, until recently, she notes, Ontario had not approached that threshold. Linda also says it is too easy to be mesmerized by the challenge of a supercharged Canadian currency. In fact, if you look at the strong loonie from a holistic standpoint, it is entirely positive for Canadian companies. The higher currency means our companies are worth much more—their assets are valued more highly in world markets. Also, she is in better shape to buy U.S.–dollar denominated assets and technology, and Linamar has been a very active acquirer in recent years.

She has an interesting way of putting it: when the dollar moves up, your costs really don't increase at all. They remain fixed in Canadian-dollar terms, but your international selling price changes. You still have to focus on cost control, no matter what the level of the dollar is. "The rise in the dollar has just highlighted where we've let our costs get out of control. Your costs are just as inefficient as they always were."

In many ways, Linamar offers a survival guide for the Canadian manufacturing industry, as it is buffeted by Dutch disease and the near collapse of the traditional North American auto industry. Like many North American auto parts companies, Linamar has opened a factory in China and it is very successful. By early 2008, it had won $175 million worth of future contracts. But Linamar's China strategy is not an export strategy. The Chinese factory makes products for the Chinese market, and for contiguous markets such as South Korea and Japan. In fact, that is a Linamar credo: "Our philosophy remains to manufacture in the country, or at least the continent, of consumption," Hasenfratz says. By not massively exporting goods to Canada from China, Linamar avoids the high cost of global logistics as energy costs soar, and maximizes the intimacy of relationships with its customers wherever it is active.

This strategy is also about the long-term vision of the company. Costs are going up all the time in China, and Linda says, it won't be very long before it doesn't make sense economically to make everything in China and ship it all over the world. "The last thing I'm going to do is decimate my manufacturing expertise in North America and Europe if ten or fifteen years from now it doesn't make sense to do that anymore."

In other words, she doesn't want to surrender all her Canadian trades, her edge in Canadian assembly and machining, just for short-term cost gains. Yet that seems to be what Canada is willing to do—let its manufacturing industry die from a combination of Chinese competition and the Dutch disease, without a coherent policy that would include trades and skills training, strategic tax policy, active trade promotion, and assistance in adding cutting-edge programs such as lean manufacturing and technology transfer from universities.

"I'm managing the business for fifty years from now, not for five years or this quarter," Linda says. When I talked to her, Linamar had twenty-five plants in Ontario out of its total of thirty-seven globally. It also operates factories in the United States, Mexico, and Europe, including in Frank's native Hungary. This is not a company that plans to overturn its global strategy just because the dollar moves up and down on a daily basis. She says the Canadian loonie's dramatic ascent from 61.79 cents only exposed areas of inefficiency that have to be fixed in the industry. "The water has slipped below the rocks," she says. "We can see that in companies in Ontario."

Also, Linamar has made a strong point of diversifying out of its original business of making power trains for cars, and that has helped it weather the North American auto crisis up to now. In early 2008, Linda was very concerned about a U.S. downturn and the possibility that a severe credit crunch could bite more deeply. Car power trains and other devices still make up about 45 per cent of its sales, but Linamar has taken its drive train expertise to trucks, construction vehicles, and, increasingly, the energy industry. Yes, this Ontario auto parts company was converting itself into an energy company. Indeed, it is a recipe for any Canadian company: above all, you must have a survival strategy for a world where energy drives every business decision.

A couple of days after I talked to Linda, Linamar announced plans to produce an energy-efficient lawn mower, based on combined electric battery and solar technology. Now, *that* is true diversification—an auto parts company making a solar-powered lawn mower to be sold at Home Depot. Linamar has established an energy division that makes things like gears for wind generators and production equipment for the oil and gas business. When I talked to her, the energy side was a nice sideline with sales of $10 to $20 million, but she saw it as a potential $100 million operation. Linda Hasenfratz was determined to be part of that oil sands supply chain, and saw the oil sands as a market, not just the virus that was causing the Dutch disease. She was adapting Linamar's machining and tooling capabilities to producing shafts for Alberta oil sites, and there were more contracts in the pipeline.

When I told her about the plight of the machine shops that had visited Nisku, Hasenfratz had no silver bullet for them. They would have to do what Linamar had done: go out and find new customers, and think beyond the normal confines of their industry. The auto industry may be shifting beneath their feet, but there were always battery-solar lawn mowers and oil field shafts.

That advice is cold comfort to Mike Ouellette, the machinist from Windsor, whom I talked to a couple of times after his trip to Nisku. He was still hanging in, but it was not easy, and he was trying to diversify into new sectors, such as aerospace.

When the federal government introduced a new tax rule that allowed manufacturers to write off their equipment purchases more quickly, Mike was pleased, but it was hardly a shot in the arm. "Write-offs are great when you are making a lot of money, but that's not happening right now," he told me by phone from Windsor. His machine shop was operating at about 30 per cent capacity but was still doing better than many of his peers. "We're struggling," he said.

When I caught up with him a year later, nothing much had come out of two excursions to Nisku, although he was doing some subcontracting for a project in Alberta. He bid on an oil sands contract but he was 30 per cent higher than the competing offer. Too bad, he was told, but the company was sending the work out to China. There was a common feeling among the Ontario group that perhaps, despite all their words of encouragement, Albertans were reluctant to send work to Ontario. They would rather contract it to the United States, or even to Asia. Perhaps there were still bitter memories of when Ontario lorded it over the rest of the country. Perhaps it was all a residue of the bitterness over the National Energy Program. After all, there was not much sympathy in Ontario when Alberta got caught in the downdraft of the 1980s.

So much of what happens in Canada is about regional grievance and it comes back to haunt us time and time again. Here we have two regions with complementary problems—one (the West) desperately needs manufacturing capacity, and the other (the East) has an excess of capacity. You would think they could get together, but it doesn't work that way. It's as if we have two countries, or three or four or five—or even ten.

Mike Ouellette was still heavily dependent on the auto industry, and he was bracing for yet another major auto plant closing in Windsor. He was at 50 per cent plant capacity, trying to find work for his twelve employees. Personally, he has no successors—both his sons decided to become schoolteachers—and, at forty-nine, he just wanted to hold on for another ten years. "I'm financially okay" he said, but then he added: "You still need customers." And for the shell-shocked trench soldiers of Ontario manufacturing, those were hard to find, even in the bountiful central corridor of Alberta.

CHAPTER 6

SWEET SURRENDER

Montreal's long happy decline

IT IS THE MOST SPLENDID head office building in Canada, a blend of old Montreal grey stone and a sleek modern corporate headquarters, occupying a prominent piece of real estate along fashionable Sherbrooke Street. For more than two decades, the Alcan building has been a symbol of Montreal's great history as a trading centre, but also its pretensions of being an international business city in the twenty-first century.

All those pretensions were suddenly shattered in 2007. Aluminum giant Alcan was swept away in the wave of international takeovers in the mining and smelting industry, succumbing to a massive $38 billion bid by Rio Tinto of London. The high price, garnered in a bidding war with U.S.–based Alcoa, was a tribute to the bargaining agility of Alcan's president, a charming mustachioed American named Dick Evans, who has the air of a suave matinee idol but the tenacity of a street fighter.

Evans salvaged a measure of continuity for Alcan's home city by maintaining the headquarters of the London conglomerate's aluminum subsidiary in Montreal. The subsidiary would be renamed Rio Tinto Alcan, but there was no doubt of the reality: Montreal had lost another crown jewel among its corporate head offices and the ultimate decision making would move to London.

Toronto was also reeling from the loss of two of its mining titans, Inco and Falconbridge. But the buyout of Alcan was more devastating because Montreal's base of multinationals was already so shrunken—a process that began with the controversial move of Sun Life Insurance to Toronto in the late 1970s, following the provincial election victory of the sovereigntist Parti Québécois in 1976. There had been the quiet shift in the same direction by the giant Royal Bank of Canada and Bank of Montreal, both responding to the angst that gripped the Anglo-Montreal business community. In the intervening years, the powerful Bronfman family had moved the effective headquarters of liquor giant Seagram to New York from Montreal, and then in a moment of madness, shifted into media and entertainment. Then the family sold out to a French company, Vivendi—only to lose a great deal of their fortune when the Vivendi shares they had received tanked. The Montreal Canadiens, the great sports symbol of the city, the team of the Rocket, Boom Boom, and the Flower, were sold by Molson Breweries to a U.S. entrepreneur. The team, while still an icon, seems to be composed mainly of Russians and Finns, while the great Quebec-trained players are now in Tampa Bay or Philadelphia. The Molson family then merged its 220-year-old beer business with Coors, a beer-maker from Colorado. The family remains shareholders and a Molson is still chairman of Molson Coors, but the corporate headquarters is in Golden, Colorado. And the Montreal Expos, who not long ago were the best team in baseball and had contended for the National League baseball championship, are now in Washington, D.C.

It is not that corporate Montreal is dying, but it is not growing as a corporate centre. A Statistics Canada study of head office employment showed Montreal, while still the second major head office city behind Toronto, was unchanged in its number of headquarters jobs between 1999 and 2005, while Calgary was up 64 per cent and Toronto was 19 per cent higher. There are still great companies in Montreal, led by Power Corporation of

Canada, the holding company of the Desmarais family. A shrewd global investor, Power maintains its tasteful head office in Victoria Square, packed with a trove of Riopelles and other Canadian painting masters. Hydro-Québec remains the bulwark of the province's industrial policy and is empowered by its fashionable cachet of clean hydroelectric power. But other charter members of Quebec Inc. are in relative decline, including media giant Quebecor, and once-mighty forestry players such as Abitibi, Tembec, and Domtar. Even Bombardier, the great hero of French Quebec, has been up and down and up again—not the reliable global growth machine of past decades.

Now Alcan, which was an international company, never a "Quebec company," and which was once positioned to be a global consolidator, was itself taken out in a binge of industry consolidation. The company's aluminum operations will remain very present in Quebec, attracted by financially sweet power deals with the province. But the head office is gone and Montreal's Square Mile has lost a bit more lustre. With it go not just emotional loss, but service jobs, legal work, executive positions, charitable giving, arena boxes, and a host of other good things that make a city great.

Just to add to the angst, the Montreal Exchange announced it would merge with the Toronto Stock Exchange. The Montreal bourse would get to keep its hard-earned expertise in derivatives trading, but the headquarters of the combined organization would be in Toronto. The powerful Caisse de dépôt pension fund opposed the new alignment, even though both stock exchange institutions are doomed if they stay on their own. Somehow, the sale seemed more painful because it would cement Toronto's dominance. You can't help but wonder why there is so much excitement over a Canadian-only merger, when stock market consolidation is happening on a global basis. It's the same kind of narrow provincial thinking that allows Canada to persist in having ten securities exchanges.

Alcan had always been an anomaly, as a company born out of the 1951 breakup of the monopoly enjoyed by Alcoa, the U.S. aluminum giant. It has often been run by Americans—indeed, it was practically managed out of former CEO Travis Engen's home in Connecticut for a few years. But Montreal warmed to Alcan because the company was committed to Montreal. It had actually acquired foreign rivals, such as the French company Pechiney and the Belgian firm Algroup, making it the world's second-largest aluminum supplier and leading to the illusion that it could not become a casualty itself. But it did, and it tore out the still faintly beating heart of head office Montreal.

So how does a great commercial city decline? Slowly, painfully, it seems, and not for a single reason but for a sea of change—in politics, markets, and entrepreneurial fire. The benefits of geographical location can suddenly become liabilities, as the relative prices of goods and services, and thus the terms of trade, shift. In Canada, a relatively young country, commercial power is in a state of constant evolution and there has been a gradual westward shift as the country has opened up to settlement and resource extraction.

Consider Halifax, which at the time of Confederation was a financial centre to reckon with. It bred entrepreneurs, industrial companies and financial institutions; after all, this was the birthplace of not just the Bank of Nova Scotia but the Royal Bank of Canada. Halifax was a victim of changing geopolitics. It had benefited greatly from its North-South trading relationships with the United States and the Caribbean. But when Nova Scotia joined Confederation and the United States moved away from free trade, Halifax cast its lot with Canada, with East-West trade and a railway system that gravitated power to Montreal and Toronto. Only recently, with the revival of North-South trade as the dominant commercial traffic, Haligonians have re-embraced the concept of Atlantica, a commercial hinterland that links Atlantic Canada to the densely populated U.S. Northeast.

They have also learned the value of being a deep-harbour gateway into North America from India.

As Halifax declined, Montreal emerged as the country's leading commercial city, extending its status as a trading entrepôt in the days of New France and the fur trade, into the age of the railroad and to the great mansions of the Square Mile, built by names like Holt, Stephen, Van Horne, and Redpath. Its dominance in the 1800s to early 1900s was often the product of political corruption, double-dealing, and conflicts of interest everywhere, but it created a powerful commercial city, the headquarters of such defining companies as Bell Canada, Canadian National, the Royal Bank, the Bank of Montreal, Molson Breweries, and Canada Steamship Lines.

When I joined the financial journalism game in the mid-1970s, Montreal was where a lot of the action was. Rue St. Jacques was in elegant decline but still a shining brand name as a financial capital. But this was before the Parti Québécois victory, the departure of Sun Life and the rise of a countervailing force, the cluster of entrepreneurial firms that Torontonians like to call Quebec Inc.—Bombardier, Cascades, Quebecor, Power Corp., Transcontinental, National Bank and others.

Yet even though it is still the number-two head office city in Canada, it no longer has the critical mass of corporate work that spawns giant law firms, consultancies, or corporate service firms. Some of the head offices that do remain, such as those of Bell Canada and Air Canada, are the product of restrictive company charters and political considerations, rather than market forces. There are still traces of the grand old textile and garment firms, with names like Peerless, Parasuco, and Gildan, but these are increasingly global players with diminishing imprints in Montreal.

Yet walk out on Sherbrooke Street and or head to the Plateau, the trendy area where hipsters and university students hang out, and you cannot conceive that Montreal is in decline.

This is a city of great lifestyles, although not of great multinational companies. After all, where would you rather spend a weekend, in downtown Montreal or in downtown Calgary? But to sustain this lifestyle, you need corporate head offices and you need a proprietor class that is willing to buy immortality by funding galleries, museums, and hockey teams. You do not want to create a hollowed-out lifestyle city with no commercial base. That can only be sustained for a short period. And you don't want to lose a baseball team like the Montreal Expos, which left the city because it is not rich enough and does not have enough wealthy people to rent boxes or support Major League Baseball. Montreal does not like losers and, as the team's fortunes ebbed, the fan support dwindled. The clearest symbol of Montreal's plight is the empty Olympic Stadium on Pie IX Boulevard built by Montreal's once-lofty ambitions, but now a derelict victim of its decline.

Montreal today is a city of arts, culture, and style, but it is not a financial centre and much less of a national or international business centre. I believe the city made an implicit choice to live this way—that in Quebec and in Montreal some things seem to be more important than baseball teams and head offices. The priorities are language, culture, social structure, parental leave, day care, and a certain élan—a way of living. The separatist threat eroded Quebec's competitiveness but it was not the critical factor in its decline. Together, Quebec as a province and Montreal as its signature city have chosen to be marginal by not improving the deteriorating infrastructure and not fixing the oppressive regulation, staggering tax rates, and inefficient health care. Quebecers have been able to live comfortably thanks to federal government largesse, a core of strong public institutions and surviving industrial operations—in pharmaceuticals, aerospace, and even in the remnants of the garment trade.

Indeed, the downward cycle that has gripped Montreal is also the harbinger of what could happen to its successor, the city of Toronto. With commercial vibrancy having shifted from Halifax to Montreal and Montreal to Toronto, will there be another shift to Calgary?

Even if there had been no language issue, no decline in head offices, Montreal would have faded in importance. It is part of the human spirit to move in search of opportunity and, in Canada, the movement has been westward, away from the rigid social strata, stagnant elites, and slow growth of the East. Entrepreneurial activity seeks a vacuum. David O'Brien represents that trend. Born in Montreal to an Irish-Canadian family, he went to a tough school and, at nine years of age, got into boxing and was a local champion. His father was a successful lawyer, the youngest of thirteen kids, not all of whom had survived childhood. David's father was the only one of his family to go to university, and he put himself through school by writing for newspapers back in the days when Montreal had a brace of them.

Things were much easier for the son. David O'Brien went to Loyola College in Montreal, now Concordia University, and to McGill Law School, and became a trial lawyer in his home city. But he always thought it would be fun to get into business, maybe by running a big diversified company like Canadian Pacific, which had evolved from its railway base and huge land concessions to own hotels, communications, and energy assets.

O'Brien started doing more and more commercial law, and picked up some good clients, such as the Royal Bank. He got involved in the first financing of Petro-Canada, the controversial federal energy company, and when he had a chance to move to Calgary to become the oil company's general counsel, he grabbed the opportunity.

"This was when the migrations were occurring out of Montreal, with the Royal Bank and Bank of Montreal, and I decided

my legal career in Montreal was going to peak at thirty-five, and
that wasn't a very good prospect," O'Brien recalls.

"I either had to go to a growing law firm in Toronto or Calgary, or I had to find a way out of law and into business. I decided if I were to move into business, and move my family, I
would change direction and the best way I could find was as
general counsel of Petro-Can."

O'Brien became part of one of the most massive talent migrations in Canadian history—the movement of smart Anglophone
people out of Montreal in the wake of the 1976 Parti Québécois
victory. It was a signature moment in the decline of Montreal,
the rise of Toronto, and the new strength of the West. As Montreal
lost thousands of bright people, it lost its momentum. O'Brien's
move to Calgary led to a stint of corporate jobs until he found
himself as president of Calgary-based PanCanadian Petroleum,
a Canadian Pacific subsidiary, in the 1980s. He then rose to CEO
of the parent company, Canadian Pacific, thus fulfilling his
dream as a young man to head the conglomerate. Ironically, he
arrived in time to blow it up. In 2001, he accomplished the mon-
umental breakup of the ungainly CP conglomerate, spinning out
its coal, hotel, energy, shipping, and rail units into separate public companies. The strategy unlocked huge value and O'Brien
became a shareholders' hero. When the CEO of PanCanadian
suddenly resigned, O'Brien slipped back into that job and pulled
off the mighty merger of PanCanadian with Alberta Energy, thus
creating a Canadian oil and gas colossus called EnCana.

O'Brien has thus enjoyed one of the most successful Canadian corporate careers of his generation, the kind that lets you
ease back into nice plum directorships. In his early sixties, he is
chairman of EnCana and the Royal Bank of Canada, a bank that
was once based in Montreal. He keeps a home in Calgary and an
apartment in Toronto—arguably the two cities that still matter
for Canadian business. And what's the future of his hometown
Montreal? "It's going to be a very attractive provincial city with

a lovely touch of the Old World that you don't find in other cities," O'Brien says gently.

They call it *la ville savante*—the smart city—and that will be its future role, he says. Education, style, and creativity will abound. "It has its own charms but is it going to be a major industrial financial centre? No. It's going to be a regional centre." At one time, the energy bosses in Calgary used to make regular visits to Montreal to meet financial institutions and investors. "Ten to fifteen years later, very few did," he says a bit sadly. Montreal is irrelevant in that regard.

He says power is definitely shifting west. "If you look at it in the sweep of time, in the late sixties and seventies, you could see the power shifting from Montreal to Toronto and that is one of the reasons I ended up leaving," he says. "And then gradually there were more power shifts to the West. If this commodity cycle were to continue another fifteen to twenty years, Calgary would be a very, very powerful force on the national scene, easily second to Toronto if not pushing Toronto."

That would seem to be a good bet as long as the Chinese economic surge continues, as long as oil remains politically sensitive, and as long as environmental issues don't overwhelm the economics of energy. "Those are a lot of ifs," O'Brien concedes. "But Calgary wasn't even on the radar screen in the 1960s, and forty years later, it is now the second most powerful centre in the country.'

That means the economic decline of Montreal could become even more pronounced because people and capital are so mobile. And fixing Montreal is not as easy as it sounds. The transfusion of federal money has helped contain taxes somewhat, and that has been a factor in attracting and keeping highly skilled and highly mobile professionals. But the Quebec infrastructure, its roads, bridges, and public buildings are in dire shape. The schools, arguably the city's and province's ace in the hole, are bending under a hefty financial burden.

The decline of Quebec and Montreal was underlined in a recent book by Jacques Menard, Bank of Montreal's Quebec president. The book, titled *Si on s'y mettait* (loosely translated as Let's Get On with It), is a call to arms for a Quebec that is in danger of losing its brightest young people to the rest of the world. And nowhere would that be felt so dramatically than in the province's elite business city, Montreal.

My *Globe and Mail* colleague Konrad Yakabuski described the book as a *cri du coeur* that warns of the potential exodus of young francophone Quebecers, despite the common belief that they are more interested in language and culture than their English-speaking counterparts. Mr. Menard's research found that half of Quebecers between the ages of eighteen and thirty-five say they like the idea of working in a foreign country, compared with 43 per cent in the rest of Canada. And 45 per cent say they would not hesitate to leave Quebec to work somewhere else if a better opportunity came up.

In some ways, those are encouraging numbers because they puncture all those myths about Quebecers' isolation and the lack of job mobility. But it also means that in the push and pull of the modern global economy, Montreal could be faring in the future even more poorly than is widely thought.

In a global marketplace, where people, information, and capital move freely, there is not a good enough reason for any company, executive, or skilled professional to choose Montreal as a place to live, work, and do business. Michel Patry, the principal of the prestigious HEC Montréal, the province's hundred-year-old landmark business school, lives with these pressures every day. The decline of head offices in Montreal is particularly troubling, even for HEC, which enjoys the status of the province's leading francophone business academy. The city, he insists, still has very strong industries in the information technology, pharmaceutical, bioscience, and aerospace sectors. It also has a vigorous video game and software development sector. The universities are strong, comprising four major institutions of which two are leaders in research—McGill and Université de Montréal. But if you look at the aggregate number of global or even Canadian head offices, it is of real concern, he says.

What's more, that feeds into a larger crisis. "We have those assets but the whole educational sector is largely underfinanced and tuition fees are ridiculously low," he laments—and anyone viewing the physical plant at, say, McGill, Montreal's great anglophone university, would have to agree. Government has not invested in universities to the same extent as in the rest of the country, and tuition is kept unnaturally low. If you are staking your future on human talent, on the ready supply of culturally adept, smart people, it is self-defeating to starve your universities. Patry says the same kind of underinvestment has afflicted roads, public transit, and the arts. Years of neglect have created a crisis in which catch-up will be a long painful undertaking.

"There is a growing feeling in Quebec that we have to reconsider how we do things and the way we allocate effort," Patry says in a *Globe and Mail* interview. He says the so-called Quebec Model, with its strong statist role, needs to be examined, as Quebec and Montreal try to find their way in a context where money flows freely and human capital is very mobile.

"I live that every day as a recruiter," says Patry, who grew up in central Montreal, in the shadow of the Jacques Cartier Bridge, where his father ran a grocery store. He says that twenty years ago his own school, HEC, was very much like the Montreal Canadiens, a magnet for talented young Quebec academics who invariably came home to show off their skills.

"You looked at very bright French-speaking Canadians who had been to universities of Stanford and Michigan and they all returned to Quebec. So you could sort of draft them.

"It's not the same anymore. Talk to these graduates today and they say, 'Look, I have offers from Denver or other American universities or in England and France. I will start there and maybe come back to Quebec.' Our young bright French Quebecers are very mobile. I'm not sure we have fully taken that into account."

At one time the pull of lifestyle and culture was stronger that it is now. "You have to have value and to have something competitive to offer if you want those resources to stay with you." When it is suggested that Montreal is a nice place to live, but perhaps it coasts a bit on that reputation, Patry readily agrees.

"I am told that all the time—it's a nice place to live, arts and entertainment are wonderful, it's fairly non-violent, with very few racial or linguistic tensions. Yet we cannot coast on that. That goes only so far because when people talk about Seattle, Boston or London, that is the competition you face. I guess we have to seriously consider how to improve our effectiveness."

Patry, as a scholar, is an expert in regulation, and he feels the heavy regulatory burden would be a good target in which to start building a new Quebec. "There is a lot of bad regulation," he says. "We have a way with such regulation in Quebec. The state is very active, a lot of good intentions but . . ." His voice trails away, frustrated at where to begin.

⌀

To uncover the reality of the Montreal of the twenty-first century, it is best to get away from Sherbrooke Street, or the stylish Plateau, and travel to the northeast, beyond the traffic-clogged Autoroute Métropolitaine and into the gritty Saint-Michel quarter, a working-class area of wrought-iron porches and strip malls. This is where two of Montreal's most successful companies are located—within twenty blocks of each other. Over the past five years, I have spent some time with both these companies on assignment for the *Globe and Mail*, and what I found was a study of organizations moving in opposite directions—at least in terms of their presence in Saint-Michel. Both are finding their business models rocked by the reality of a turbocharged dollar and by China.

One of them, Cirque du Soleil, the company that reinvented the circus, is bursting at the seams with new shows and a seemingly endless demand for hard-bodied performers and artists. Its three buildings in Saint-Michel sit at the heart of the country's most unlikely industrial cluster—a mini-city devoted to the circus arts. The other company, Peerless Clothing, is also bustling—after all, this drab building on Pie IX Boulevard is the headquarters of the largest clothing manufacturer in North America, the world's tailor with an output of more than 80,000 suits a week, and a company that has thrived on North American free trade. But the factory in Montreal is in relative decline as most of its men's suits are now being made in China and the dollar eats away at Canadian operations, which in the past have hired generations of new immigrants from Haiti, Asia, and Africa. "We have two priorities, creating success in the company and keeping jobs in the country," says Tony Nardi, Peerless Clothing's straight-talking corporate controller, in a *Globe and Mail* interview. "Now they are moving in opposite directions."

In an age of Alberta and the oil sands, of a surging China and India, Montreal remains, at its core, an economic island of thread and circuses. The thread part is unravelling, as the garment trade, once the heart and soul of industrial Montreal, is undermined by a rising dollar. Yet the circus is thriving, part of an arts-and-culture scene in Montreal that has given the world Céline Dion, the band Arcade Fire, the Formula One Grand Prix, the jazz festival, and the Cirque itself, as well as a number of smaller circus troupes. Not to mention the four major universities that have turned the island of Montreal into a youth culture, a 24/7 carnival of smart, young, sexy people.

The Cirque is part of an information-and-arts sector that in 2006 employed about 100,000 people in Montreal, according to Statistics Canada. This number is far below the 245,000 jobs created by the manufacturing sector. But manufacturing has lost tens of thousands of jobs, while the arts have been stable and, in some areas, growing strongly. It is a startling reversal because the garment trade, in particular, was one of the industries that contributed mightily to the vibrant industrial life of twentieth-century Montreal. The needle trade, the legendary *shmatte* trade of Jewish Montreal, survived the rust-belt deterioration that destroyed other industries, and has hung on—by a thread. More recently, manufacturers have pushed into the style business, shifting up-market and performing high-end design activities in Montreal.

The transition has not spared the new Canadians who inhabit the Saint-Michel quarter. Once a farming community, the quarter was torn up in the early twentieth century to create garbage dumps and gravel quarries to service the growing needs of the metropolis. Its materials helped build modern Montreal, including the Autoroute Métropolitaine. And as the quarries ran out, manufacturing settled in, drawing on a rising population of immigrants who settled into the tidy bungalows and low-slung apartment buildings. Today, about 60,000 people live in the quarter, 42 per cent of them immigrants, and many of whom got their first Canadian jobs working at Peerless Clothing. At Peerless, they took English classes, learned new trades, and even officially became citizens in ceremonies held in the plant. Many of them quickly moved on to new jobs, but Peerless gained a reputation as a kind of nurturing place for new Canadians.

Today, the district is more renowned for its new players—the Cirque, the National Circus School, and Tohu, a community centre with performance spaces, partly funded by governments and an association of circus performers. Yet Cirque du Soleil chief executive officer Daniel Lamarre is not thinking about Montreal as his market, but of Asia, particularly Macao, the city-state on the China coast that has overtaken Las Vegas as the world's gambling supercentre. In his view, Macao still lags far behind Vegas in top-calibre nightclub entertainment and so the Cirque is putting a permanent show into the territory. "If it works, we will have perhaps a dominant position there, as we have in Vegas," Lamarre says.

The Cirque was founded twenty-five years ago by a couple of friends, both street performers in Montreal. One of the friends, Guy Laliberté, had left his middle-class home at fourteen. His father was an Alcan vice-president but young Guy became a fire-eater and a circus entrepreneur. He bought out his partner and built a billion-dollar fortune on lithe acrobatics, a finger on the popular pulse, and a huge dollop of Las Vegas glitz. The Cirque is a big player in Vegas. In fact, Vegas is the ideal venue for Montreal's great middle-brow entertainment exports of the twenty-first century, the Cirque and Céline. Now the Cirque has a touring show in Shanghai and big hopes for permanent sites in Tokyo, Macao and Dubai. It is not thinking of a low-cost Asia, but an Asia of rising middle classes with disposable incomes that are ripe for the Cirque's brand of theatre that has taken the circus concept beyond sawdust and animal acts. That vision has attracted the government of Dubai as a minority shareholder in the Cirque which some Quebecers feel is just the precursor to a full takeover.

This expansion will not be at the expense of Montreal, Lamarre insists. Every new show in Asia produces jobs in Montreal, where the Cirque does its creative and development work before it sends its spectacles on the road. Montreal is part of the Cirque's identity and its brand, and represents a huge investment. Still, Lamarre sounds like any harried Canadian exporter when he says the Alberta-charged dollar is affecting him in a major way. Ninety per cent of the Cirque's expenses are in Canadian dollars while more than half its revenue is earned in depreciating U.S. dollars. So would the Cirque shift some jobs out of Montreal? "It would be the smart business decision, maybe, but it will be the wrong decision for us because we will lose this spirit that we have here," Lamarre told me in an interview for the *Globe and Mail*. That spirit is essential to the Cirque's culture, he argues—and it's highly visible in the diverse crowd of athletic, tattooed and sometimes pink-haired people who roam through its reception area.

That eclectic spirit was the vision of Laliberté, who moved his circus business to a Saint-Michel landfill site in 2000, out of downtown Montreal. As the company grew, he recruited Lamarre, a former reporter and public relations executive, to run the business while Laliberté remains the creative sparkplug. I have watched Lamarre's wardrobe change over the years, from subdued brown suede jackets in his early years at the Cirque to zany striped garments that give him the look of a funky ringmaster—which, of course, in a way, he is.

And the company he co-heads has grown substantially in Montreal. The Cirque has built three connected head office buildings, as well as a residence with 125 rooms to accommodate touring artists from all over the world. It is now a $700 million business that employs about 4,000 people, of whom more than 1,500 are in Montreal. At one time or another, most of its people pass through Montreal. As new productions are added, employment numbers will rise, and those additions will be based in Montreal, at least in the initial periods of their employment. In essence, Montreal has run away to join the circus, but the reality it has left behind is troubling.

Only fifteen minutes away from the Cirque du Soleil, at Peerless Clothing, Elliot Lifson and Tony Nardi are engaged in a lively debate that's replayed over and over in Montreal's garment industry. What is the future of Peerless's manufacturing operations in Montreal?

Nardi, the corporate controller, broods over what he sees on Peerless's financial statements. Peerless is a private family company, but if it were a public company with twitchy shareholders, the Montreal operations would be a quarter of its current size, Nardi argues. "Dollar to dollar, it makes no sense to keep this factory open," he says at one point. "You make the same suit overseas and you make twice the amount of money."

Lifson, the vice-chairman, is an ebullient veteran of the Montreal garment industry. He argues that the head office and factory on Pie IX Boulevard is a repository of knowledge and expertise that Peerless must nurture if it is to maintain its global pre-eminence in men's suits. I must admit I am a friend of Elliot Lifson—it is hard not to like this happy warrior of the needle trade. On my visits to Peerless, Elliot has been my tour guide through the organized mayhem of this frantic, sprawling polyglot factory. He comes out of a Montreal garment family, teaches management at McGill, and has been a passionate defender of the industry against brutal economics, negligent government, and wacky tariff regimes, which have penalized companies for importing raw textiles for manufacturing in Canada, but not finished clothing. It's been a killer situation for any company that wants to manufacture here.

I have also seen this huge factory on Pie IX Boulevard decline in employment numbers in the face of Chinese and other Asian competition. At my most recent visit for the *Globe and Mail*, Peerless had three Montreal managers travelling to visit factories in China. It was evidence, Lifson says, that the company relies heavily on its homegrown management to bolster its import capability. Without the Pie IX factory, Peerless could not make smart decisions on Chinese manufacturing, he said. But the fact remained that the managers were examining manufacturing sites in China, not Quebec, Ontario, or even North Carolina.

Elliot's view is that manufacturing can thrive in Montreal if it moves up the value chain, and Peerless has been successful in doing that. So has Jack Victor, another Montreal suit-maker that managed to avoid producing any garments in China by maintaining its high-value, quality image. Also, importing suits from Asia involves longer distances, extra inventory and bigger warehouses—and as the price of oil spirals upward, the costs of moving stuff over long distances can be oppressive. Meanwhile, a Canadian operation can provide fast turnarounds for North American retailers. But Peerless competes heavily on production costs—it is a contract supplier and not a brand name on its own, as is Cirque du Soleil.

Peerless's owner, Alvin Segal, has been adept at playing the global-trade game. He saw the 1989 free-trade agreement as a lever to open the U.S. market. Today, Peerless sells 80 per cent of its production into the United States under such labels as Calvin Klein, Ralph Lauren, Izod, and various store brands. Then, in the early years of the twentieth century, Segal saw new writing on the wall: China was entering the World Trade Organization, creating a major import threat. The Canadian dollar was beginning its fast upward ascent. At that time, none of Peerless's production was outsourced to offshore manufacturers. But in 2007, about 65 to 70 per cent of its suits came from Asia, and many of them were shipped directly to a mega-warehouse in St. Albans, Vermont.

Such nimbleness has allowed Peerless to remain successful, and its annual sales, undisclosed but likely more than $500 million, have grown considerably. The Montreal factory has been the net loser. Although operations have been bolstered by overall sales growth, the Montreal production numbers will likely continue their decline, unless the economics of fuel pricing create conditions for a comeback. Peerless may still be making suits on Pie IX Boulevard in ten years, but its managers cannot predict the exact shape or size of that operation.

The hope is that as the city loses more of its once-vibrant needle trade, it will adapt by moving into a new world of value-added manufacturing, including a resurgent aerospace industry. The other hope is that it will fill the gap with high-end services— the creative sector, video game development, arts, and entertainment—indeed, replace manufacturing with circuses.

And what is wrong with that? Montreal has made its choice and will live with it. It will always be a dynamic place, an educational centre, and a cultural haven in the francophone world. It will try to sell its verve and talent to the world. Montreal's most important tycoon today is not Laurent Beaudoin, the venerable builder of Bombardier's transportation empire, but that son of an Alcan vice-president, Guy Laliberté, the great builder of spectacles. That appears to be Montreal's quintessential business of the twenty-first century, as a place that does not make things but makes events. Can a great city subsist on circuses? That is yet to be determined.

There is a little bit of Alberta in downtown Montreal, in a mundane office building, just at the edge of Chinatown. With every upward twitch of the oil price, with every barrel of dirty crude produced in Fort McMurray, the company that occupies this building becomes a more attractive option in the global energy spectrum. This is Montreal's version of EnCana—a homegrown champion—but it is classically Quebecois: government-owned, bureaucratic, sometimes clumsy and opaque as an organization. It is an instrument of industrial strategy, but more than anything it is a creature of Quebec's geography, which has given it a surfeit of rivers that can be harnessed for clean, renewable energy. If Quebec has any competitive advantage over Alberta, it is in the vast supply of water—fast-flowing river water that can be harnessed and dammed and turned into megawatts and shipped to markets in Canada and, most profitably, the United States.

The company that manages this great gift is the massive Hydro-Québec power utility, and it is run by a man who may be just as influential in Canada's energy game as Rick George, Randy Eresman, and the branch-plant CEOs of Imperial Oil or Shell. He is Thierry Vandal, the slim, elegant sheik of Rue Ste-Catherine. Montreal's fortunes ebb and flow, Quebec's economy is generally stagnating, governments come and go, both separatist and federalist, but Hydro-Québec rolls on like its rivers. It is a reminder that physical geography, above all, counts in an economy like Canada's. Hong Kong or Singapore may excel as flourishing islands of capitalism without the benefit of resources, but this sprawling country is all about trees, rock, sand, and water. Success in Canada is all about how you manage your geographic good fortune, and Alberta and Quebec enjoy uncommonly good luck—Alberta in its fossil fuels and Quebec in its free-flowing rivers. They offer two distinctly opposing models, one defiantly private sector, and the other, just as defiantly, state-owned.

Finely built, elegantly tailored, and movie-star handsome, Vandal is often described as the second-most important man in Quebec after the premier, but he is unfailingly humble. "Hydro-Québec is a large corporation in Quebec but we have a shareholder—it's the government," he says.

So it's clear who the boss is? I ask.

"Voilà," he says, with a smile. It is also clear he is a unique kind of Quebec manager, so much so that he may not be the utility's CEO for long. You can't help thinking a political career may be in Vandal's future. Even as you read this, he may have embarked on another destiny.

Vandal suffers from none of the parochialism that afflicts a lot of the Quebec elite. He was born in Germany to a Quebecois mother and to a Franco-American father of Quebec origins. His father's family, like that of many other French Canadians, emigrated to Massachusetts and settled in Easthampton, not too far from Lowell, Massachusetts, where that other famous Quebec-American, Jack Kerouac, the author of the beat classic *On the Road,* was born.

Vandal's father also hit the road—back to Canada where he joined the military, got married, and moved the family to a Canadian military base in Germany, where Thierry was born forty-seven years ago. The family moved around a lot, living for a while in Winnipeg, Quebec City, and Ottawa.

The young Thierry, fluently bilingual, got his engineering education at the Université de Montréal and, during the summers, joined the trek of young Quebecers to work on Hydro-Québec's James Bay facility, *le grand projet* of its time. He is part of a generation that was moulded by René Lévesque's nationalization of the private power companies to create a massive provincial utility. René's "children" grew up with Hydro-Québec as the central engine of economic development, part of the trinity that also included the Caisse de dépôt pension fund and the Desjardins caisse populaire movement.

And now Vandal plans to pass his own legacy to a new generation wise in the ways of wind power, battery technology, and $100-plus per-barrel oil. "I hope that people will look back and say that these guys—myself and my team—they did a great job," Vandal muses. "That we took the *flambeau* [the torch] and passed it on to the next generation. The organization that we turn over is going to be a little more efficient, a little more profitable, a little more successful commercially than the one we inherited."

He dabbled a bit in Liberal campus politics as a student, but Vandal's first job after engineering school was in Halifax with Shell Canada. Then he moved around between Toronto and Montreal before leaving Shell for Gaz Métropolitain, the big Quebec gas distribution company. He did well there, and came under the mentoring eye of the CEO André Caillé. When Caillé went over to Hydro-Québec in the 1990s, Vandal followed.

Caillé's mandate was to fix Hydro-Québec, an institution

that had lost its way in an era when traditional utilities, from Ontario Hydro to BCE, were dazzled by new technology, including the Internet, and disillusioned by their own staid, mature businesses. So Hydro-Québec made a big move towards becoming a telecommunications carrier. It was a disaster. Vandal was part of the team that got the company back on track as a mainstream power utility. When Caillé had finished his job, Vandal succeeded him as CEO.

He reached the top at a time when energy can no longer be considered a uniform, undifferentiated commodity—not when oil is $100 a barrel or more. Energy is a product as rarefied as a bottle of fine wine, and it costs about as much. It is a highly segmented industrial product—it can be manufactured, it can be refined, it can be clean, it can be dirty, it can be green, it can be brown, it can be hydroelectric, it can be hydrocarbon—and increasingly, consumers will demand the kind of power that most appeals to their needs, their convenience, and their environmental tastes. The power that sells in California is not the same as what will sell in China. The successful vendor of energy is a company that can position itself with a brand and identity that appeals to the most discriminating tastes. It is what Vandal understands when he talks about Hydro-Québec's role as a renewable-energy company. It is all about hydro, wind, and battery power—and maybe a little nuclear. This is market positioning and branding for a green era, and it is something that Alberta's oil sands don't quite get yet. Yet they will have to, if they want to sell energy to increasingly fussy segments of the U.S. market. Hydro-Québec exports billions of dollars' of power to New England every year and it has plans for a major transmission line into Ontario's congenitally screwed-up energy market. And you're not going to hear any gripes about Dirty Hydro from the environmental crowd.

Yet Vandal admitted to the *Globe and Mail* that he totally misjudged the market for nuclear energy. "I was among others who were convinced that nuclear would disappear, that the day of nuclear is behind us, and here we are either in the midst or outset of a nuclear renaissance." Now that he is proven wrong he has no plans for new nuclear investments, beyond refurbishing the single plant Hydro-Québec owns. Vandal likes to quote Napoleon who said that all politics are basically about geography. And in Quebec, "we have a geography that is well suited to water, but also to wind and other potential renewables. With water and wind we can see ourselves far out in time, so the question of nuclear is not a question that we need to address from the perspective of investing—but it is one we are addressing from the impact on our markets."

Vandal believes that expensive oil will ultimately spell the precipitous decline, perhaps the end, of the internal combustion engine. He talks about hybrid autos going to the next step—developing cash-back hybrids that connect to the power grid but also become a source of power at certain times during the day. Using the Internet and global positioning systems, these electric cars can operate as moving power plants that attach to the power grid in an efficient way. "The car of the future will not only draw from the grid but push back during those very short periods when you actually need that burst of power. It recognizes that people use their cars very little, maybe an hour a day, and the rest of the time it is stationed somewhere where you can probably plug it in."

Vandal also keeps a close eye on Hydro-Québec's polar-opposite model in Alberta. He remembers his father working for the Canadian military in western Canada and coming home with stories of these massive tar sands, which would be a huge future source of energy. Clearly, the son sees Hydro-Québec offering the clean alternative to the dirty oil of the Athabasca. He bristles when reminded of Hydro-Québec's image problems for strong-arming native groups and pushing through mega-projects that alter the northern Quebec terrain. Cloaking itself in green seems strange for a company that despoils northern lands.

"I will challenge you on the word despoiled," he snapped at me in an interview for the *Globe*. While acknowledging that some portions of the habitat are different than they were back before the 1970s, the land has not been laid to waste, he insists. He brings a lot of outsiders to James Bay—bankers, environmentalists, and aboriginal leaders from across the world. He insists he has never heard a word on the flights back about how Hydro-Québec is being heavy-handed with natives or the environment.

The geography is different than in other areas of intense hydroelectric development, such as Brazil's Amazon region where the flooding of rivers damages biodiversity and soil formations. "In terms of flooding, yes, it has happened, but if you go around James Bay, there are no fewer fish habitats or fish numbers than before," he says. "Yes, you are installing a dam but you are making sure fish habitats are more productive than before and making sure the aboriginal communities have more access to fishing and hunting lands than ever before."

Vandal complains that there is another myth about Hydro-Québec, that it has touched every river in Quebec with its hydro development. "But the number of rivers in Quebec measures in the thousands and we're present on only fifty rivers," he says.

Yes, but fifty rivers is a lot of intrusion and there will be more. Hydro-Québec is tackling its next big project, the $5 billion Eastmain project that will divert the Rupert River in northern Quebec and create four new dams and seventy-two dikes and flood 188 square kilometres of forest land along the Rupert. After all, Canada is a land of mega-projects—in Alberta, in Quebec, and in Newfoundland. Engineering always trumps rivers and lakes. And Thierry Vandal is betting that his mega-projects are shaded green, not the black colour of the Athabasca sands. In early May 2008, he signaled Hydro-Québec's ambitions by announcing, with Premier Jean Charest, a $5.5 billion investment in wind power—the largest wind energy tender ever awarded in a single block in North America, a move that would propel the utility into the front ranks of the world's wind power developers. In a juxtaposition that seemed to validate Vandal's vision, Hydro-Québec's initiative came the same week that Syncrude apologized for the death of 500 ducks on its tailing ponds. In the marketplace of world opinion, Vandal's stock is trading higher than that of the oil sands giants. In the future, that may be the most important marketplace of all.

CHAPTER 7

PLAYGROUND OF THE PETRO-RICH
The colonization of British Columbia

TAKE A WALK AROUND Lakeview Meadows, an enclave of timber-framed million-dollar homes scattered across a hillside overlooking Lake Windermere in eastern British Columbia, and the first thing you notice is that almost all the cars in the driveways are from "Wild Rose Country." They all have Alberta licence plates and they are nice cars—BMWs, Mercedes, expensive SUVs, high-end minivans. These homes are largely occupied by retired and semi-retired oilmen or by affluent young Calgary families who want a weekend place in the country.

In Invermere, B.C., Frank Kernick, the Lakeview Meadows developer, has created one of the most popular getaway places for Calgary energy executives west of, well, Canmore, Alberta, another stunning mountain town just over two hours to the east, which is Kernick's home base and where he is building another big project aimed at affluent Albertans.

Kernick has done very well by the oil sands, even though they are fifteen hours away from his Invermere development. He has capitalized mightily on the spinoff wealth effect. He came to the shores of Lake Windermere a decade ago to buy a weekend place on a lake for his own young family. Lakeside property is at a premium in this part of the world, particularly outside the protected areas of the national parks, and Kernick found 44.5 hectares on a hillside that was unimpeded by native land claims or any other complications. And it had private access to Lake Windermere.

He saw huge potential in the sandy soil, bought the land and developed 280 lots, just in time to catch the wave of wealth-creation spawned by booming Calgary and crude oil at $U.S. 100 a barrel. Ninety per cent of his lots were gobbled up by Calgary buyers, who proceeded to build a collection of some of the nicest timbered houses in the West. And the nicest of all is the one down the hill near Lake Windermere, which Frank Kernick built for himself. "It ended up perfect," he said.

Indeed it did, not just for Frank Kernick, but for all the inhabitants of Calgary West, the playground of the energy elite in the gorgeous Columbia Valley, where the places have names like Windermere and Invermere, evocative of England's Lake District with its cozy cottages, gently rounded hills, and placid lakes. There is nothing cozy about the rugged mountains that rim the valley as it extends down the east side of British Columbia before the river turns west towards the Pacific.

This stretch of eastern B.C. is a kind of western version of Ontario's Muskoka. It is a colony of Calgary's nicer neighbourhoods, in the same way that Lake Muskoka and Lake of Bays are colonies of Toronto's Rosedale and Forest Hill. Also on Lake Windermere, oil services magnate Hank Swartout has a golf course, hotel, house, and condo development. Billionaire oilman Clay Riddell has a place on the lake in Invermere. Calgary cable baron Jim Shaw used to have a place in Windermere but he sold it and moved west to Lake Okanagan, that other playground of the Alberta elite. For much of the year, he runs his Calgary communications empire almost by remote control, summoning his Calgary-based executives down to the Okanagan house for meetings about once a week.

Calgary's oil people are used to thinking big, and now they are applying this appetite for scale to recreation communities, some of them in Alberta but many more outside the province.

These are places where Calgarians go to relax, to retire, and sometimes to die. While Palm Springs is very popular and Scottsdale and Tucson are in vogue, greater Calgary now stretches west to include large tracts of British Columbia—Radium, Fairmont, and the ski town of Fernie, extending all the way to Kelowna, a popular Okanagan retirement community that feeds off that same energy-wealth dynamic. A Calgarian flying by WestJet to Kelowna can land in the B.C. city before he or she officially leaves Calgary—thanks to the magic of the hour-earlier time zone. It takes longer than the hour-long flight to Kelowna to get from some suburbs of Calgary to the city's downtown core.

Brett Wilson, the wealthy Calgary investment banker who has become a major land investor in the West, describes his portfolio this way: "I am long in oil but also long in real estate in Kelowna because Kelowna is influenced by the disposable dollars in the oil patch. Without WestJet, Kelowna would be this little place you drive to once in a while. But WestJet developed Kelowna for Calgary."

That is part of a much broader trend in which the wealth coming out of the great Alberta energy complex is spilling over into British Columbia in myriad ways, says Dan Muzyka, the dean of the Sauder School of Business at University of British Columbia. It's reflected in Albertans' purchase of second homes in B.C., but also in the massive natural gas developments in the northeastern area of the province. It can also be seen in the improvements of highways, ports and other transportation infrastructure for the movement of Alberta's resources to the West Coast and beyond. Economic forces do not recognize artificial boundaries, Muzyka says. "I am getting more and more a sense that the West is actually doing what people thought it would do for the last twenty years, which is to grow up and become more integrated."

British Columbia is feasting on this integration, but the story is more complex. It is British Columbia's happy fate to sit at the confluence of three great economic engines—the Alberta energy economy, the Chinese export powerhouse—in both people and manufactured goods—and the West Coast software, media, and film culture. It helps too to be the playground for people from other places in the world where the climate isn't so gentle, the mountains aren't so beautiful, and the skiing and hiking aren't as spectacular. After making big money in hardscrabble Fort Mc-Murray, Grande Prairie, or even Calgary, affluent Albertans flock to the areas around Victoria and the gorgeous Comox Valley. Even Vancouver, a metropolitan area of two million people, is dominated by its status as an urban colony for the world's affluent economic refugees, whether they come from Shenzhen, Mumbai, or Beverly Hills.

The pattern is the same whether you are in the Gulf Islands or on the Sunshine Coast northwest of Vancouver—people want to come here, if not to put down roots, at least to get mellow or get in shape. It creates an amazing protective bubble of prosperity in a province where, in fact, there is incredible hardship stemming from the decline of a once-powerful forestry industry, a tangible goods-producing industry that is bleeding huge puddles of red ink. British Columbia is, thus, both paradise and hell, depending on your location, your training, your age, your industry, your wealth. These tensions make it a difficult place to govern. On one hand, it is subject to the vagaries of a resource economy, with one commodity going one direction and the other into the dumps. At the time I was writing this book, it is oil and mining up, forestry down, a situation only exacerbated by the collapse of the U.S. housing market. Towns like Prince George and Port Alberni, where a generation of forestry workers is out of work, are suffering badly. But it is good times in communities that feed off natural gas discoveries, or anyplace where rich Albertans are moving in. So when the resources in the ground are risky and volatile, can a region or a province flourish because it is simply attractive to people—mobile, fun-seeking, and talented human capital from the world over?

Guy Turcotte thinks so. He is betting his considerable wealth and engineering talent on the mountainous terrain that skirts the Alberta–B.C. border. If you are an investor, you could do worse than follow the enterprising Turcotte. This shy Alberta farm boy has been on the ground floor of every big idea in the oil patch for the past twenty-five years. He took a bet on natural gas when the industry was still in its infancy, and watched it take off. He took a flier on a pipeline project that paid off big-time. And he was the executive who developed Western Oil Sands, a partner in the Athabasca Oil Sands project near Fort McMurray, before selling the company in 2007 to Marathon Oil for $6.5 billion.

"The oil sands opportunity is the biggest opportunity in the world, by probably a factor of ten bigger than the next one, in energy and wealth creation," says Turcotte, whose grandiose visions seem incongruous in a man who is so low-key and modest he has taken personality tests that reveal him to be a complete introvert.

Now Turcotte's attention, which has long been directed at both conventional and oil sands development, is focused on real estate, although he continues to maintain passive investments in energy, including wind power in the gusty south of Alberta. Not far from Frank Kernick's Lakeview Meadows, Turcotte has developed the Eagle Ranch Golf Resort overlooking the Columbia River, where he plans to bring 500 housing units on stream. According to the project's website, Eagle Ranch is the work of Turcotte's company Stone Creek Properties, "whose sole purpose is to create world-class resort properties in Mother Nature's most breathtaking place while preserving her delicate balance."

Turcotte is part of the new wave of middle-aged oil barons who, having made their fortunes, want to leverage that same engineering know-how and entrepreneurial drive into the next big strike. He has come a longer distance than most, emerging from Chauvin, Alberta, near Wainright, close to the Saskatchewan border, where he grew up on a farm with his eight siblings, a father from northern Ontario and a mother from a Quebec family transplanted to Alberta.

At eighteen, he took off for the big city, visiting Edmonton for the first time to attend the Northern Alberta Institute of Technology, where he took a diploma in natural gas technology. After he graduated he decided to get an engineering degree but the University of Alberta cancelled the summer math course he needed for admission. So he ended up at the University of Tulsa instead—a broadening experience for an Alberta farm boy. He later picked up an MBA from the U of A.

Turcotte has a knack for making money. After a couple of years working for the federal small business bank, he bought one of its borrowing clients, a woodworking business that he later sold for a profit of $50,000. That profit, and some stock market winnings, helped bankroll his first energy venture in 1981—a natural gas company that, in an act of hometown chauvinism, he called Chauvco after his birthplace.

He sold Chauvco to U.S. energy company Pioneer Natural Resources for almost a billion dollars in 1997, pocketing about $26 million for himself. By that time, he was already the prime mover behind the $3.7 billion Alliance natural gas pipeline that was being built to bring gas out of pipeline-starved northeast Alberta. The pipeline ran within a few miles of the old Turcotte homestead.

Turcotte figured he would now have some free time on his hands, but that was not to be. He was approached by some former Canadian managers of Australian resource giant Broken Hill Proprietary. They were savvy mining engineers who had the idea of helping Shell develop the promising Athabasca oil sands project, but they clearly needed a seasoned executive to help them raise money. They approached Turcotte and he took over what became Western Oil Sands. He brought new investors into Western Oil Sands, including the Richardsons of Winnipeg.

When the oil sands company was sold to Marathon in 2007, he was finally free to develop what had become his obsession for more than fifteen years—mountain real estate. It appealed to Turcotte's money-making instincts, but also to his engineer's sense of making things work, of tinkering and trying things, just as he had done in the oil sands.

The Eagle Ranch project started to take shape in Invermere, but Turcotte's grand obsession is a chunk of property that he had part owned for fifteen years, when he first walked across a stunning stretch of forest on the slope overlooking Canmore, Alberta, then a modest mountain town with some tourist cachet. He and a group of partners, who included the late transportation tycoon Bud McCaig and oilman Gordon Stollery, bought the land and, over the years, his company began to develop the site, called Silver Tip, for some private homes. Turcotte eventually bought out his partners.

While Invermere's Eagle Ranch is a nice golf course project, Turcotte saw the Canmore land as a concept for the ages. He travelled to Europe to try to find the right design for the upper reaches of his property. He targeted the villages of the Alps, moving from Switzerland, to France and then into Italy. He had never been to Tuscany, and he loved Siena with its grand square and town hall. His imagination was stirred by the long skinny villages atop the Tuscan hills. It was a fine day when he motored out to the village of San Gimignano and to the forest of medieval towers that had made it the darling of a million tourist postcards. Turcotte found his answer in the town square, the archways, the timber-framed buildings, the outdoor market. "This place just felt right," he says. "It felt timeless. It's probably a thousand years old, but this architecture looks as good today as back then. We took three thousand pictures." And he brought them all back to Calgary.

He decided to build the New World version of San Gimignano, a half-mile-long village of squares, towers, and stone abodes on the side of the Rocky Mountains. Turcotte still keeps an investment interest in his pipeline company and an Afghan oil venture. His offices are a little cubbyhole on 17th Avenue SW in Calgary, but his dreams are of building timeless monuments. Building plans are scattered over his desk, and he has a picture book of Tuscan towns with bookmarks opening to striking photos. He has hired eight architects, including Italian and French designers.

"This is probably one of the most complex things I've had to pull out of the ground," says the man who built grand pipeline and oil sands projects. "But it is very neat because it has a lot of complexity and my mind likes working on things that have challenges."

He is thinking that it will cost $1.5 billion over the next decade to build his dream village, which will contain 1,300 residential units. "We want this thing to still be around 300 or 400 years from now," says Turcotte, who is fifty-five years old. Critics will say that a Tuscan villa looks wildly out of place in the natural rustic beauty of a Canadian mountainside. But Turcotte argues that the designs are eternal and universal, and he will build using local stone and wood.

Will this be his final legacy? "If you want to call it that," he says. "I've been involved here so long that I really didn't want to screw up the village. Because this piece of dirt is so spectacular." And it takes an oil sands engineer to know great dirt.

If Albertans own a growing share of eastern B.C., the Comox Valley on Vancouver Island, and the Okanagan Valley in the interior, one man can be said to control the rest of the province. He is known as Jimmy, a small happy warrior who is B.C.'s last great tycoon, an owner of forests in the north-central Skeena, grocery stores in Fernie, and tourist sites all the way to Niagara Falls, Ontario.

Jimmy Pattison will have turned eighty in 2008, and he hasn't changed his work habits since he was eighteen, hustling his way through college by selling cars. He is still pushing hard, still checking over income statements, still staying in inexpensive hotels as he travels by business jet across the continent, keeping his eye on his $6 billion empire of forestry, fish, supermarkets, billboards, and tourist sites. He owns a place in Palm Springs that used to belong to Frank Sinatra but still comes home to North Vancouver and takes his big boat for a jaunt around the Gulf Islands.

Jimmy Pattison, a Saskatchewan kid who grew up poor and moved to the West Coast when he was seven, is one of the last links to an old Vancouver that boasted a coterie of homegrown titans who had their base camps in the lower B.C. mainland. The great families have faded—the MacMillans, Woodwards, Bentleys, and Gibsons, among others. When I asked Pattison if he was indeed the last of the West Coast titans, he gave that trademark aw-shucks Jimmy smile and said: "I don't think so but anyway ... you can say what you want." Which I think means: it's not that far off the mark.

Perhaps the only B.C. titan who approaches Jimmy's stature is Vancouver mining baron Norman Keevil. But Keevil lost his big chance in 2006, when his company Teck Cominco could not nail the financing to take over Inco, the Toronto-based nickel giant, thus losing the battle to a Brazilian company. It meant a squandered opportunity to create a nickel and base metals giant in Canada, and it was a huge blow to the entire country. It would have put Vancouver on the map again as a head office centre, but that was not to be.

There is also Brandt Louie, the scion of a 110-year-old Chinese-Canadian family dynasty that controls retailer London Drugs, a charter airline, supermarkets, and assorted other businesses. The son of the dynamic builder Tong Louie, Brandt Louie is the best known of the low-key Chinese business community that is powerful but without a public profile to match its economic clout. This is a group to watch over the next decade. As for the old forestry barons, they are slowly leaving the scene and there are no replacements—except perhaps Jimmy.

He remains the last important businessman to call Vancouver his permanent home. While his empire spans North America, and he is aggressively buying U.S. assets, more than 60 per cent of his $6 billion of annual revenue and $3.3 billion in assets are generated in Canada. That includes a wide swath of the B.C. economy. He employs, directly and indirectly, close to 20,000 people in the province, and creates countless more jobs for suppliers and partners.

This is all very impressive and yet it is a drop in the bucket compared with the heyday of MacMillan Bloedel, a forestry company that at its peak from the 1950s to the 1960s controlled 30 per cent of the B.C. economy. Its founder, Harvey Reginald MacMillan—known as HR, much like Pattison is just Jimmy—came out of rural Ontario to become British Columbia's chief forester before moving into the private sector and buying up companies until he was the top dog on the West Coast.

Not only that, he and his related families involved in MacMillan Bloedel, such as the Southams, Foleys, and Flavelles, were the big swinging titans of the city. They funded new parks, art galleries, and university chairs. Over the years, MacBlo has taken on almost mythic status, so much so that it is generally agreed that the most tragic date in Vancouver's history, the date that rivals the launch of the NEP in Calgary, was October 28, 1999. That is Vancouver's day of infamy, the point when shareholders approved the sale of MacMillan Bloedel to U.S. giant Weyerhaeuser Co.

It tore a major head office out of Vancouver, but also ripped away B.C.'s most venerable company, the cornerstone of its economy. That was the culmination of a long painful process that had begun almost thirty years earlier when MacBlo passed from its Vancouver founding families to outside investors. The gradual loss of local control culminated in the 1981 takeover by Noranda Inc., a conglomerate based in Toronto. It was never the same. The Weyerhaeuser deal eighteen years later and the final loss of the head office simply confirmed that trend of decline in Vancouver, in the forestry industry and in the B.C economy. In the politically charged B.C. environment, many observers blamed the decline on sour labour relations and the high costs of taxes and regulations, but it was a host of things that brought B.C. down.

MacBlo itself was unimaginative and uncreative. It did not seize the opportunity to get bigger, so that when it was sold, it was the twenty-fifth-largest forestry company in the world—hardly a position of competitive advantage. Sources in the forestry industry say MacBlo simply failed to step up as a major consolidator, leaving it vulnerable to takeover. Indeed, it exhibited the same pattern of listless timidity that has allowed the Canadian mining industry to fall into foreign hands. Its management was not alert to new opportunities—for example, it clung to its forest base in B.C.'s high-cost coastal area, and failed to make inroads in the interior, as other companies did.

The one major plus was its research group, which had developed *parallam*, a revolutionary form of engineered wood. Parallam has been one of the major innovations in the industry, but the research group was closed down, not by Weyerhaeuser but by Tom Stephens, the Denver-based restructuring ace who, in the late 1990s, was brought in to improve MacBlo's financial results and ultimately sold the company. "There was a mere skeleton left in Vancouver at the end," says Otto Forgacs, the former vice-president of technology, in an interview he did with me for the *Globe and Mail*. Since then, Weyerhaeuser has built on the old MacBlo innovation to develop a strong market presence in engineered wood.

Since MacBlo was sold in 1999, the erosion of head offices in Vancouver has rolled on unabated, as many major companies have fallen to outside buyers. Between 1999 and 2005, Vancouver lost 30 per cent of its head office jobs, the largest percentage loss among major Canadian cities, according to Statistics Canada.

The end of MacBlo simply mirrored a wave of changes in B.C. It was no longer a head office centre and it wasn't the forestry province it used to be. The southern hemisphere, and the southern U.S., had taken over. Then it was hit by a number of shocks, including a softwood lumber trade dispute that restricted exports to the key U.S. market. There followed a devastating decline in the newsprint market, that was both cyclical and structural. Next the mountain pine beetle tore into huge swaths of forest. Add to that a crippling downturn in the U.S. housing market that by mid-2008 was threatening to inflict a global recession. With these body blows to its most important industry, British Columbia should be on its knees.

And yet, strangely enough, it isn't. Vancouver, in particular, has prospered, with some of the highest incomes, the richest real estate, and the highest immigration rates in the country. Indeed, that has been part of its success: the influx of smart, often wealthy people—some from Alberta, but many from Asia, Europe, and the United States—to live in what is among the world's most beautiful major cities. Vancouver's lifestyle has also attracted a different kind of labour force, a lifestyle-seeking knowledge worker, not with pinstripes and a BMW, but hiking shorts and a mountain bike.

And this kind of worker has attracted a different kind of business—environmental, youth-oriented, knowledge-based, creative. The quintessential Vancouver company of today is not a forestry head office but an apparel company that makes yoga gear, or a co-operative that sells outdoor clothing and equipment.

Vancouver is the only place in Canada to which employers come because of the labour force, rather than where the labour force comes because of the employer. The oil sands represent the old resources model in which Newfoundland workers flock to a boomtown on the Athabasca River to make $100,000 in no time flat and then get out of town as quickly as they can. But B.C.'s Lower Mainland is the new kind of boomtown, where people are the valuable resource. Workers used to come to B.C. from Ontario, Nova Scotia, or Saskatchewan to work in the forests and mines—and, to some extent, they still do. But now employers come to B.C. to mine the smart, cool workers who proliferate in Vancouver, Victoria, the Okanagan, and the islands.

The ultimate role model for this kind of migration is Electronic Arts, the largest video-game maker in the world, which is based in Redwood City, California, but operates a campus carved out of a hillside in suburban Burnaby, B.C., with a breathtaking view of the mountains on Vancouver's North Shore. Spend a few minutes in the complex's vast lobby and you know you are not in Fort McMurray. There are all the amenities, including a full soccer field, a beach volleyball pit, and interior and exterior basketball courts. It looks like a well-groomed college campus, rather than a development branch of a U.S. multinational.

With 1,500 people, the Burnaby facility is the largest of three Canadian studios operated by EA, which also has a studio in a high-rise in downtown Vancouver, where what may be Canada's richest cultural export, the $2 billion driving game called Need for Speed, was created—not Group of Seven art, not even Cirque du Soleil, but a video game. The world is truly changing.

Electronic Arts is not always an easy place to work, especially when deadlines approach for launching new games. The U.S. parent has incurred a class action suit for the extreme work hours it expects of its people. But in the vast Burnaby campus, there is a West Coast vibe to the place. Everyone is walking his or her dog, from whippets to mongrels, all of which are welcome in the workplace as long as they can behave. And the place where they work is no assembly-line factory but is chopped into about fifty small development areas, each of which operates as a single business devoted to game design.

Electronic Arts is part of a burgeoning new media industry in British Columbia that consists of 1,100 companies, ranging from the tiniest one-person operation to giants like EA. The video-gaming industry in Vancouver has been a growth industry since the early 1980s when there was a proliferation of game designers. One of them was Don Mattrick, who founded a company called Distinctive Software in the basement of his parents' home in Burnaby. In 1992, Mattrick merged his company with California-based EA, and, for many years, was an executive with the U.S. company, helping spearhead its growth in Vancouver and internationally.

Instead of becoming a branch plant, EA in Vancouver has become progressively more important as a source of game development. The parent company has invested heavily in the new campus, as well as the downtown location. The reason is that Vancouver has a large supply of smart young people who like to play video games. They are a source not only of employees but also of the army of game testers who vet every new hockey, football, or action game. In all, there are about eighty-five Vancouver game studios, generating about $1.4 billion in annual revenue.

They are populated by people like Rory Armes, who you would think would finally be thinking of doing something useful at the age of forty-five, instead of playing video games. "Every day I wake up and say I have to play more," says Armes, the Electronic Arts general manager who oversees the Vancouver development sites as well as a companion site in Montreal. Armes is the perfect example of the kind of person who calls Vancouver home: he has worked in the business for twenty years, but he still exhibits the hyper-enthusiasm of the kid gamer. His favourite line when he comes into a meeting is: "Wouldn't it be cool if . . ." He actually talks about the "spitballing" of a creative idea.

Mattrick has moved on. In 2007, he jumped to Microsoft as senior vice president of interactive entertainment. He said he would live in Vancouver and commute to the Redmond, Washington, home of Microsoft. In fact, his new employer is commuting the other way, widening its imprint in Vancouver by opening a development centre to draw skilled high-technology workers from around the world.

Microsoft's reasoning reflects Vancouver's other great strength: it is the entry point for thousands of students with computer science degrees, many of them coming to Canada from India, China, and the Asia-Pacific region. Microsoft Canada president Phil Sorgen told the *Globe and Mail* that: "Vancouver has a very strong connection and a very strong link to that part of the world."

It is a striking manifestation of Vancouver's biggest competitive advantage—it is close to Asia, not just in geography and shipping lanes, but in its spirit and the composition of its population. Microsoft simply follows the trail to Vancouver blazed by other technology companies that have located studios there— whether EA or Walt Disney Co., or the French firm Vivendi. The post–9/11 crackdown on U.S. immigration and the backlash against foreign technology workers have boosted Vancouver's status as a home of smart people—and it's a short flight from L.A.

This status will only be augmented by the 2010 Winter Olympics, which is a perfect kind of B.C. event. It is triggering a cascade of infrastructure improvements, so that, for example, Whistler should become much more accessible as the Sea to Sky Highway undergoes a radical upgrade for the games. In fact, B.C. is reaping the rewards from two simultaneous infrastructure waves: one is flowing from the Olympics, and the other reflects its positioning as Canada's Gateway to the Pacific and ultimately to China.

So, of the old B.C. titans, only Jimmy remains, running his North American businesses from his small downtown head office with its staff of eight. He is a collector of businesses all over North America, but Jimmy is committed to his hometown. He is really a softie about Vancouver, hard to believe for a guy who as a car dealer used to fire the last salesman on his charts every month. He salvaged the Expo 1986 World's Fair in Vancouver, and he has been picking up more shares in the forest giant he controls, Canfor, when the stock was in the dumps. For Jimmy, it is all about buying when a stock is in disfavour, because he is a long-term thinker. And he has been very long-term in his vision for Vancouver and B.C.

In the midst of the subprime debacle in the winter of 2007–2008 he told me he was looking at new investments: "We are looking now on a selected basis, but either way [the market] goes, we're ready for it. When I say ready for it, if things take a real serious dive, well, that's the opportunity. Opportunity comes when things are at the very worst and everyone's fearful—including me."

It is classic Jimmy, who in his sunny upbeat way is a master of telling reporters what they think are deep insights but on closer examination, are smoke and mirrors: Buy low, sell high, Jimmy says. Where have we heard that before?

In British Columbia, he is bigger than all outdoors and he is in the final run of his great career. When he goes, the Pattison Group will likely be broken up because Jimmy does not believe in family dynasties. He has two daughters who do not work for the Pattison Group and one son in the business, but Jimmy Jr. will not inherit control of the company. When Jimmy Sr. passes from the scene, B.C. will lose its last tycoon and the province will be smaller because of it. It will lose another great character, and B.C., once a province that grew characters as profusely as Douglas firs, will be much poorer.

It will not be an apocalyptic crisis like the loss of MacBlo. There will be no sense that the soul has been ripped out of the province. As British Columbia has lost head offices, as its forest industry has eroded, it has actually become more affluent and more successful. That is because of branding. It has managed to brand itself as one of the most attractive places in the world to live. When Alberta's oil men tire of Edmonton's endless winters, or Calgary's barren downtown, they come West.

Is that enough in an age of mobile capital and labour? It's a pretty good start, as long as it is accompanied by smart taxation, trade, and industrial policies. When B.C.'s Liberal government imposed a carbon tax in a recent budget, the first in Canada, it was a pioneering step, a bold move that was broadly applauded. However the carbon tax plays out in an age of expensive oil, it was, above all, a branding maneuver. It positioned B.C. as a progressive, environmentally activist, twenty-first-century jurisdiction. It appealed to its most important customers—the smart people who would want to live and work in a city like Vancouver or Victoria—or in Kelowna, for that matter. Alberta hasn't figured that out, which is why it is in danger of losing its millionaires. Calgary has lots of head offices, lots of money, lots of smart engineers, but it isn't a place where people, if they had their choice, would avidly want to live. Neither are a lot of other affluent places in the world. For the first time, B.C. may be assuming its natural role in Canada—as the brand name for new ideas. And one of these ideas is a closer economic relationship with the emerging powerhouse to its immediate east.

※

The Calgary financier Murray Edwards once described to me the travails of one of his holdings, a mining company called Imperial Metals that operates a couple of mines in British Columbia. In the late 1990s, Imperial was planning to open a new copper/nickel mine in northern British Columbia and it needed a milling operation to go along with it. So it heard that one of Noranda's mines was closing down in the Gaspé region of Quebec. Imperial would buy the milling equipment, break it up in pieces, load it on trucks, and ship it across the country. The one problem was the loads would have to be oversized and they would have to get special authorization to travel over every province's roads. Thus began a bureaucratic voyage through the intricate hell of Canadian provincial regulations. First up was Quebec, which, according to Edwards, approved the passage, as long as Imperial would use Quebec welders and tradesmen to cut up the equipment so it could be loaded. Imperial felt it could go along with the plan.

Ontario said okay, as well—provided the convoy had an Ontario Provincial Police escort and the company paid the overtime. No problem with that. They got to Manitoba, which was pretty relaxed about the whole thing: pay $1,000 for the permit and put the proper flashing lights on the vehicles. In fact, it was similar in Saskatchewan and Alberta: get the permit, be safe.

Then the company went to B.C. This was the province that was going to garner a new mine, new jobs, new revenues. B.C. said it would not let the oversized vehicles on its roads. One can imagine it had something to do with the mountains, but the Imperial people said they had found a route that was not heavily travelled, and they would move the oversized loads between midnight to 4 a.m. Surely that was acceptable?

"No, it wasn't," Edwards recalled. So Imperial Metals had to relocate the oversized loads to Grande Prairie, Alberta, where it paid to have the equipment cut up into even smaller portions. Total cost for this extra work was hundreds of thousands of dollars.

Moral of this story: assume that in Canada, governments will bite the hands that feed them. Assume that the country operates as a bunch of little fiefdoms, and that for years, B.C. was one of the worst.

Edwards pointed out that this story is a decade old and things are getting better in B.C. and elsewhere—but they have not been solved. Getting rid of interprovincial barriers of all kinds would be a great first step to making all of Canada work better. Trade has become more of a north-south affair, and the United States, at least until the subprime fiasco and its fallout, has been a massive bonanza for many companies. But with Alberta, B.C., Saskatchewan, and Newfoundland in ascendance, and everyone else in the tank, surely we should be thinking about breaking up the old rigidities. It is hard to believe that, in an age of an integrated Europe, of NAFTA, and the World Trade Organization, we do not have a real Canadian common market.

In fact, there is a movement gathering force that would do just that, and it has its origins in Alberta and B.C. It is one more manifestation of the integration of these two powerhouse provinces, which will become more pronounced in the future. For the moment, at least, B.C. has a Liberal premier, Gordon Campbell, who is a kind of a mixed Alberta–B.C. kind of politician—fiscally conservative with a dash of environmental brio you don't find in energy-dominated Alberta. And the government of Alberta likes more open provincial borders to deal with some of its shortages of labour and materials. The result is TILMA, a short form for the British Columbia–Alberta Trade Investment and Labour Mobility Agreement, signed in 2006, that seeks to unite the two provincial economies in a common market that allows goods, services, and investments—and, it is hoped, labour—to move more easily between the two.

If fully realized and exploited, it would create Canada's second-largest economy with 28 per cent of the national gross domestic product, compared with 39 per cent for Ontario and 20 per cent for Quebec. It would be a market of 7.7 million people, a touch ahead of Quebec's 7.6 million but behind Ontario's imposing 12.7 million people. The special charm of TILMA is the liberalizing spirit and the anti-protection bias. Unless a provincial measure is clearly identified as an exception to the free movement of goods and services, it is subject to the rules of the agreement and therefore exposed to competition. And there is a tough dispute resolution process to give the agreement some real bite. One of the key thrusts of the document is that occupational standards in the two provinces will be reconciled so that labour can move easily across the border.

TILMA is not perfect and too many things are still exempt. There are difficult transitions ahead, and it will take a long time before every sub-trade, every profession, is open to free movement across the border. It is clearly a work in progress. But the days may be over when trucks carrying hay from Alberta to B.C. will have to unload and reload their cargos to meet B.C. regulations. It is a real start and both governments should push forward. "You will get the slipstream effect," says Daniel Muzyka, the UBC business dean. "When Alberta's economy pops up, it provides huge demand and TILMA's going to allow B.C. to link into that much faster. It's going to be quite dramatic, a true integrated free trade zone."

The real challenge will be taking it across the country, in much the same way as Murray Edwards' load of milling equipment. There have been attempts for decades to break down provincial barriers, and they have crashed against provincial lassitude or outright opposition. There is talk about taking this nationwide in a series of bilateral agreements. Saskatchewan is a certain candidate, as Manitoba may be. In fact, a Manitoba-Saskatchewan combination has been discussed in the past, going as far as talk of potential unification. But this kind of piecemeal approach would require dozens of bilateral province-to-province deals before Canada would get a common market.

Some would go even further than TILMA towards entire economic integration. J.R. Shaw is a communications tycoon who is based in Calgary—his son is the aforementioned Jim Shaw—but a good part of his cable TV empire, the second largest in

Canada, is in British Columbia. His first cable franchise outside Edmonton was in the lush Okanagan Valley. For J.R., close integration with B.C. is not just as a nice thing but a necessary thing because Alberta will need this link when its own resources begin to decline. The boom will not last forever and, for land-locked Alberta, B.C. can be a vital window to continuing prosperity.

"If I were the politicians in Alberta and B.C., I'd be looking for a merger between the two provinces," says J.R., whose folksy way of talking belies a razor-sharp business mind. "You'd have a major force; you'd develop more secondary industries. You've got the coast; you've got the ports, the imports and exports." There might be problems with who gets the capital city and all the public servants, Shaw allows, but together Alberta and B.C. would be a balanced and sustainable economy. On its own, Alberta is largely a resources province, but B.C. offers an extra dimension in tourism, mining, and the cosmopolitan energy of Vancouver and its knowledge industry. B.C.'s forestry sector is badly battered, but it has strong mining and energy resources. Above all, British Columbia is the gateway to Asia—a status tht it finally seems to appreciate—and that is its ace in the hole.

Would the West then be as powerful as Ontario? Shaw chuckles that he wasn't really thinking about who is on top: "I grew up in Ontario—I'm pretty sympathetic to Ontario." This is not, he says, a reprise of that famous 1980s Alberta bumper sticker: "Let the eastern bastards freeze in the dark." He adds that "we're one country first, but from an economic point of view, shouldn't these two provinces go together? You've got a common border, common mountains, common things—I think it makes eminent sense." And, indeed, it does.

CHAPTER 8

EAST MEETS WEST

Memory and myth along the great divide

ASK JIM GRAY ABOUT THE National Energy Program, the most hated institution in Alberta history, and he will practically spit out the words: "October 28, 1980 at 4 p.m."

That date—that time—is etched forever in the memory of the veteran Calgary oilman. It was the moment he learned that Pierre Trudeau had unveiled the NEP, a sweeping policy arsenal enabling Ottawa to impose its grand plan on the energy industry, to enforce Canadian ownership of energy assets, and, in the view of the Calgary oil industry, to confiscate wealth that belonged to Albertans and to the foreign investors in their resources.

In the war of words that followed, Gray was a passionate and charismatic figure, one of the most bitter and vociferous enemies of the NEP and defender of Alberta rights. Now in his seventies, having long ago sold his energy company, Canadian Hunter, he remains energized and outraged by the events of over twenty-five years ago.

He was my first interview for this book—in the breakfast room of the Royal York Hotel in Toronto, that bastion of eastern supremacy—and it set the stage for my research. Jim Gray is the personification of Alberta: resentful, touchy, proud, with a long memory—but also entrepreneurial, passionate, caring, a coach to hundreds of young Albertans who are learning his community-minded values. And, oh yes, he was born in Kirkland

Lake, Ontario, but, then again, Alberta is as much a state of mind as it is a geographical entity.

He is living evidence that Alberta is still a churning cauldron of grievances, particularly among a generation of people who survived the NEP; lived through the savage downturn that followed in the oil and gas business; and lost businesses, houses, and fortunes. They are the people who will never quite believe in another oil and gas boom, even one as seemingly resilient as that generated by the oil sands, and who will never again trust Ottawa and eastern Canada. When they vow never to piss it away again, what they really mean is: "We'll never let Ottawa piss it away again."

They can now feel some satisfaction in knowing this might be finally Alberta's moment—in fact, the West's moment. Jim Gray sees Canada as a sprawling dysfunctional family with Ontario and Quebec as the big brothers who are constantly beating up their younger sibling, Alberta. In fact, this sibling analogy is repeated to me over and over by Albertans. The kicker is, suddenly the younger kid has grown up and is threatening to take over the house. But will the older kids accept him? Will they once again try to seize what belongs to him? Or will the younger one have to leave home to prove himself?

If Gray is a survivor, he is also a captive, caught up in many of the myths that inhabit the soul of modern Alberta, even as it seems poised on the edge of maturity and leadership. Alberta is a province, a geography, a climate, but most of all it is an elaborate mythology. And it is also the target of mythology, in all the preconceptions—indeed, misconceptions—held by non-Albertans, particularly in Ontario and Quebec. If this country has any chance of surviving and achieving its potential, it is important to get beyond these myths. Let's take a look at some of them, starting with the images that Albertans have of themselves:

Albertans are cowboys.

This is true for about ten days in July every year, when all of Calgary turns into one big orgy of Stetsons, blue jeans, and checkered shirts—and, increasingly, pink shirts to advance the battle against breast cancer. In Alberta, "Yahoo" is not an Internet search engine but a common greeting during Stampede Week.

In reality, Stampede is mostly an opportunity to have fun, to forget yourself, to indulge in civic self-congratulation, and, for many, to get laid. Calgary investment banker Bob Dinning once told a journalist that the motto for Stampede Week is: "Drink triple; see double; act single."

Oh, there are a handful of real cowboys left and the rodeo and chuckwagon races are still a big hit. Some men and women really get into it, vying for the most extravagant shirt, the biggest hat, the most elaborate brocade on a jeans skirt. The best place to watch elite Calgary come out in style is at the Hays breakfast at Heritage Park where you might see secretive billionaire Fred Mannix in an Australian wax overcoat or Stephen Harper looking ridiculous in a western shirt. And who's that guy serving Sillabub, the inexplicable concoction of juice and motor oil served up at the picnic? It's none other than Stéphane Dion looking like he wished he was somewhere else.

There is a bit of a cowboy mentality in the politics, but more importantly, there are many prominent Albertans with cowboy roots—that is, rural roots that they embellish and glorify long after the manure has been scraped off their boots. The Stampede is a healthy reminder of where they come from and a necessary ritual tribute to the culture they have left far behind.

Until recently, there was also a bar in Calgary called Cowboys, a hoary and horny monument to rampant testosterone that hit its peak every Stampede week as thousands of young people pour through its doors. It was where Prince Harry came when he was serving at CFB Suffield and romanced a twenty-two-year-old waitress by the name of Cherie Cymbalisty. It is perhaps symbolic that Cowboys, in typical style, was demolished right after the 2007 Stampede to make way for an office tower. This is the real Alberta that lets nothing, not even a shrine to ersatz cowboy culture, stand in the way of commerce. Perhaps Albertans believe they are still living in this cowboy culture and so why fight to preserve its phony artifacts?

The reality of modern Alberta is that two-thirds of its people live in Calgary and Edmonton and they are more likely to wear suits than chaps. Alberta is increasingly industrial, capital intensive, urban, white-collar, and well educated. They will come back to the new Cowboys as it rises nearby because this is a harmless myth and it is good for tourism.

Albertans are mavericks.

There is a permanent exhibition at the Glenbow Museum in Calgary that proclaims this is a province moulded by independent thinkers, contrary dudes—indeed, mavericks. The exhibition—and the book that inspired it by Aritha van Herk—are outstanding guides to Alberta mythology, but remember that a maverick is a stray, unbranded cow that wanders away from its herd. This concept of maverick assumes that the rest of the herd acts like cattle—docile, unquestioning, easy to lead—which at times, to outsiders, seems to describe the Alberta electorate. How quickly Ontario residents forget that their province was run for forty-two years—from 1943 to 1985—by a seemingly impregnable Conservative dynasty called the Big Blue Machine.

The maverick myth does contain some reality. In the early days, Alberta was populated by people who didn't quite fit in back home—in strife-torn Ukraine of the late-nineteenth early-twentieth century, in stuffy Ontario of the 1950s, or the over-crowded tenements of Scotland. The early days of European settlement saw the arrival of remittance men from Britain, younger sons of well-off families, who would not succumb to family expectations. Many of the icons glorified at the Glenbow went against the grain—Métis guide Jerry Potts, irreverent journalist Bob Edwards, evangelist premier William Aberhart, and Eric Harvie, the lawyer whose quirky collection forms the heart of the Glenbow Museum exhibits.

Every society has its individualists, even Ontario, and Albertans also harbour some irresistible pressures to conform. In today's Alberta, there is a powerful tendency to hew to the party line, rather than strike out on one's own. And there are powerful forces driving this socialization—the Stampede, the anti-NEP sentiment, the family-friendly culture, the tradition of volunteerism. When people come off the plane from Toronto or Winnipeg, they seem to morph instantly into red-meat, anti-socialist, anti-Ottawa Albertans, no matter how lefty they were back home. In fact, some would suggest the Glenbow should have a companion exhibition to the mavericks, called the Mind-Meld— how Albertans get to think the same way on so many issues.

Yet travel a little more widely in Alberta, particularly outside Calgary, and you will find considerable diversity of opinion. Albertans disagree greatly on the environment, for example, despite easterners' view of a monolithic antipathy to any kind of ecological controls. There is a deep divide between the views of rural and urban, and north and south, Calgary and Edmonton. The province in fact seems almost paralyzed on how to spend its surplus cash because there are so many warring agendas. The energy royalty debate was a startling example of how much rural Alberta hates the Calgary energy establishment and how much Calgary misjudges the rural communities. There will be more of this diversity of viewpoints as immigration from the rest of Canada and the rest of the world continues to soar.

Many Albertans are violently apathetic about the nasty game of politics. They love family, the outdoors, community giving, but they dislike the machinations of party politics, the constant compromises, the ambiguity, and the devious processes in which they always seem to end up the loser. They portray themselves as innocents in a complex world that always seems to be run by Quebec politicians and Ontario bankers.

Or, in many cases, they are so consumed with making money that they have not picked up their heads to see what is happening in the world. Certainly that is the case with many new Albertans. In the last provincial election, there was a 21 per cent voter turnout in Fort McMurray and only 40 per cent in the province as a whole. That is the product of two unfortunate mindsets—One: "I'm not going to be in Alberta long, so why bother to get involved?" Two: "That is the way it is, and I can't change it."

Albertans are more entrepreneurial.

The announcer at the National Rodeo Championship in Edmonton put it best: the bronco riders who mount the most ornery beasts will taste one of two things—"Money or mud." That sums up Albertans' view of their business culture. They are go-for-broke types who swing in the saddle between riches and rags.

Outsiders will point out it is plumb easy to be risk-taking and adventurous when you have the biggest energy resource in the world under your feet. How can you not help being entrepreneurially successful? This is a no-win argument. Ontario is also sitting on terrific mineral deposits and rich farmland, and is buttressed by geographical fortune—proximity to the big U.S. market. That's what drove its manufacturing industry, its vast auto parts and auto assembly plants until the recent slowdown, and its financial services sector.

Nancy Knowlton, who with her husband owns Smart Technologies, a Calgary high-tech manufacturing company, explains that she had to expand her manufacturing in Ottawa because Ontario has one big geographical edge over Calgary: "In Ottawa, you're a two-day truck drive away from the largest U.S. population of people. Here in Calgary, we're a two-day drive from the largest U.S. population of deer and elk."

You just play the hand you're dealt, and no one region is better or worse at creating great companies. Albertans have done remarkably well with the hands they've been dealt. Look at the outstanding entrepreneurs who have come from somewhere else—Clay Riddell, the boy from North End Winnipeg, who has rolled the dice time after time in the Alberta oil patch and ended up a billionaire with a big stake in the Mackenzie Delta and a bunch of high-end Calgary eateries. J.R. Shaw left the shelter of a nice family business in southwestern Ontario to build the number-two cable TV franchise in Canada. Murray Edwards was born to a less-than-affluent Regina family, and now dominates the oil patch.

For many restless types, Alberta offers an escape valve, a fresh start, a new opportunity with a lack of establishment and parental restraints. In Alberta, they are less likely to ask what school you went to, what your mother's maiden name is, what clubs you joined, and where your family lives. They may, however, ask you how much cash you're earning in the oil sands—it's about what you are doing now, not what your family did back then. There are more up-from-the-bootstraps strivers and fewer family dynasties. The only multi-generation family wealth that matters much in Alberta are the Southerns, who have built their empire on utility trailers and now own utility companies, and the Mannixes, whose private business dealings are guarded with fierce intensity. Otherwise, wealthy people tend to have risen from poverty to extreme affluence in one generation. The province is simply too young for dynasties, and the boom-and-bust pattern in the oil patch means it is not uncommon to win and lose fortunes several times in a lifetime—to piss it away and win it back.

If the province is such an easy place to make money, why doesn't everybody come out here? In fact, Alberta is more likely to attract a certain breed who like wide-open spaces, the sense of freedom, the low tax rates. It is that openness that drew Bob Dhillon, the Japan-born son of a Sikh trading family that had lost all its wealth from political confiscation in Liberia, West Africa. After growing up in Vancouver, he set up shop in Calgary, buying and renovating apartment buildings, because it is an open society, and maybe even a little redneck, a spirit that he gleefully embraces.

"When I talk to young guys from Ontario, when I ask what they want to be when they grow up, they all want to be part of a corporate organization," Dhillon says. "They say, 'I want to be an investment banker or senior vice president of CIBC World Markets, or head mortgage guy, or work for Price Waterhouse.' You ask an Albertan and he'll tell you, 'I want to be an entrepreneur.'"

The culture attracts a certain type of person, and this type feeds the culture, which propels a cycle of constant renewal. For many years, this culture was embodied by the wildcat oilman, drilling and striking it rich, losing it all in the NEP, and rising back up again to make another fortune. Forget that it was the gyrations in the world price of oil, the machinations of geopolitics, that have driven these cycles. What is important is that people believe this myth.

Now, like the cliché of the cowboy, the myth of the wildcatter is a quaint anachronism. The oil patch is becoming a manufacturing industry, run by accountants, engineers, and financiers, not by guys with pickup trucks and a little knowledge of geology. There is still risk, but it is corporate and institutional risk, and it is managed continually.

The quintessential Alberta business person today is no longer a wildcat driller but two upwardly mobile engineers who run the province's major pipeline companies—Hal Kvisle of TransCanada and Pat Daniel of Enbridge. The head offices of these two powerful, rival companies face each other across a Calgary street. And the two guys in the corner office share eerily similar careers. Both come from families of ordinary means—Kvisle from a Norwegian farming background in Innisfail, Alberta, and Daniel, the son of a municipal recreation employee in Red Deer. Both have engineering degrees from the University of Alberta.

They embody the Great Alberta Meritocracy—poor boys who grabbed the brass ring after navigating through the industry's maze of mergers and acquisitions over the past twenty-five years. Of course, they share another requirement of any top energy executive in Alberta—each once worked with the ubiquitous Dick Haskayne, the benevolent godfather of the industry. Kvisle and Daniel are not mavericks or cowboys. They are great technocrats, smart corporate managers, visionaries even in plotting the intricate networks of pipe that span the continent like spiderwebs. They embody the button-down reality of today's oil patch.

Albertans are rugged outdoors people.

You could not live in Calgary, Edmonton, Drumheller, or Lethbridge without being overwhelmed by the sheer beauty of the place, the proximity of mountains, coulees, foothills, and prairie, all within a half-day's drive of each other. You cannot sit in an office building in Calgary with a view of the rippling peaks without being moved. In fact, the proximity of urban centres and the most beautiful landscape in the world is the great promise and potential of Alberta. It is a visual paradise, a feast for the senses, but also a city with great possibility.

The climate does define Albertans to some extent. You have to be tougher to endure a long, cold winter in Edmonton—or the extremes of remote High Level, where it seems to be minus 40 the entire year. You have to be adaptable to go through a winter of Calgary chinooks, snow and cold one day, warmth and melting the next. Pioneering Albertans also possess an urge to subdue the elements. This is a huge tug-of-war for many Albertans—both to preserve and control. It is a classic western paradox that can often be found in the same person, in the same community.

Preston Manning, the former Conservative politician who writes eloquently about Alberta's "natural capital," talks of the split personality of the ranchers who live in the exquisitely beautiful southwest of the province.

"If you hire the political science guys to study them, they say they are rock-ribbed fiscal conservative ranchers who have resisted government involvement in their sector more than any other part of agriculture," says Manning. "But they have this almost fanatical commitment to conserving the fescue and the aquifers on that land so they are green as grass.

"So what is that? Are these blue environmentalists or green conservatives? What are they? They have integrated in their heads these two concepts. They can't provide a theoretical model but they have proven those two concepts can co-exist."

The closeness of the outdoors, the mountains, also gives a sense of still living on a frontier. In reality the frontier is fast disappearing. Many Albertans still have what might be called a "whoop-up mentality." Fort Whoop-up was an outpost of American whiskey traders in the 1870s on the site of today's Lethbridge. The existence of this lawless bastion attracted Ottawa's attention and the first Mounties marched into western Canada with the aim of closing down this embarrassing blot on the new nation. In a sense, the Mounties' march was the NEP of its time, with an eastern government moving against an Alberta institution—albeit a rather tainted institution.

There is something about Albertans that still embraces this glorious whoop-up image of a wild unregulated West, resisting the attempts of the so-called civilized East to restrain their conduct and ability to make money. It is this same spirit that loves the concept of Fort McMurray, the whoop-up of the twenty-first century, a lawless and unregulated frontier without a plan. In the end, many Albertans feel, you let the market work and the problems will solve themselves.

Alberta is a young society.
True, but it can't get away with this image much longer. The province is now more than a century old. The *we-are-oh-so*

young attitude has created a temporary boom-town feel, as if nothing is going to last and so why bother building a real society. Now it is time to grow up and think about the kind of province Albertans want to create.

The image of the adolescent Alberta is often invoked to explain why there has been so little investment in architecture, arts, and culture. This is not an excuse for being casual or haphazard. Many Albertans recognize this and are building for the ages, exemplified by the Bow, EnCana's new head office building in Calgary (even after cost-saving compromises to its glorious design), or the gigantic medical complex in the four-block area south of the University of Alberta in Edmonton.

The East is evil.

Okay, this is true. Albertans have had to endure the calumny of the NEP, the condescension of the federal Liberal Party, and attacks by bankers and intellectuals alike. Their paranoia has some justification, but Albertans have to get over it. Otherwise they will live in an eternal Oz, perpetually repeating over and over that the Wicked Witch is dead: "Pierre Trudeau is gone, Pierre Trudeau is gone . . ."

They have to understand the East as much as try to erase the East's misconceptions of the West. The East is not a hotbed of monolithic socialism, but a diverse political culture, like their own. And even if it were entirely socialist, they shouldn't take it so personally. It's not about them—it's about ideas.

Yet many westerners have funny conceptions of this huge expanse east of Winnipeg. This was driven home to me at the University of Alberta, where in late 2006 I was treated to a discussion on the province's finances by Shirley McClellan, the then finance minister in the dying days of the Klein government.

McClellan had risen from her farming roots in central Alberta to the second-highest job in the province. Business-looking in a black pantsuit and striped blouse, she gave a thoughtful analysis of why the Klein government did what it did or, more precisely, why it didn't. She defended the lack of a plan to deal with the explosion of oil sands development and population in Fort McMurray. "I'm looking for the scholars and business leaders and economists who said we were going to get this kind of growth," she said.

Fair enough, I thought to myself, until the discussion took a weird, almost surreal turn. She began to talk to me about the need for Ontarians to get out more, a point on which I heartily agreed. Then her conversation veered into a tirade about a family relative in Toronto who was "far to the left." She said "they just don't get it in Ontario," as if the province were teeming with socialists, which is as simplistic as any Ontarian's view of Alberta as a bunch of bloodthirsty right wingers. The underlying message: the East is leftist, the East is bad.

There is an absolute nature to many Alberta opinions, and there are politicians who are ready to exploit it. That is what allowed Alberta to let itself be run by one of the most appalling administrations in Canadian history—the third Klein government, of which McClellan was a key part. That's the one that had no more imagination than to give $400 to every Albertan at a time when there was an infrastructure gap in Fort McMurray, a desperate need to twin Highway 63 north of Edmonton, and schools in dire need of repair. Yet here was this $1.4 billion giveaway whose only impact was to further feed the flames of inflation in Alberta and envy in the rest of Canada. Alberta business people who were travelling in Asia were approached by local business people with an air of disbelief and mockery: "So you are the people who are so rich you have nothing better to do than give away a billion dollars?"

There is a view in eastern Canada that the Klein government was ultra-right wing. Wrong, it was pretty moderate. Certainly, it did attack the deficit and debt in its first term, a move that most Albertans applauded. But, having been rewarded with a third term in office, the only thing it stood for was regional resentment and a kind of lazy anti-planning ineptitude that hurt Alberta and Canada in so many ways in the eyes of the world. Alberta was largely absent from national decision making, except to complain. Canada needs an engaged Alberta at the table.

The NEP is dead. Long live the NEP.

It is often said that Canada has not suffered through a civil war, like the United States, but the storm over the NEP in the 1980s came as close as anything we've ever known. It was a war of words and rhetoric, not of guns and shooting battles. Forget about Quebec's various dalliances with sovereignty. That is not a real insurrection in the making so much as an implicit strategy by a very shrewd linguistic and ethnic group to bargain for a better deal in Confederation. And it has been a successful strategy.

So what was the NEP all about? Now it seems almost quaint in its goals to redistribute some energy wealth to the rest of the country and Canadianize the oil patch. In its purpose, it was an attempt to redress an economic imbalance. But, whatever its substance, many Albertans saw it as both a power and money grab by a grasping federal government that was aiming at nothing less than to destroy a distinctive way of life.

The NEP's worst sin was trying to force more Canadian ownership on the oil patch. Canadian champions emerged to take on debt and buy the domestic assets of U.S. companies. But in the bloodbath of high interest rates and plunging oil prices, these debt-laden Canadian champions, such as Dome Petroleum, tanked, and the assets ended up in foreign hands again. It was a ham-handed interference in the market, and Alberta has reason to be unhappy. What would have been a severe recession in any case turned into a rout, with people losing homes and walking away from businesses.

So the eighties and nineties were Canada's civil war, Alberta vs. Ottawa. There was no issue of slavery to muddy the moral waters, but there was a lot of moralistic chatter on both sides. It was a clash of belief systems, of centralization vs. provincial rights, and a powerful industrial heartland in Ontario and Quebec vs. a region dominated by a single industry—in this case, energy. The thinking in Calgary was: if you attack that industry, if you try to confiscate it, it signifies an attack on what is rightfully ours. While the U.S. Civil War pitted Washington against a declining U.S. South built on the economics of cotton, this was Ottawa against an Alberta that was temporarily hobbled but is now rising again. It is the rise of the Dixie of the North.

In this standoff, oilmen like Jim Gray and political provocateurs like Ralph Klein were the firebrands, but Peter Lougheed was the Alberta version of Robert E. Lee, a reluctant combatant who was pulled into the conflict. Lougheed, like Lee, was the epitome of regional aristocracy, as close to nobility as anyone in a very young Alberta could be. He could easily have shared that classic western sense of grievance, because his family's home in downtown Calgary was taken in the Dirty Thirties to settle tax arrears. But he is a proud Canadian who embodied all the tensions that Albertans feel about their country, and he artfully guided Alberta to as good a deal as it could get.

The NEP was not the only killer of Alberta's 1970s boom, but it has been the one event that stokes the myth of Alberta mistreatment. This rhetorical Kool-Aid is consumed by almost every new Albertan, people who come from Halifax or Kitchener and two hours after arriving with no knowledge of the NEP, are complaining about it as if they lived through the 1980s. It has changed politics, destroying the Liberals as a factor in Alberta federal politics and tainting their provincial brethren to the extent that some people argue the provincial Liberals would sweep the province if they would just change their name. It worked for the scandal-ridden Conservative Party in the province next door, allowing the "Saskatchewan Party" to reclaim power. So why not call the Liberals the Alberta Party?

What is clear is that any strong action against the oil patch by the federal government would be interpreted by many people as a second coming of the NEP even if it is perpetrated by an Alberta Conservative prime minister. "That is a reality to Alberta that you discover in your first ten seconds here," marvels Clive Mather, the British oil executive who headed Shell Canada for several years. "There isn't a conversation in the oil patch but that at some point, the issue of the NEP is raised. Through all the conversations that went on around the most recent announcements on climate change, the NEP was ever present in the room."

In fact, there was real hardship during the 1980s, which was not entirely the product of the NEP. High global interest rates contributed to the collapse in asset values. Randy Eresman, now president of powerful EnCana, had to put his young career on hold in the depths of the 1980s slowdown, and went back to university, which in the end benefited him immensely. Irv Kipnes, now a major developer and liquor baron in Edmonton, was effectively bankrupted by the recession. Brett Wilson, the influential head of FirstEnergy investment bank, saw the value of his home dip far below his mortgage value. He would have walked away if his employer, then Imperial Oil, hadn't been holding the mortgage.

But some fortunes were made in the perverse logic of the NEP. A Saskatchewan-born oilfield services tycoon named Hank Swartout used the 1980s to snap up distressed assets in his services industry. He likes to joke that he went to the banks not for free toasters, but to pick up cheap rigs, which he used to build Precision Drilling, the world's biggest oil-field services company.

Stan Milner, the Edmonton oilman, never liked the cut and thrust of the Trudeau government and he shifted his activities to the United States well before the NEP was brought in. He established an office in Denver and he bought a U.S. drilling operation. He also dropped all his acreage in the Arctic, which had become a favoured region of the Trudeau nationalists. It was a smart move. Milner was practically unscathed and came out of the 1980s with a stronger company than most energy bosses. "I was always nervous about the Trudeau administration," Milner says. "I always said my success came because we did everything opposite from what they talked about."

Brett Wilson says the NEP served as a handy scapegoat for all the anti-eastern, anti-Trudeau feeling that was already rampant in the province. "The well-intentioned NEP came along and the Albertans tend to use it as a lightning rod for their hatred," Wilson says. Alberta was living in a bubble economy, and the NEP was one of the needles that popped that bubble. "It was the straw that broke the camel's back. It wasn't everything, and yet people describe it as everything."

The plunging global price of oil and the upward spike in interest rates were much more powerful forces than federal policy, but this is rarely acknowledged in Alberta. "Nobody ever explained to me how the NEP crashed Texas," muses Tim Hamilton, a Calgary headhunter and a prominent local Liberal. Yet he acknowledges the power of the NEP as a symbol, in the same way that freight rates or the CPR used to be focuses for anti-eastern feeling. It takes generations before something as powerful as the NEP is cleansed from the consciousness.

Indeed, ask George Gosbee, the thirty-seven-year-old investment banker, if he still gets hot and bothered over the NEP, and he says: "It was a kick in the head to Alberta, but I don't think you will ever see anything like it again." He was only thirteen years old when it happened, but "I remember seeing all that about what Petro-Canada stands for and Pierre Elliott Trudeau ripping up Canada. I saw it growing up in Calgary." In fact, it may be the children who came away most scarred by the NEP. Kids playing hockey in the 1980s would suddenly notice that their friend Joey from next door was no longer on the team. When they would ask the coach what happened, they would learn that Joey's dad had lost his job with an oil company and they couldn't afford hockey and hockey gear anymore. It was a pretty common scenario, and it left its mark on young Albertans' psyches.

The enduring power of the NEP—both the symbol and the reality—can be seen in the response of Roger Gibbins, one of Alberta's most thoughtful public intellectuals, sitting at the boardroom table at the Canada West Foundation, the Calgary think tank he runs. He feels a repeat of the National Energy Program is always out there as a threat, and Alberta's new wealth is compounding that threat.

"We haven't had a lot of experience in Canada dealing with huge inequities of wealth," he says—particularly inequities on the upside, rather than on the bottom. The country has lots of programs to lift individuals, communities and provinces up to a national average—and rich Ontario has served as the major contributor to balancing regional inequity, extending back to the 1930s when the federal system actually bailed out Alberta.

Now Alberta's wealth is rising well above the rest of the country and Ontario is no longer in shape to carry the equalization burden, as its manufacturing falls into disarray. "I don't want to suggest a conspiracy theory with the NEP but there is a political challenge in federal states about incquities of wealth," Gibbins says. "How much variation can you sustain within a common economy and political system? At some point, we may be pushing that limit."

For Gibbins, the challenge is how Albertans can forestall the East coming after its money and thus inspiring a new anti-Ottawa frenzy. That can best be accomplished if all Canadians feel they are sharing in the Alberta boom. The health research arm of the Heritage Fund is the kind of spending initiative that makes Canadians think they are getting a deal from the oil sands. "If you're filling up your SUV in downtown Toronto and you're paying $1.40 a litre for gas, you're not shaking your fist and saying, 'Goddam those heart surgeons in Edmonton,'" Gibbins says.

His organization has pondered a number of ideas, such as the Canadian equivalent of the Rhodes scholarship, a national scholarship program to bring the best and brightest into Canada, which would be a gift to the country from Alberta. But there are also bigger things that could be done, such as taking the lead on clean coal technology that would help Ontario with its harrowing power problems.

He says the fundamental challenge remains "whether Alberta can find a way to exercise that national leadership, as opposed to just painting a big target on our chests ... The challenge is to find things we can do in Alberta that other Canadians will look at, and think, 'yes, that's really a good thing for the country.'

"We have two regional economies that are only loosely linked to one another and the global changes are good on one side and bad on the other. The question is how Alberta handles those opportunities without causing resentment and anxiety in the rest of the country. If we don't come up with things we can do that are seen in that positive way, then we exacerbate the threat."

Jack Mintz, the former University of Toronto economist who has moved to the University of Calgary, says there are two things that can split up a federation: a steep difference in preferences, such as the favourable treatment accorded Quebec; and differences in fiscal capacity, which is the state of Canada in 2008. There are inevitable tensions when the country goes from several affluent provinces, led by highly populated Ontario, to one very rich province, Alberta, with the others clustered around the average. The fiscal gap can break up the country if there is too much of a disparity and there is a growing fear in Alberta that central Canada is about to pounce on its surplus wealth.

But if there were another NEP, would Alberta really separate or is that threat just an overly dramatic bargaining chip? Randall Morck, the respected finance professor at the University of Alberta, has no doubt: in case of a new NEP, there would be pressure for separation. Alberta could easily see itself joining the American union. It is not expressed as a threat but as a simple fact of life. There is a sense that Alberta doesn't spend a lot of time thinking about this. It is a reality.

Many Alberta moderates believe the NEP was not the apocalyptic event that it is often portrayed to be. But they also take the possibility of separation seriously because Albertans no longer believe that separation would hurt their standard of living. In fact, many believe it would help, because they currently see a net loss of benefits to Ottawa. Federalist economists can demonstrate that the Confederation equation is very good for Alberta, but the argument is hard to win because it gets caught up in inflammatory rhetoric.

There is one litmus test to gauge the sentiments of Albertans: ask if they are Albertans first or Canadians first. As I roamed around the province, I found strong opinions on both sides of the question—but there is no doubt where Peter Lougheed stands. "Deep down, these people are Canadians before they are Albertans," he states with no hesitation. It is different than in Quebec, where most people are Quebecers first, he says. Look at most of Canadians outside Quebec and they put Canada first and their province second.

"That is probably the saving factor for our country in all of these things. I've seen it on issues—I've seen it when I've taken too strong a position in Ottawa. I've seen it happen when I've made a compromise such as after the NEP. We argued we were Canadian before we were Albertan. It's the fact that has made it different in this country."

This was impressed on me during the war in Afghanistan when the most fervent expressions of pride, and of sorrow at the soldiers' deaths, seemed to come from westerners and easterners, people outside central Canada. Perhaps they were suddenly confronted with tangible, vivid, often tragic, reminders that they were Canadian—and of why they were Canadian.

Lougheed has seen this before in the sweep of Alberta history. "When I was a kid, I couldn't get over all the big brothers we had who enlisted in 1939. There was a certain excitement factor and it was so prevailing. That sort of thing permeates through the years."

It would be a good beginning just to challenge some of the outsider myths about the province. For instance:

Albertans are dumb.

This is one making the rounds a lot these days and it is just plain dumb thinking. In fact, Alberta is getting smarter all the time. The Alberta workforce, for example, has the highest average education in the country. But there is this paradox that the province also has the highest high school drop-out rate. What it means is that plenty of educated people are coming to Alberta to work, but many young Albertans are leaving school early to make easy money in the oil patch. People worry that a generation of young Albertans will be left high and dry in terms of skills, when the boom is over and the easy money is gone.

There is also a strong anti-intellectual streak in Alberta, particularly in rural areas, but that is not unusual in Canada. This streak of know-nothing populism finds expression from Newfoundland to B.C., including in wide swaths of Ontario.

In the past, Alberta has not been stellar in intellectual leadership, but now the province is bursting with think tanks, university institutes, and public intellectuals. The most influential thought leaders in Canada may be the conservative thinkers in the University of Calgary's political science department who laid the intellectual foundation of the Reform Party and today's Conservative Party.

There are many more of all political stripes in this new

generation of public intellectuals—Roger Gibbins, Todd Hirsch, Randall Morck, Indira Samarasekera, David Schindler, David Bercuson, Reg Bibby, and Andrew Nikiforuk, to just skim the surface. There are wry social commentators like Todd Babiak and political pundits like David Taras. And just follow the road travelled by Preston Manning, the son of a premier and the father of the Reform Alliance movement in western Canada, the movement that spawned the current prime minister. Manning has evolved from a maverick politician into a true public intellectual of the right, who is trying to narrow a serious knowledge gap in electoral politics. With his Manning Centre for Building Democracy, he is now providing a training ground for conservative politicians to prepare them to assume a life in politics.

All westerners are rich oil people.

Many are, and the wealth creation has been breathtaking. But agriculture was left out of the party until the recent explosion in the price of grain and other commodities. Livestock has remained a difficult market and now cattle farmers must pay the higher costs of feed from a booming wheat price and staggering energy costs. Many small communities outside the Calgary-Edmonton corridor have been punished by the high costs of labour, spurred by the oil sands. It is hard to get help on feedlots and beef ranches when even menial energy jobs pay five times as much.

The forestry industry is on its knees from devastating commodity prices and insect infestations. It is a nasty ecological cycle: the oil sands are feeding a greenhouse gas phenomenon that is making the earth warmer and making it easier for the flourishing of pine beetles that are changing the forestry face of the West.

And now it is conventional oil and gas that are hurting because of the decline of the basin and the escalation of costs. It is a lopsided wealth in western Canada, with the oil sands driving the growth and the rest of the region trying to cope with the costs.

Alberta is the West.

Yikes! Don't try telling this to Saskatchewanians, Manitobans, or British Columbians. The political traditions are so different, their ethnic composition and their histories have diverged. And yet very often, we in eastern Canada use the term "West" when we really mean Alberta.

From the time of Fort Whoop-up, Alberta has been the most American province in attitude, and it partly reflects where many of its people came from. Many are employees of the multinational oil companies whose branch offices are based in Calgary or have operations throughout the province. Calgary often feels more like Houston or Denver, and many Albertans feel more at home in those cities than in Toronto or Ottawa.

Underneath the libertarian soul, however, there beats a very socialist heart in Alberta. Socialism? Albertans? It's just that they don't see government as the main agent of their collective community activism. Preston Manning says if an Albertan wants to solve an international relief crisis, he does not go running to the government. "Albertans don't consider politics as a way to get things done. In this town if you want to help Afghanistan, you won't go to see a politician. A guy like Jim Gray will eventually get around to the government but he first says 'what can we do? Can we get money together, and set up a private thing?' There is a whole lot that is small-p politicial here, but not always visible."

Albertans are a monolithic political mindset.

Despite the political conformism, there are interesting nuances. The Conservative Party acts as a big tent for all kinds of strange people, both of the left and right. Provincially, Alberta has a Progressive Conservative government. So the real election came during the 2006 Tory leadership convention when you had a big government centrist (Jim Dinning), an Alberta separatist and libertarian (Ted Morton), and a Mackenzie King kind of mushy pragmatist (Ed Stelmach) who was inoffensive to the other two camps. In the leadership race, won by Stelmach, 133,000 people, including many Liberal and NDP supporters, became Conservative Party members in order to support or block a particular candidate. By the time the real provincial election came eighteen months later, many of the voters had tuned out. You can't help feeling sorry for the Liberal leader, poor Kevin Taft, a smart, hard-working guy who will never be premier.

Sometime, Alberta will experience the inevitable tsunami that will drive the Conservatives out of power. It happens every thirty to forty years, and the province is already overdue. Preston Manning says it is not the established opposition parties that topple the government in power. Too often, they have the taint of being losers. It is an out-of-the-blue outlier, such as the Socreds when they knocked off the United Farmers, or the Lougheed Conservatives who toppled the Socreds. Somewhere out there, a butterfly's wings are flapping and there will be chaos. We just don't know when.

Energy wealth is a zero-sum game.

Somehow the rest of Canada has to get beyond the politics of envy. I once told Randall Morck that the title to this book might well be: "How the West Has Won." His response was, "I didn't know there was any war." It was a revealing comment because it suggested I was falling into the old eastern concept of Canada as a zero-sum game. In fact, Alberta's success is Canada's success. Oil exports are the tide that should lift us all. Despite the economic distortions, all Canadians should be able to share in the bounty. Now, if only the Alberta government would take up the environmental side of the bargain.

Peter Lougheed wonders why more isn't made of the huge supply chain spreading from the oil sands to the rest of Canada.

Why isn't the Alberta government making more of the fact oil sands players spend $5 billion annually in the rest of Canada, the fact that the oil sands will add $100 billion to Ontario's GDP over the next decade? Alberta is so rich a market that, just as every company should have a China strategy, it should have an Alberta strategy, and, increasingly, a B.C. and Saskatchewan strategy.

It also means pushing back against the old Canadian idea that when one province rises, everyone else falls. For a non-Canadian and a non-Albertan, Clive Mather wholeheartedly embraced the country, the province, and all its bounties. This British executive, who called Calgary home for three years as he ran Shell Canada, loved the mountains, the great outdoors, the huge tradition of giving. He and his wife were fixtures on the volunteer scene, particularly in supporting help for troubled youth. But there was one thing he could never get about Canada. "If I have one regret about Canada, it is this propensity to dash to a provincial refuge in the face of the bigger picture," he told me the day before he left Calgary for retirement in southern England. It's the same on every issue—the economy, taxation, and the environment—and he sees it particularly in sports. "There are times when you think that people would rather the U.S. triumph at something than another province. It is a systemic weakness in the country.

"On a personal level it [provincial difference] is just irrelevant because people come from wherever. Half of Alberta comes from Saskatchewan or Ontario. Many of our Shell people migrated across when we moved the head office from Toronto in 1984. So if you go to Fort McMurray you might just as well be in St. John's or Nova Scotia or wherever. But the reality is that people rush to this provincial difference and it is a weakness because it isn't healthy long term for the country.

"It's not for me to imagine the solution to this, but the more often we can think in national federal terms rather than provincial, the better," says Mather, who as a British citizen has had to deal with this kind of thinking in reference to Scotland's national aspirations.

This attitude, he agrees, is a glorification of small differences. "And people love it, don't they?" he says, smiling. His great concern is that some politicians are only too eager to exploit these provincial differences because it is an easy route to popularity and to winning elections. While he does not name names, it's not hard to find examples, all the way from Calgary to Quebec City and St. John's. You know who you are. It's time for us to ignore the politicians and the radio talk jocks, and listen to our own hearts.

PART TWO

NEW LEADERS

CHAPTER 9

MEET YOUR NEW BOSSES
Who's heading the new Canada

TO DISCOVER THE HEART and soul of Alberta business, drive into the industrial northwest of Edmonton, an unappealing area of low-slung factories, distribution depots, and exhaust-spewing trucks rumbling down wide avenues. Look for the corner with the Gasland pumps, the convenience store, and the bland-looking office building across the parking lot. Go up to the second storey of the office building and you will find the headquarters of a small industrial and real estate empire, commanded by a tousle-haired millionaire named Cal Nichols.

Walk into Nichols' office and, except for the Edmonton Oiler memorabilia, you'd have no idea you were in the presence of an influential entrepreneur, civic leader, and National Hockey League governor. But for the past decade, the sixty-five-year-old Nichols has been the face of the Edmonton Oilers ownership, the titular head of a thirty-seven-member consortium that bought the team in 1999 when it seemed to be headed for Houston, which would have robbed Edmonton of its pride and joy *and* its most powerful brand.

Nichols is more than a hockey team saviour and NHL team director. He is a high school graduate from small-town Saskatchewan, who made a fortune in oil and gas by building energy trading, distribution and service station businesses that he sold off to bigger players. He has parlayed that windfall into a tidy collection of real estate, retail assets, and automated teller machines that he puts into colleges and shopping centres. Through it all, he has remained likeable, straight-shooting Cal Nichols, the kind of guy you'd join for a beer after a pick-up hockey game. In other words, he is the ideal representation of the new western aristocracy.

Canada, meet your new bosses: the western business leaders of the twenty-first century. There are thousands of Cal Nicholses in Alberta and, particularly in Edmonton, the home of unpretentious tycoons who struck it rich by finding and drilling for oil, and by servicing and manufacturing equipment, pipes, wire, and rigs for the oil patch. They're the kind of people who populate the Nisku business park—not billionaire-rich and certainly not ostentatious, but very quiet, very comfortable, with enough money for a ranch-style house in an Edmonton suburb, golf vacations in Scottsdale, a cottage at Pigeon Lake south of Edmonton, or a chalet at Canmore. On their own, these people are not mega-wealthy like the Thomsons and Westons in the East, but collectively they are a force to be reckoned with. And their wealth can only grow in a commodity-driven economy, while the great families of the East are in danger of relative decline unless they can hitch a ride on that same resources bandwagon.

To understand how the West will evolve, you could do worse than study its business leaders, who are like no other in Canada—straightforward, no-nonsense, pragmatic, just like the hard-nosed grinders they admire in hockey. Edmonton's greatest hockey player may have been smooth, cerebral Wayne Gretzky, but it was sharp-elbowed, dangerous Mark Messier who best reflected the blue-collar business ethos. Or more recently, it was Ryan Smyth, the gap-toothed, stringy-haired opportunist who in his Oiler days muscled his way into the slot to pick up garbage goals. It ain't pretty but it sure is effective.

These images matter because leadership styles matter. A region's business leaders set the tone for the entire community.

They create strong companies that generate good jobs and reward investors. They provide leadership in civil society that gets
things done. They are major benefactors and volunteers, driving the causes, the philanthropy, and the creation of a livable
community. They inspire the innovation that breeds sustained
wealth; and they are the ambassadors who present the image of
the region and the country to the world. The West has always
been about business, first and foremost, and business leadership is even more important now, because the stakes in the
game are a lot bigger, as the oil sands have developed into a
$100 billion bonanza for investors, suppliers, tradespeople, and
labourers.

It is good for a region to have lots of money, but how it uses
this money is critical. The wealthy westerners are perhaps the
most important people in Canada right now because they direct
the proceeds, the surplus cash, from the energy boom. Of course,
other people make money from resources, including plenty of
central Canadian investors who hold EnCana and Suncor in
their portfolios. But the westerners make their money every day
from the commodity bonanza and then they decide how to
spend it. They decide if it goes to Palm Springs golf courses,
Caribbean islands, new hospitals in Red Deer, or a new chair at
the university. Or will it go into venture capital, which is still extremely undeveloped in Alberta and Saskatchewan? They deploy
private money for public good or, in many cases, they take it
away and spend it somewhere else in the world, in the perennial
style of the nouveau riche.

The western business class is growing up. Unlike its counterparts in the East, it is still largely first- or second-generation
money, not the inherited wealth of several generations. The fathers and mothers of today's mega-rich were not business people, except to the extent ranchers and farmers are business
people. Because they are new to business and have built their
own companies, they tend to be more entrepreneurial than their

eastern counterparts—even those who are hired-hand professional managers rather than owners.

In Alberta and Saskatchewan, the leaders have not been offshore immigrants, and they are not women, although both those
groups are starting to make their mark. Kathy Sendall, the senior vice-president for North American natural gas at Petro-Can,
minced few words when she was asked if she was someone who
went against the western grain. "The obvious surface thing is
that I am a female in a generally male-dominated industry. I've
taken to calling it a gender-challenged environment.

While women are not making much impact yet, the character of this elite is changing. This is the first generation of business leaders who are largely born in the West, rather than in
Ontario, Quebec, or the United States. You might think that
makes them more western-centric. In fact, they are more confident, less touchy about their role in Confederation than their
predecessors, who always felt they were living in the shadow of
their siblings who stayed at home in Toronto or Montreal.

Many of the older ones did not get beyond high school—Cal
Nichols, for example—or they went to technical college, like oil-
field services tycoon Hank Swartout. A good many went back to
school after a few years of experience under their belts and with
a few dollars in their pockets. There is no sense that education
is the only key to a successful life. Hard work, opportunism, and
riding the energy cycles are just as important as a Harvard education or an establishment pedigree.

Educational levels are rising in the elite—witness the increasing status accorded oil sands scientists like Columba Yeung. But
the classic well-educated western business leader is an engineer
who maintains his roots on the farm—someone like TransCanada's
CEO Hal Kvisle, who comes into the office on Monday morning
not with soreness from driving a golf ball but with scraped hands
from horsing around fence wire on his farm north of Calgary.

In Alberta, the energy titans are very different than the CEOs of banks or industrial firms in the East. Their mindset was formed in rural communities. They are predominantly products of small-town Alberta, Saskatchewan, or Manitoba. In Saskatchewan, there is still a strong representation of Americans in senior positions while Manitoba tends to have homegrown products in its executive chairs. But in all provinces they tend to be engineering types because energy is an engineering industry, and that creates both pluses and minuses. These people are smart, can-do types who often lack vision of the kind of society they want to build and they may be devoid of strong people skills. They built the western economy and it reflects their pragmatic, optimistic but often narrow vision of what the world can be. They take huge calculated risks on a mining project in the oil sands but they are reluctant to let the imagination run free in their plans for development in Calgary, Red Deer, or Edmonton. You see it in the boxy buildings in downtown Calgary and the endless strip malls and factories on Edmonton's main corridors. (Lethbridge has perhaps the most interesting Alberta downtown, including a restaurant housed in an old water tower and a spectacular cliff-side university.)

If a Calgary CEO has any business training at all, it may be in the form of an MBA or a commerce degree from the University of Calgary or Alberta, or a short advanced management program tacked on to engineering background. Meanwhile, an MBA from Harvard, or perhaps the Ivey School at the University of Western Ontario or one of the other high-end academies, such as Rotman or Schulich, carries immense clout in Toronto. Indeed, the Harvard Business School class of 1970 is considered the best business network that Canada ever produced. It yielded, arguably, Canada's most successful manager of the past fifty years, Richard Currie, who built Loblaws into a powerhouse retailer— and the best investor, Gerry Schwartz of Onex. It also generated a major arts and media manager in Peter Herrndorf, a top telecom boss in Wes Scott, and a star investment manager in David

Knight. It is a remarkable group, evidence of the power of the Harvard degree to mould leaders and lifetime relationships. But it is rare to find a Harvard MBA leading a company west of Lake Superior—the best-known example may be Peter Lougheed, who was a politician and not a CEO.

As a result, there are fewer old-school ties. Western executives are less pleased with themselves than their eastern counterparts, but they also lack the cohesive network of former classmates around the world. For the western guys, the networks are built around the companies they worked for and people they have known as they climbed the ladder in the oil patch. Dome Petroleum, a blazing comet in Canada's energy history, may have been an ultimate bust, but it spawned dozens of executive careers for men who were touched by the charisma and genius of Dome visionary Jack Gallagher. In a sense, the Dome experience was the Alberta equivalent of a Harvard MBA: it seemed to mould leaders. Other networks have developed around singular business leaders, including Dick Haskayne, the popular dean of the oil patch, Bill McGregor and Stan Milner, both revered Edmonton oilmen, and, increasingly, Murray Edwards, the hub of the making-money-with-Murray crowd.

As the oil patch has gone through its gyrating cycles, the company names have changed but the relationships remain. It is clearly personality and friendship that drive western business networks, not elite institutions or alumni clubs, such as Harvard, Ivey, or Upper Canada College. It is truly who you worked with, not where you went to school.

There is some major private family wealth in Alberta and it is very powerful. The Mannixes are in a league of their own, a quiet forceful presence in industry and charity. They are the Irvings of the West. Like the New Brunswick billionaire family, they simply do not talk to reporters, and they keep their own counsel. I was not able to break through the walls. Ron Southern, the second-generation entrepreneur who built the Atco utilities empire, has developed his Spruce Meadows complex south of Calgary into a world-class equestrian centre and the site of an important gathering of global thinkers. Now his daughters, Nancy and Linda, are taking command.

It is a small enough community that everybody knows everybody else. In Calgary, they meet in the Ranchmen's Club or the Petroleum Club, and the Stampede remains a core networking institution. In Edmonton, it is an entirely different crowd, and they have the local Petroleum Club, university events, and golf clubhouses. The energy bosses tend to be moderate political types, not extreme right wingers, as eastern stereotypes might suggest. There are even some Liberals. However, the strongest component seems to be centrist Conservatives in the mould of Jim Dinning. As well, the income trust fiasco has bolstered the ranks of flaming libertarians, who are opposed to tax and regulation and devoted to God and family.

But the real religion in the West is NHL hockey, even more so than in central and eastern Canada. Hence, power and influence reside in the ownership of hockey teams. In fact, the composition of ownership in hockey teams can tell you a lot about a city, its elite, and its business style. Take Toronto, where the owner of the Maple Leafs is a sports conglomerate, Maple Leaf Sports and Entertainment, which also owns the Toronto Raptors basketball team, the Toronto FC soccer team, and the Air Canada Centre. Maple Leaf Sports in turn is controlled by the massive Ontario Teacher Pension Plan, which has $108 billion in assets under administration. Its holdings include BCE, the owner of Bell Canada and other communications assets; a stake in CTVglobemedia, the owner of the CTV network and the *Globe and Mail*; and the Cadillac Fairview real estate interests. So Maple Leaf Sports is an investment, not a personal passion.

The presence of Teachers in the ownership group reflects the investment muscle of pension funds, private equity, and institutional money in central Canada—indeed, in the entire Canadian economy, including the oil patch. Funds drive so much economic activity now. Besides Teachers, the institutional titans include the $52 billion Ontario Municipal Employees Retirement System and the mighty $155 billion Caisse de dépôt et placement du Québec. Such powerful institutions do not exist in the West. Alberta has the Heritage Fund but, in the typical Alberta style of spend-now, save-later, it has never been allowed to draw sufficiently from the province's energy revenues to grow into a major investment force. It has been a lost opportunity that has deprived the West of a vital tool—especially in an age when state-controlled sovereign funds from Asia, Europe, and the Middle East are roaming the world for deals.

Maple Leaf Sports' minority owners include the Toronto-Dominion Bank and ctvglobemedia itself, whose largest shareholder is David Thomson, the third-generation scion of Canada's richest family. Indeed, the most important figures in Toronto business are Jim Leech, the Royal Military College–trained ceo of Teachers (who also has a Queen's mba), and Geoff Beattie, the lawyer who manages the Thomson family's holding company and engineered family-controlled Thomson Corp.'s takeover of Reuters. These are not entrepreneurs, but they are powerful custodians. The other individual investor in the Maple Leaf consortium is Larry Tanenbaum, a sports-, media-, and construction tycoon who represents established Toronto-family money.

In other words, Maple Leaf Sports is a perfect reflection of its city, where ownership is dominated by institutions, investment managers, and old money. Maple Leaf is a highly valued company and, although it is private, it appears to generate strong returns for its owners. But the Maple Leafs' success on the ice has been less than stellar. The ownership says it is no less determined to win the Stanley Cup than the owners of the Oilers or the Calgary Flames. The Leafs are an icon, not only in Toronto but across Canada. But hockey is not the only game in town in a city where baseball, soccer, basketball, football, music, theatre, and the arts battle for the entertainment dollar. And Maple Leaf Sports is as dedicated to making money from real estate investment as to building sports winners. The passion at the Air Canada Centre is for capitalism, not hockey.

In Calgary, the Flames are the biggest show in town, and the owners of the Flames automatically become media celebrities. You cannot hide from your duty to bring a winner to the town. Unlike in Toronto, there is no institutional ownership. Instead, the hockey club is owned by eight very wealthy people, most of them self-made energy magnates. They are led by Murray Edwards, perhaps the city's richest person, and by the venerable oilman Harley Hotchkiss, another one of the personalities around which the Calgary elite coalesces. Hotchkiss is a legendary businessman whose steady hand as NHL governor helped guide the Flames and the NHL through difficult years. There is also billionaire energy magnate Clay Riddell; Edwards' oil sands partner Al Markin; Saskatchewan-born oilmen brothers, Doc and Byron Seaman; investor Alvin Libin; and the family of the late transportation baron Bud McCaig. This group is the very core of the city's business establishment. They reflect the emergence of an ultra-wealthy Calgary elite with its own billionaires and near billionaires.

Contrast these eight outsized tycoons with the Edmonton Oilers' thirty-seven owners, the quiet millionaires who banded together and kept the team in Edmonton. These affluent but not overly rich owners have been toasted as heroes because they saved a glorious franchise from being shipped south. In Canada, the loss of a hockey team is like a death in the family. Winnipeg has still not recovered from the spiritual loss accompanying the departure of its beloved Jets to Phoenix in 1996. Anyone who has seen filmmaker Guy Maddin's quirky ode to his home city, *My Winnipeg*, senses the tragedy that still cloaks the city more than a decade after the departure of the Jets. It would have been even more devastating for a franchise as storied as the Oilers, winners of five Stanley Cups between 1984 and 1990.

While the Flames are the biggest thing in Calgary, the Oilers tower far above any Edmonton institution—and that includes the University of Alberta and the West Edmonton Mall. To really understand Edmonton, you have to sense the symbolic and financial stature of the Oilers. The hockey team is the central brand, the spirit, the thing that makes Edmonton different from Calgary or Toronto.

You're caught up in Oiler spirit the moment the giant derrick hits the ice at the Rexall Place arena and the players skate out from under its tentacles. The big screen plays videos of people working in the oil sands, on construction, giving the sense of a can-do kind of town. The videos flash with signposts along Alberta highways, reading Camrose, Edson, and Lac la Biche, all towns in Edmonton's hinterland. It is a glorification of rural life, of small farms, and oil rigs. The crowd is a cross-section of Edmonton society—university professors, gals in tight pants, blue-jeaned oil rig workers, nouveau entrepreneurs, old wealth. It is a much more real experience than Toronto's Air Canada Centre, which is populated by suits who sit on their hands and count their dividends in their minds.

At the southern entry point to Edmonton, there is another conspicuous oil derrick plunked on the highway median and a sign that declares "City of Champions." And that was once the truth: in the 1980s with the Oiler teams of Gretzky, Kurri, Messier, Coffey, and Fuhr. It was one of the great sports dynasties, and a number of their star sweater numbers are dangling from the ceiling. But in 1997, the city almost lost its beloved Oilers when eccentric owner Peter Pocklington was in deep financial trouble. The Alberta Treasury Branches called its loans and forced him to put the Oilers up for sale.

Edmonton has had its share of maverick business guys—and Pocklington was certainly out of the ordinary, enlisting psychics for business advice, running for the leadership of the federal

Conservatives, and watching his empire dissolve in a sea of bad decisions. Some, though, have skated closer to the line than the quirky, colourful Pocklington. Bernie Ebbers, who is in prison for defrauding investors in WorldCom, the U.S. communications giant, was born in Edmonton and delivered milk there before heading off to school in Mississippi and starting a telecom company that bled billions of shareholder value. In late 2006, a scoundrel named Michael Ritter was sentenced to ten years in prison for masterminding elaborate fraud and pyramid schemes that bilked investors of tens of millions of dollars from investors across North America. And Ritter was the former chief parliamentary counsel for the Alberta legislature.

But the largest fortunes in Edmonton are usually the quietest. The Ghermezian family built the West Edmonton Mall, the biggest mega-project in Alberta before Fort McMurray, but the family, with roots in Iran, has zealously protected its privacy. The elders live in the U.S. South while a new generation runs the mall and invests in Saskatchewan energy, while retaining an enclave of homes high above the river in Edmonton. The wealthiest Edmontonian today—perhaps the wealthiest Albertan—is the reclusive Daryl Katz, owner of the Rexall pharmacy empire, who is petrified of having his picture in the paper. Yet he has built a monster house on the river valley that has made him the subject of gossip and speculation.

Pocklington, on the other hand, was a very public millionaire, whose adventures and mishaps were fertile fodder for the media. When he had to sell the Oilers, it was high-profile negotiation that almost lost the team to Houston. Fortunately, another classic Edmonton persona emerged, "the blue-collar millionaire," the terminology used by Cal Nichols to describe himself and the thirty-six other moderately rich folks he assembled to buy the Oilers and keep them in Edmonton.

Some of these millionaires are well known locally, such as Tim Melton, head of the family development company Melcor;

Jim Hole of the Lockerbie and Hole construction fortune; technology entrepreneur Bruce Saville; and Todd Macfarlane, the comic-book designer who was born in Calgary but now lives in Los Angeles. They were not big names even in the rest of Alberta. Many are ordinary guys, Nisku and Lloydminster types with trucks and backhoes, and Cal Nichols is typical of the breed.

The story of what happened to that ownership group is a case study in Alberta's business evolution over the past decade, from a province of small-town entrepreneurs to a playground for corporate billionaires. I spent a little time with Cal Nichols at perhaps the most important juncture in his life as an Oilers owner. For two weeks in early 2007, he and the other team owners had been quietly negotiating to sell the team to Daryl Katz, and the deal had come apart. The story of the negotiations and the lapsed deal had broken in the *Edmonton Journal*, in an article by columnist Gary Lamphier. In his story, Lamphier made it clear that Nichols, usually an accessible guy, had not been returning calls. Nichols told me he liked Lamphier as a person but he wasn't about to do his talking through the press. He was into damage control, with some owners wanting to cut and run but others still committed to the Oilers.

There was chaos in his office that day, as he hosted a couple of old friends from Saskatchewan who had known him from the early days as an Esso dealer. His son Ken popped in to celebrate a business breakthrough in his own enterprise, which is running cash machines. Cal kept taking calls from Oilers owners responding to the press coverage. It's what made his job so hard, but it was clear he revelled being at the centre of a hurricane of public attention. He was spending three hours a day on Oiler business and receiving not a dime in pay.

Nichols' roots are typical of the Group of Thirty-seven. They extend back to Paradise Hill, Saskatchewan, where, as the son of an Esso dealer, he went into business for himself at nineteen.

There was no thought of going to university. "I don't think I was smart enough. I wasn't a good student. I used to bring my dad's fuel truck to school and as soon as I was done I would deliver fuel. I was more interested in that than I was in school."

Growing up in Saskatchewan, Nichols always had the idea that there was another paradise across the provincial boundary in Alberta: "I had an uncle in Edmonton and when I visited him I crossed the border and wondered how come all the roads in Alberta are paved. How come everyone has a flush toilet? In Saskatchewan, we don't have all these things. I thought maybe I'd better go there and find out."

He eventually ended up as a regional Esso manager in Edmonton, part of the twenty-year stint he spent with Imperial Oil. The oil company gave him his education through on-the-ground experience and special courses. But one day in the 1980s, a colleague noted that Alberta was about to deregulate its gas and oil distribution. The two men founded Northridge, an energy trading company. Then they went on to create a vertically integrated supply chain with their own chain of gas stations called Gasland.

Nichols owed a lot to Edmonton, the town that made him rich. He sold Gasland to Husky Oil for good money and he kept a lot of the real estate. He was an Oiler ticket-holder through the years of Gretzky and Messier, but the economics of the game had changed. The free-agency system, whereby players could sell themselves to the highest bidder, was hard on Canadian hockey clubs that were handcuffed by the low Canadian dollar through the 1990s. The one salvation was a league subsidy program that would dole out money based on ticket sales. In 1995, Nichols was part of the ticket-selling initiative in Edmonton. That was when the team became his calling.

So when Pocklington put the Oilers on the block in 1997 and the team was close to moving to Houston, Nichols stepped forward with his ownership group. They made a $5 million deposit with little time to spare, and bought the Oilers for $100 million.

The team has been on a roller coaster. It made a stirring return to the Stanley Cup finals in 2006, riding the polished toughness of free-agent defenceman Chris Pronger. But Pronger stayed only a season, and demanded a trade away from Edmonton—ostensibly because his wife, an American, hated the place. Pronger's departure seemed to kick the stuffing out of Edmonton's self-confidence. Then came the trade of hometown favourite Ryan Smyth. The arena was an icon but it was eroding; its imprint was small and, frankly, it is in a desolate location.

All these things are so deeply felt in Edmonton because the team is such a family affair. "This is not a normal private business—it is a public trust," Cal Nichols says. Sometimes the nasty business of hockey put strains on this family. Mike Comrie, for example, is a local boy, a slick hockey player who had one good year for the Oilers, then one ordinary year, and, because of a quirk in the rules, he could test the free-agent market. He wanted a lot more money than the small-market Oilers could pay.

It happened his father was Bill Comrie, the legendary retailer who built the Brick Warehouse into the icon of low-cost furniture and noisy TV ads. The Comrie family was popular in Edmonton, and feelings ran raw as Mike battled in the media with general manager Kevin Lowe. At one point Comrie was asked to ante up some of his money to help fund his own trade. He was eventually traded to Philadelphia and has since moved on to Ottawa and the New York Islanders.

The controversy cut deep. "It was a rupture in the family but it was also fuelled by the economic environment that existed," Nichols conceded. Comrie had always been adroit in his contract moves and had used a labour arbitration precedent to gain free agency earlier than was the norm. "I don't know if Mike Comrie has improved his life by a whole lot through the twists and turns he's taken," Nichols said. "There have been a lot of family relationships at stake with him. I don't know where that will get you in the end. It's not about money, because he will inherit all that he will need."

Bill Comrie had left Edmonton, having taken Brick public through an income trust offering. He was living in Los Angeles, but kept a place in Edmonton. He comes back, but is no longer a presence at the Oilers' games. Asked if he has seen Bill in the arena since the incident, Cal said: "Not that I know, I don't think so. It's so sensitive."

When I caught up with Cal Nichols on a spring day in 2007, the Oilers were occupying all of his time. He said the owners were not about to sell, but added that he never says never. It was wise thinking because Daryl Katz did not get to be the wealthiest Albertan by giving up easily. Katz grew up in Edmonton and practiced law but spent a lot of time thinking about the pharmacy industry, the profession of his father. He knew the industry was going to consolidate and it seemed like a good time to buy assets. He built a large empire, reputedly valued at more than $2 billion, that spans the Rexall, Pharma Save, and Guardian brands. Katz has a tough-guy way of talking, and once told me that his major recommendation to entrepreneurs is to be absolutely tenacious and never give up on an idea or project. Really grit your teeth and jump into it, he says. "We are often underdogs but we are tenacious."

By fall 2007, the tenacious Katz has raised his price to $188 million. Cal Nichols finally supported the Katz bid and quit as Oilers chairman. The ownership group was in chaos, divided between sellers and holders. "I looked at all the steep hills to climb and the amount of gas in my tank and I didn't think I was up to it," Nichols told the *Globe and Mail*. Within a month, Katz had hiked his offer to $200 million and the team was finally sold. The thirty-seven owners did well, doubling their investments in most cases, and Cal Nichols walked away with $13 million.

Optimism was growing in Edmonton that with a single

owner with deep pockets, the team would finally spend enough money to be a contender. But as an outsider, I felt the sale of the team to Katz robbed Edmonton of one of its cherished myths— the idea that a city can be built on the backs of hard-working people who drove around in pickups, not Porsches. The Oilers' sprawling ownership group typified Edmonton's unpretentious, unvarnished style of leadership, which made it different than New York, Toronto, or even Calgary. Now the Oilers would be owned by just another billionaire (although Katz is at least a local boy and he isn't a soulless pension fund). They would be little different than the Flames who were owned by eight plutocrats and whose public image was personified by billionaire financier Murray Edwards. In defiantly blue-collar Edmonton, it was like selling your soul, while perhaps gaining a Stanley Cup.

CHAPTER 10

WELCOME TO EDGARY

The city life that waits at the end of the line

IT IS A STIFLINGLY HOT DAY in mid-May, the kind of smelly, oily weather that Toronto seems to experience more and more these days, even in the springtime. The oppressive heat doesn't wilt the enthusiasm of a delegation of Calgary civic and business leaders who have descended on Canada's largest city to meet people, give speeches, and preach the gospel of Calgary to the unconverted. The idea is to forge economic alliances in Toronto, spreading the message that there is enough money being made in Calgary to share the largesse with the rest of the country. The Calgary companies are saying they need Ontario's help because their own businesses are stressed out by the demands of an over-heated economy.

The high-profile lunch on the Sutton Place Hotel's thirty-third floor is full of good humour. Beneath this surface bon-homie, some Ontario business people believe they detect a steely message from their Calgary confreres: "Look out, Toronto, we're coming after you. Your city is crumbling and what's more, it's becoming an unliveable, smelly, smog-enveloped monument to old, dying industry. We need you, but more than that, you need us—because we've got the money now."

However valid the Torontonians' paranoia, the Calgarians' visit was a clear statement that "we have arrived"—in the same manner as the Calgary alderman who rode his horse through the lobby of the Royal York Hotel during the Grey Cup celebrations of 1948. Calgary is saying it has come of age. There are no tacky cowboy trappings—these are serious business people and, in the view of some of their hosts, they have come to eat Toronto's lunch in more ways than one.

It is hard to see Calgary and Toronto as natural rivals. Toronto has more than three times the number of people, at least ten times the number of skyscrapers, a Major League baseball team, and the headquarters of Canada's five major banks. Toronto sees itself as a world-class city; not long ago, Calgary was straining just to get attention as the leading city in Alberta. Make no mistake: this is the rivalry that will meet head-on for national supremacy in the years to come. Toronto still has at least twice as many head offices, but Calgary is on the move. It is recognized as one of the world centres of energy finance with a critical mass of investment bankers. It has some of the world's best oil and gas consultants and engineers. Calgary has the brains in all the right spots for a resource-driven planet. The petro-boom is driving a massive expansion throughout western Canada, and Calgary is the West's head office capital.

Don't expect Toronto to fall into precipitous decline. In fact, it will remain an important *regional* finance centre and the headquarters of the Canadian entertainment and media industries. It will maintain its cachet as one of the world's most liveable big cities. But Calgary's huge wealth advantage should allow it to close the gap, if not in population, at least in education, health care, quality of life, and its dazzling wealth. The Calgary Economic Development website reports that Calgary already has the highest density of millionaires in the country, with 183 people per 100,000 in population pulling down million-dollar annual incomes. That's more than twice the density in Toronto and, even better, more than three times the number in equally despised Edmonton. That adds up to about 2,000 millionaires. Some local officials suggest this is underestimating the true number and there may be as many 22,000 millionaires in Calgary, a town of a million people. And there are at least a half-dozen billionaires, including Clay Riddell, Murray Edwards, Ron and Fred Mannix, Ron Southern, and probably a few more, like Ron Matheson, Hank Swartout, and the Seaman brothers, who are testing those limits.

This of course pales beside the Toronto mega-rich, for Toronto is the home of David Thomson, who according to *Forbes* magazine is the world's thirty-first richest person with $19 billion in net worth, and Galen Weston, the 132nd richest with $7 billion. Toronto, with its media and financial head offices, is the city Calgary aspires to be, just as Toronto aspires to be New York. But Calgary wants to be a western kind of Toronto, packed with head offices and cultural institutions, but without the pretensions and the snooty elite, the clubby atmosphere, and the sense of entitlement. Calgary wants to solve the riddle: how can you be a wealthy, high-class city and retain your open, friendly personality?

Calgary figures it has lots of models of how not to act. One Calgary investment banker told me a story that is typical of how Calgarians view Toronto. A native of Ontario himself, he sent one of his sons to a fine private school in Europe that was heavily attended by the sons and daughters of the Toronto business elite. The son became close friends with some of these young people and, when they all returned to Canada, he was invited up to a Muskoka cottage for a weekend. Suddenly, the young man found himself no longer among people he liked, but in a stifling society where bloodlines, family ties, and who you know, not what you know, are the admission tickets. He was clearly overwhelmed by the sense of privilege. He headed back to Calgary where he asked his father, only partly joking, if it were possible to revoke his Canadian citizenship.

Yet Toronto, for all its fine old families, is going through its own crisis. All around its southern Ontario hinterland, in places like Oshawa and St. Catharines, manufacturing is being hammered, and much of it will never come back. It also faces a funding shortfall that hamstrings its municipal government and threatens to deny people basic civic services. Various polls indicate that Torontonians have less confidence in their economic future than at any time in recent memory. That was underlined by the right-wing Fraser Institute's report titled *Is Toronto in Decline?*, which used census data to paint a picture of an erosion of economic clout and a declining civic confidence.

"Management occupations have been bleeding away from the city," said the report, spearheaded by former Alberta politician Preston Manning and ex-Ontario premier Mike Harris. The report did not have any prescriptions for this decline, other than point to a survey suggesting Torontonians blamed City Hall. Many would no doubt blame Harris' own savage downloading of municipal services while he was premier for a good deal of the malaise. But a new industry is clearly sprouting in central Canada—Toronto declinism. It is epitomized by the graphic image accompanying the *Toronto Star*'s coverage of the report: a huge cobweb spangled across the Toronto skyline.

Even as it struggles to fund its daily services, the city is living through a golden age of philanthropy—a kind of wealth amid the chaos, a modern version of a crumbling Rome. As the city's self-confidence is hurting, its aging and middle-aging plutocrats—such as Izzy Sharp, Peter Munk, Michael Lee-Chin, Robert McEwen, and Gerry Schwartz—are giving money to build great buildings and institutions, monuments to their public-spiritedness and their desire for immortality. It is the age of public building: the controversial Michael Lee-Chin Crystal, designed by Daniel Libeskind, at the Royal Ontario Museum; the Sharp Centre at the Ontario College of Art and Design, which looks like dice on toothpicks; a striking new opera house; and a Frank Gehry–designed expansion of the Art Gallery of Ontario. A cluster of new hospital wings are forming in the area around the College Street–University Avenue intersection—as well as MaRS, a lively incubator of small technology start-ups.

In other words, Toronto can still show Calgary how to do it. In an age of monument building, Calgary isn't even out of the starting gate. Calgary was built by people who believed they did not need a city that was a cathedral. They wanted a useful place, a place to work and make money, and then get on the next plane to Palm Springs. Their cathedrals lie to the West, in the craggy mountains and the playgrounds of Banff, Canmore, Invermere, and Fernie.

Many of Calgary's office buildings are utilitarian branch-plant boxes erected as outposts of companies based in Toronto or Houston. As a frontier town, Calgary has a feeling of impermanence—that you are moving on to the next bigger house, the next bigger office building. There was no need to make them memorable because they would soon be torn down, flotsam in the tidal wave of entrepreneurship. And if you were an engineer or geologist who grew up on a farm in rural Alberta or Saskatchewan, you really preferred to be on your spread in Carstairs or Gleichen, rather than strolling down a city street.

In fact there is a great city straining to emerge in Alberta, but it is not Calgary or Edmonton—it is Edgary, the combination of the two. Together they have two million people, only four hours or so apart along a busy corridor of commerce. And if Calgary didn't have Edmonton, it would have to invent it. Calgary is white-collar, oil-industry head office, centre-right in its politics; Edmonton is blue-collar, oil-field services, refineries, and centre-left in its politics. While Calgary is easy to figure out—it's about money, the making and spending of it—Edmonton is a place of infinite complexity, a strange brew of hard hats, civil servants, and university professors. Downtown looks bombed out, but the city boasts an interesting cultural fabric around the university and Old Strathcona. There is great wealth here, but it is deceptive—it comes from guys with trucks, chains, pipes, and generators, with machine shops in Nisku, pulling down a million a year in Fort McMurray.

The two mayors are a reflection of their cities. Calgary's "Bronco Dave" Bronconnier is all upfront salesmanship, a gregarious former construction-company owner who clearly has eyes on the provincial Liberal leadership. Edmonton's Stephen Mandel is as complex as the city he runs, with the ironic smile of a wry intellectual. He is also a former real estate developer who has known punishing financial losses. He was once a part owner of a baseball team in Tucson that bit the dust.

Did I tell you the two cities hate each other?

With *a passion*.

The rivalry is like Calgary's relationship with Toronto, only more intense. Calgary resents to this day the fact that it was outslicked by its northern rival in the choosing of the provincial capital in the early 1900s. The two cities fight over hockey, football, education funding, political leadership—you name it. For an easterner, it is as puzzling as the symbolic resilience of the National Energy Program grievances.

Harvey Weingarten, president of the University of Calgary, who was born in Montreal and worked many years at McMaster University in Hamilton, says he has never seen anything quite like the Calgary–Edmonton feud in its debilitating effects. "I actually think the Calgary–Edmonton dynamic is one of the things that inhibits the progress of the province in a serious way," he says. "If we don't somehow overcome it, it is a serious limitation on the ability of Alberta to accomplish things and to realize its potential."

To capture a sense of this duality, just read the columnists in the *Calgary Herald* who rail against the provincial education dollars that, they insist, are being sucked into Edmonton. Even the Conservative leadership campaign in 2006 was a regional play, with Edmonton and much of rural Alberta throwing their votes to Edmonton-area farmer Ed Stelmach in order to gang up on Calgary, which backed local boy Jim Dinning. The regional jealousy meant Alberta squandered a great opportunity because the eloquent, visionary Dinning, a man who had wanted to be premier since Grade 11, would have a great asset in advancing Alberta's cause at the national level. Instead, the province got Stelmach, a nice guy but not the person to make Alberta forget Peter Lougheed.

Viewed together, these two cities possess a commercial vitality that is unrivalled in Canada. If there were a way to link the two, say, with a high-speed rail corridor, Edgary would be the one city that could rival Toronto in its drive, its creativity, its industry. In fact, the two Alberta cities already function as a single entity in terms of complementary strengths and weaknesses. Now, if only they could get over the silly bickering.

Downtown Edmonton is not pretty. There are no nearby mountains or foothills, and its core is still hobbled by a monster suburban shopping mall. Yet it enjoys a funkiness that Calgary can only aspire to. One thing that really rankles Calgarians is that Edmonton is the superior cultural city. It has a great museum, an art gallery—to be housed in an interesting new building—and a major theatre, the Citadel. Some of that comes from being the provincial capital—hence, another source of Calgary bitterness. Edmonton has spawned a strong, small theatre scene, flowing out of its pioneering fringe festival. Calgary's arts scene is much thinner, although there is some adventurous theatre, such as the One Yellow Rabbit troupe.

Despite its voluntary enthusiasms, Calgary is still devoid of striking cultural institutions and its major museum is housed in an annex of a convention centre. The downtown still largely dies at night as the office crowd heads for the burbs—and the burbs are sprawling out of control. This cannot be a serious city until it gets serious about arts and culture.

Calgary used to have an excuse. Many of its corporate leaders lived in the city for only five-year terms. They were Americans from big U.S. or European oil companies who would send their executives to Calgary for five-year appointments to the Canadian branch office. Calgary was not a place to spend an entire career. Top executives rarely put down roots, and their philanthropic and artistic commitment reflected a limited adherence to their adopted home. In no time at all, they were back in Houston, Denver, Dallas, or Pittsburgh. There are no excuses anymore. Now there is serious homegrown money in Calgary, reflected in the billions of dollars of in-the-money stock options held by the city's oil chieftains. Will this money stay in Calgary or go south?

Calgary does have a highly educated population and a strong engineering mentality, but it has not been able to develop outstanding artistic leaders. Could William Thorsell, the Alberta native who heads the Royal Ontario Museum, have unfolded his vision in Calgary? Could Albert Schultz, who has built the Soulpepper theatre complex in Toronto over the past decade, have done the same thing had he been in Calgary? Or could the late Richard Bradshaw, who spearheaded the building of a new opera house in Toronto (although the opera house had been decades in the planning and making, which suggests even self-proclaimed world-class cities don't get what they want overnight), have accomplished the same in Calgary? None of these cultural entrepreneurs would probably have made it in Calgary. So that raises the question: Can a middle-aged gay man from Los Angeles change Calgary and its view of itself?

I meet Lance Carlson in his office where he presides over the Alberta College of Art & Design, which clings to the side of the hill overlooking the Bow River and the Calgary skyline. There is a mantle of snow hugging the trees and you can get a glimpse of the mountains. It is, in short, a spectacular place to work, but Lance doesn't want to be here. He wants to be downtown, in Calgary's benighted eastern downtown, where he can engage the city that has adopted him. There is a plan to move his school, sitting in a leased building on the Southern Alberta Institute of

Technology campus, to a site in the East Village, a down-on-its-luck area east of city hall that today is mainly occupied by panhandlers, addicts, and street people.

Carlson rode into town in 2004 as ACAD's president and has initiated a whirlwind of change. A man with two academic disciplines—anthropology and design—he was born in Los Angeles, but has worked in cultural institutions across the U.S. Now he wants to change Calgary—not only to build this downtown campus but also to educate Alberta's elite into realizing there is a greater purpose to life; that this city has to be more than just a place to make money and then disappear to Victoria or Scottsdale.

He sees his role as more than an educator and something akin to a cultural catalyst who can help Calgary find a greater purpose beyond filthy lucre. "We have the money and resources, so I feel there is a moment right now of huge possibility," says Carlson, a man with a perfectly trimmed light beard, a tightly shaved head, and a quiet precise Zen-like way of talking. "The key right now is to make the right decisions. I think if Calgary and Alberta make the right decisions for a cultural vision, there is the potential for enormous gains."

Carlson has turned ACAD into a continuing forum on the future of the modern city. His innovations have included the concept of the Intelligent City, a colloquium ACAD has sponsored that draws heavily on his design thinking. He has founded the Institute of the Creative Process, a zesty think tank of innovation. With his Stirring Culture lecture series, he has brought thinkers to Calgary, such as smart-city guru Richard Florida and author and *New Yorker* writer Malcolm Gladwell. (Florida himself had been recently lured to University of Toronto by ambitious business dean Roger Martin.)

And for his Smart Night fund-raising gala, he invited Daniel Pink, the evangeslist of right-brain creative thinking in a left-brain corporate world. The session with Daniel Pink in early 2007 was one of ACAD's most successful events because it truly challenged the left-brain engineers who dominate Calgary's elite. Pink argues that creative, inventive thinking has to be injected into organizations to balance the analytical thinkers who have run companies and governments. This is going to be the key competitive advantage of this century, he argues. Many of those left-brain thinkers were in the audience that night. The crowd totally bought Pink's thesis. All around the room there was the sense that Calgary was built on great engineering thinking, but now it has to stoke its imagination.

Carlson is betting that Calgary may just be the continent's rising new urban star, a city that really understands the new economy. Indeed, the city is a little-known high-tech haven with 3,200 technology companies and close to 80,000 knowledge workers. More fittingly, Carlson sees the link between culture and economic development. He poses a question that has enormous implications: Can Calgarians finally learn to love their city? "Is Calgary going to be a city where people make enormous amounts of money and then buy homes elsewhere?" Carlson asks. "Someone says 'I want to go to the Calgary Opera and support it, but if you really want the opera experience, go to New York.' That kind of thinking is a real issue here."

He admits that the pull of the mountains, the WestJet flights to Palm Springs and Kelowna, are a big challenge for Calgary. "How can we create an experience that is compelling enough that you want to be in Calgary? You have to love the city. That is a design problem: How do we create an experience?

"If you're a law firm or a college or oil and gas firm, you have to structure the meaning of the experience of the people. What is the purpose of Calgary? What is the meaning of being in this place?" That, he argues, is the link to economic development: "Why would anyone want to live or work here?"

Fortunately, he has encountered people who do make that important connection. He reels off the names of executives at Enbridge, Nexen, and FirstEnergy Capital. "People are ready for this stuff, ready for the purpose. I think it is about: How do you create a fabric of cultural life that provides people with purpose?"

My wife visited Calgary during Stampede Week and loved the friendly people and the openness. Accustomed to Toronto's Queen Street West, she asked where the older sections with small theatres, galleries, and offbeat shops were. There was really nothing like that, although the potential clearly area exists in an area like Inglewood and perhaps in the East Village. If it all comes together, a new ACAD would be part of that.

Carlson's vision is engaging the new millionaires, including George Gosbee, the young investment banker who agreed to become the chairman of the Alberta College of Art & Design. Gosbee has been involved with charities and philanthropy since the early years of his meteoric career, but held himself back from full engagement because he could not see examples of dynamic leadership. That changed when Carlson came, with his vision of taking ACAD to a new level. In turn, Carlson has become a cultural mentor to Gosbee, who now has aspirations of being a great art collector. Carlson has accompanied him on buying trips to Los Angeles.

Gosbee agrees that, in the past, the words "Calgary" and "culture" didn't belong together. "There are not a lot of words that come together with Calgary other than oil and gas. You can substitute a lot of words there for art. That's where I think I can add to it, and why this is such a great vision."

Gosbee says Calgarians have gone through so much economic turmoil over the past three decades that they have lacked the confidence to support the arts consistently. A lot of fortunes were quickly lost and quickly made and lost again. Now a new generation, with its wealth comfortably pocketed, is feeling confident. "You're seeing lots of guys my age involved in a lot of different projects and that's what's needed."

If the young are getting engaged, what about the rich boomers who are set for life? Mike Robinson, the eclectic thinker who is the former head of the Glenbow Museum, won-ders what will happen to the people who made truly great wealth in the boom. As mentioned, Calgary is traditionally a transient city where people come to make money and, as soon as they hit retirement, head out the back door to other climes. "When you recruit people to a province using the model of the work camp, this is where they come to work and make money and build up their poke," Robinson says. That has been the pattern through-out Canada, whether it is the Klondike or Fort McMurray.

What happens once you've built up your poke? Where do you go? He sees people like himself heading out to the West Coast. He is from B.C. and keeps a place on B.C.'s magical Sun-shine Coast as well as an apartment in Calgary. Others are cash-ing out and heading home to Saskatchewan or Nova Scotia. "The evidence before me is that a lot of people I know are re-turning to the rivers of their birth. They hear the bell ring and they go back to the Fraser River." They are like salmon in their habits: "They smell that water and they swim up and they spawn."

Robinson, who left the Glenbow for an unsuccessful foray into provincial politics for the Liberals, asks: Does Calgary have the critical mix of amenities to retain boomers at retirement? The evidence is definitely mixed, he says. When he goes to par-ties, he hears a lot of talk about how long it takes by float plane to get from Vancouver to Gabriola Island and how much it costs to buy a kayak. There is little chatter about what it's like to spend retirement in Calgary, and support the cultural institu-tions that have taken root. He contrasts that with the scene in Montreal, which, for all its financial constraints, retains its af-fluent retirees. They become what he calls "cultural flâneurs," people who love their neighbourhoods, their local restaurants, and the arts scene. Instead, Calgary people leave and that is a problem. And the people who stay and take aesthetic risks get roasted for them.

To understand the complex yearnings of the new Calgary, consider the life paths of two middle-aged men who care passionately about their city. One is farmer and rancher Tim Harvie, who lives on the city's outskirts and is the scion of a great old Alberta family. The other is Fred Woods, an oilman who would be classified as nouveau riche. These are two guys who don't seem to have a lot in common. I found them aligned on one important point—they want to build a better Calgary by preserving the best parts of the past, a past that they feel is being threatened. They are approaching this challenge in dramatically different ways.

I met Fred Woods at a Stampede party held by FirstEnergy Capital, an orgy of great food, beer, and guys and gals with cowboy hats and healthy appetites for business networking and, in some cases, old-fashioned sex. The FirstEnergy party in 2007 was known as FirstRowdier and there was nothing subtle about its intent. The admission ticket came complete with lists of recommended pick-up lines. For women, the conversational ice-breaker might be something like: "How BIG is your oil company?" and "Your belt buckle is SO BIG!" For men, the killer lines might be "I'm the sheriff 'round these parts" and "My horse is also quite cute." The party, held at a downtown hockey-themed venue called Flames Central, is a who's who of the oil patch, with a few politicians and cultural bigwigs thrown in. I was introduced to Fred, garbed in cowboy hat, checkered shirt, and blue jeans, and his wife Rosanne, but I was struck by their reticence amid such a party-hearty atmosphere. They were not having a good time. I yelled a few greetings to them over the country-rock band playing in the background, but we never really connected. They looked like deer caught in the headlights.

Little did I know that a few days earlier they had become the poster children for excessive, tasteless Calgary oil wealth. I had been travelling in the south of the province when the *Calgary*

Herald had run a front-page photo of Fred and Rosanne in a different context: standing with their kids in front of their nice Mount Royal home, explaining how they were planning to build a $10 million dream home, with an area of 1,300 square metres, that, they said, would be based on the design of the legendary Fairmont Banff Springs Hotel, turrets and all, as well as elements of the long-gone home of Canadian Pacific Railway builder Sir William Van Horne. They would tear down their own considerable mansion, as well as demolish the house they had bought beside it, to build an ersatz late-nineteenth-century dwelling, with a slide for their kids built on a spiral staircase, an open-air kitchen, and a gymnasium with five-metre ceilings. "We just had that vision of it being our castle," Rosanne naively confided to the *Herald* reporter.

Suddenly Fred and Rosanne were the targets of a notoriety they did not welcome. Calgarians were appalled by the couple's questionable taste, their showiness, their craving for attention, and the East was snickering at these crass Calgary arrivistes, who drove tasteless big cars with tacky vanity slogans ("Gore-Jus," declared Rosanne's new pink Caddie.) They were even pilloried for having a lot of Christmas-tree lights.

So, no wonder Fred and Rosanne were a bit wary of a reporter at a Stampede party. When a few months later I caught up with Fred in his office at Midnight Oil, he was still a bit bruised. I too didn't know what to expect, certainly not the quiet guy I met, someone who had risen from a humble background to become president of a medium-sized oil and gas company. He was still overwhelmed by the negative reaction and puzzled by the *Herald*'s decision to slap the picture on page one. He was clearly uncomfortable, but mainly wondering why he was being derided for being just honest and forthright.

If Fred Woods is uncomfortable, he should not be—not for having dreams of making Calgary a more interesting city. Calgary is merely having a case of growing pains and he got caught in the middle of a seizure of civic schizophrenia. Calgary should congratulate itself that it has a Fred Woods, a thoughtful guy with money who is passionate about the city. Fred is hardly the village idiot. He explained that over the years he had become a student of architecture conservancy, particularly the work of H. H. Richardson, the Boston architect whose château style inspired not just the statuesque Banff Springs (Bruce Price was the actual architect), but also the Château Frontenac in Quebec City and countless other urban landmarks. Fred is obsessed with preserving pieces of an era that is long past in Calgary, whose monuments have been torn down in an orgy of progress. "Architecture is a snapshot of the times," Fred says, and there are too few snapshots of the late-nineteenth- early-twentieth century.

In meeting Fred, I discovered a serious person who reads widely about history and current affairs. He was cracking David McCullough's biography of John Adams and gave me a copy of *The Black Swan*, the highly prescient book, written by a U.S. money manager on unforeseen events and how they change history—in the manner of the subprime crisis that has been racking the financial world. Fred also sat on the city's heritage authority, where he was dedicated to saving that old east-end watering hole and historic jazz club the King Edward Hotel.

A lifetime Calgarian, now in his fifties, he is the son of a furniture mover who was never around much when Fred was growing up. He took commerce at the University of Calgary, went straight into the oil industry and made some smart moves, rode the cycles and is now very well off, although he took a hit from the royalty increases introduced by Alberta's new premier. Now in his second marriage, and the father of seven children, he conducts Bible study in the early morning before he heads to work. While not a follower of any denomination, Fred has accepted that Christ is a big part of his life.

And so is architecture—creating a more complex image of Fred Woods than Calgary was ready for. He has seen his city knock down much of its heritage. His thinking is that if he could only leave some traces of this legacy, even in new houses, he would be contributing to the tone and style of Calgary, a city with no apparent memory. "I'm trying to sprinkle a little bit of that era around," he tells me.

But Calgary is not appreciative, for it is a city caught between its boom-town past and pretensions for the future. Fred Woods' vision did not fit with what it thinks it should be. It is ironic that old-money Toronto is not nearly as sensitive to such ambitions. When billionaire investor Gerry Schwartz and his bookstore-magnate-wife, Heather Reisman, tore down a neighbouring mansion in Rosedale to build a guest house and expand their garden, it got press play but was not the *cause célèbre* that befell poor Fred Woods.

For the past fifteen years, whenever I visited Calgary, I would embark on a little pilgrimage to Cochrane, twenty kilometres west of the city, mainly to visit Mackay's amazing ice cream shop, but also to get a bit closer to the mountains. With each visit, Calgary seemed to spread ever closer to Cochrane, devouring big chunks of rangeland. Million-dollar houses clung to the hills, and downtown Cochrane turned into a fake western movie set, not the genuine small town I first knew back in the 1980s. Cochrane was built on the site of the Cochrane Ranch, the great folly of the 1880s, where more than a thousand cattle died in a vainglorious attempt by greenhorn ranchers to defy nature. It is now the site of an urban park surrounded by McMansions. Cochrane's new folly is the crush of urban development across these lovely foothills.

This time, I leave Mackay's with my maple-walnut cone and head out to Smitty's Pancake House in a strip along the highway. It is a quiet Tuesday in early winter, with snow touching the hills above the Bow River as it winds its way to Calgary. Smitty's is occupied by a few retired folks and an aging cowboy who is the spitting image of actor Sam Elliott—droopy moustache, bowlegged walk, cowboy hat, and a bandana around his neck. In the corner, Tim Harvie, his sister Katie, and business partner Dave are winding up a little meeting about their cow-calf operation.

While Fred Woods is the son of a labourer, Harvie is the closest thing around Calgary to landed gentry. While Fred is planning his $10 million house, Tim decries the conspicuous consumption of the new rich. "We're living like the Romans and we're doomed like the Romans; we've got to respect where we've come from, not rape and pillage the land," says Tim, a lean compact man with the watchful eyes of a lifelong cattleman.

But there is a link between the two—both are absolutely determined to preserve the city's past in the face of sprawl and upheaval. And what a sprawl it is. With the exception of Vancouver, Canada's western cities have population densities that fall far short of some major cities in the East. It is just the way things have progressed, the function of being a small population on a vast prairie. For example, in an area the size of New York City, Calgary houses one-tenth of New York's population. It is an imprint so large that prairie towns like Balzac, High River, Cochrane, and Okotoks are being subsumed into the great maw of Calgary expansion. It puts tremendous pressure not only on water, sewage, and development, but also on the natural beauty. And yet it is the western way of urban development and a natural outgrowth of history and geography.

Tim Harvie's ranch has stood in the way of this steamroller, but Harvie decided he couldn't defy it forever. He decided to get proactive and try to guide development. So he and his three sisters sold 1,700 hectares of land to the province to create a park, including an expanse along the banks of the Bow River to the outskirts of Calgary. The cost was a bargain-basement

$40 million, about half what the land was worth, and the Harvies contributed $6 million to a trust to develop the parkland.

Near the city, the Harvie land links up with a piece of property owned by Calgary's energy godfather Dick Haskayne. He too did a deal, this time with the city. These two families, the best of community-minded Alberta wealth, have created the potential for something unique—a walking trail along the Bow all the way from downtown to the Mackay ice cream mecca. I could go for that.

And Tim Harvie hopes to plot a similar outcome for the ranchland he still owns near Cochrane. "Katie and I and Dave have a joint venture on a cow-calf operation," he explains. "I'm a grain farmer, which is my primary occupation, but in essence, we're ranching folk."

Ranching folk, maybe, but not your ordinary sodbusters. Tim Harvie's landholdings are, in some ways, a direct result of the first Leduc gusher, and yet here he is trying to limit the fallout from the latest incarnation of Leduc, the oil sands boom that has fuelled Calgary's new orgy of expansion. His grandfather Eric Harvie was a boy from Orillia, Ontario, who came to Alberta to practise law. He took some time off for a remarkable war experience in which his arm was almost blown off. After the war, he ended up with a lucrative practice working for some of the pioneering oilmen. He had married into the Southam publishing family but he was an entrepreneur on his own and over the years accumulated 195,058 hectares of leased and owned land around the province.

One of his clients owned land just south of Edmonton around the sleepy town of Leduc. The owner was in arrears for unpaid taxes and an enterprising Eric picked it up for almost nothing. All told he had about 40,468 hectares around Leduc. "It's a neat story, how he bought up land," Tim says. "It was moose pasture and people said he was nuts. He had a hunch and he got it for a song. It may have been for the gravel."

Then in 1947, a geologist with the mocking nickname of Dry Hole Hunter finally mastered the geology of the area for Imperial Oil, which drilled a well that blew up in a torrent of oil. That Leduc strike changed Alberta, it changed Canada, and it changed Eric Harvie, who became even wealthier than before. A quirky old codger, he collected artifacts that formed the basis of the Glenbow Foundation and ultimately the museum.

Much of his fortune was given to charity, but considerable land was bequeathed to his son, Neil, who was a passionate rancher, and now it is in the hands of Neil's son, Tim, and his three sisters. The family, Tim says, was raised on the idea of giving back, to question how much you really need of material things. "When I'm dead and gone, it won't matter how much I had of this land. We're such a blink in time." By creating a provincial park, he was building something for the ages.

That's easy for Tim to say, as the fifty-year-old scion of an old wealthy family. Would he deprive the new rich of a chance to enjoy their affluence? In the huge explosion of personal wealth in Alberta, the Harvies are nothing special anymore, he says, not when billions of dollars of oil riches are held in stock and stock options. And the problem he sees is not with the wealth itself, but with the conspicuous consumption—the Beemers, the million-dollar houses. There may be new Eric Harvies emerging who are prepared to give away their fortunes, but he doesn't believe they are coming forward in any proportion to wealth creation in the province.

"We're a me-first society, and preserving doesn't come naturally," Tim says.

The West's traditions are being trampled by the bulldozers rumbling west from Calgary, and, like Fred Woods, he is trying in his own little way to stop the landslide.

CHAPTER 11

FORT MURRAY

At the core of the new Calgary

IT WAS THE NIGHT THE STARS came out at the Ranchmen's Club, a 110-year-old private gathering place in the heart of Calgary. On a spring evening, the who's who of the city's business elite gathered here to do a bit of salesmanship. There was Ron Mathison, the intense energy financier and major property developer in Calgary's downtown. There was Ron Mannix, scion of the most powerful business family in the province, a secretive force in construction, oil, and coal. Dick Haskayne, the dean of Calgary energy executives who gave his name, and a lot of land, to the University of Calgary's business school, was in attendance— as were Mike Tims, the chairman of investment bank Peters & Co., and Charlie Fischer, who heads energy giant Nexen.

And above all, there was Murray Edwards, the billionaire financier at the centre of this network and the man who makes modern Calgary tick. Murray, like the others, was there to woo star economist Jack Mintz away from the University of Toronto to become an intellectual rainmaker at the University of Calgary. Edwards' old friend and mentor, prominent lawyer Jim Palmer, is the driving force behind the new university chair, which Mintz would occupy, as well as a new public policy institute, which Mintz would lead.

Mintz, who was born in Edmonton, is one of those peripatetic academics who has worked in the public service, understands capital markets, and has already run a think tank, the CD Howe Institute in Toronto. He is one of Canada's leading experts in comparative tax systems, and he has left the Howe Institute to return to his old teaching job at the University of Toronto. A bit restless, he is prime picking for a Calgary elite that, in an age of migrating academic superstars, wants to land one of its own. Mintz is being wooed by both the University of Calgary and the University of Alberta in Edmonton, but Calgary is clearly in the driver's seat with this demonstration of corporate firepower.

Months later, Harvey Weingarten, the university's president, would see the Ranchmen's Club event as pivotal in reinforcing the sense that it was not just the University of Calgary that was recruiting Jack Mintz. It was the Calgary business elite. "It was a very high-powered group sitting around that table," he recalls. "I think it was influential in his thinking to come here." It is an opinion Mintz himself endorses. Once the Calgary business elite was onside, and Weingarten and key faculty members were committed to back the institute, he was ready to jump.

Some time in the future, the capture of Jack Mintz may be looked back on as the turning point in the creation of a more ambitious, influential Calgary—a city that was no longer an intellectual and commercial outpost to Toronto, Houston, Denver, or London. And no one was more influential in the wooing than Murray Edwards, who was convinced Mintz was the ideal kind of eclectic thinker to head up the new School of Policy Studies. "He transcends the boundaries," Edwards told me later, after Mintz had agreed to come to Calgary. Edwards, a master strategist, is also thinking in a broader way about Alberta's role in national policy-making, which has often been seen as isolated, cranky, hurt, or insecure. Now that the West, and principally Alberta, have grown in economic strength and political confidence, he says, they have to create public institutes to help develop good policy.

Edwards has also become a major contributor to the Canada West Foundation, an influential, non-partisan think tank dedicated to studying the role of the West, but he is not restricted to Calgary. He has given $11 million to the University of Saskatchewan's school of business, of which he is a graduate. Now he has high hopes for the new U of C think tank and its potential for moulding better public-policy thinking and training. "If you're not willing to be part of the game, you can't complain about the score at the end," Edwards says.

He was also worried that a more complacent Alberta, and Canada, are not making good policy, after years of coasting on booming markets and a growing economy. He was contemptuous of a new provincial royalty regime that spanked the already hurting conventional energy industry. "I see political leaders talking just about where they can invest dollars or undertake new projects. I hear very little talk about maintaining a competitive economy, and it's almost like they assume this economy just happened and it will continue and I worry about that.

"You've got to have good public policy, you have to have competitive fiscal regimes, you have to have policies that don't discourage investment, such as capital taxes and non-refundable GST, " he says. "If I worry about anything in the public debate, in Alberta now, and lesser so in Canada, it is that there seems to be an assumption that the economic prosperity we are experiencing is a God-given right."

This talk betrays how, as Murray Edwards moves into his late forties, the health of the country is taking centre stage among his priorities. He wants to see a return to a competent and revered public service in Ottawa and in the provincial capitals that can be effective and respected. Like many business leaders, he is worried by the decline in status of senior public servants, which has become a downward spiral. It is becoming harder to enlist bright young people in a career that has lost its distinction. If he can help turn the tide, he is willing to bring a bit of money and clout to the table.

He also brings his formidable network, a group of younger entrepreneurs, men in their forties and early fifties who have worked with him over the years, made big money with and from Murray Edwards, and are now turning their attention to building a new kind of Calgary. The group around Murray is the most powerful determinant in how money is spent and invested in Calgary and what charities and philanthropies are supported. Their interests tend to be Calgary's interests. And they do not represent the angry Calgary of eastern caricatures, but a city that is more politically engaged, culturally and intellectually vibrant. Still a cowboy town, but a cowboy town with brains.

The old guard who made the modern Calgary are now in their seventies and eighties—revered oilmen like Haskayne, Harley Hotchkiss, Jim Gray, and Doc and Byron Seaman. They built a workable, functional, caring city, steeped in voluntarism and giving, in sports teams and recreation. The Olympics of 1988 were their high-water mark. Then the Flames won the Stanley Cup in 1989 with stars like Al MacInnis, Lanny Mac-Donald, and Doug Gilmour.

Now this is the town of Jarome Iginla, an African-Canadian star forward for the Flames, and it is the town of Murray Edwards, a kid from Saskatchewan. The outsiders have become the insiders. Then again, that is nothing new in shape-shifting Calgary, where the cast changes every week. "In Calgary old money is money that was made last week," Ron Mathison likes to say.

So that makes his friend Murray Edwards very old money. Edwards is so established, so legendary in Calgary business circles, that the only thing needed to identify him is his first name, like Elvis or Prince. "Murray" is doing this or "Murray" is thinking this way. Murray's big hand is everywhere in Calgary. He is a major investor in several landmark companies, including Canadian Natural Resources, the oil sands titan; the giant Penn West income trust; and oil-field services powerhouse Ensign

Energy Services. He owns a chunk of WestJet, Alberta's national airline, and is a co-founder and shareholder in FirstEnergy, the investment boutique.

But the new guard is more than Edwards, of course. Besides Mathison, his old friend and investing partner, it includes Brett Wilson, his even older friend from the University of Saskatchewan days; Mike Tims, an old colleague from his days at Peters & Co.; and George Gosbee, the youthful investment banker who runs Tristone Capital and devotes his spare time to building the Alberta College of Art & Design. Among professional managers of the big oil companies, there are Charlie Fischer, the CEO of Nexen, and Rick George, the U.S.–born engineer who built Suncor into an oil patch giant.

They have made their fortunes, and they are ready to make their mark in the broader community. For Calgary, they want not just a nice caring town, but intellectual leadership, cultural leadership, educational leadership, and they want to do it on the national and international stage, not as regional players.

The first thing you notice when you meet Murray Edwards is the sheer size of the man, the big beefy paw that reaches across to engulf your tiny hand. There is the physical presence that seems to fill up the room. It is not just a question of girth, and Murray's weight is known to go up and down. It is the pure brute force of the man, both intellectual and physical, that is apparent.

We are in the offices of his holding company Edco, a haven of dark wood and prairie art on the thirty-second floor of the Bow Valley Square, Tower 3, in downtown Calgary. Call it Fort Murray, a quiet redoubt in Calgary's downtown rush-hour bustle, as the hordes head for the suburbs. The office reception area is graced by two paintings by Saskatchewan artist Dorothy

Knowles, one of a twisting coulee in winter, the other of a river valley in summer. From the small meeting room off the reception area, Edwards can view downtown Calgary, Nose Hill to the north and on the western horizon, the mountains.

Edwards acknowledges he has become a bit of a public philanthropist, although he is reluctant to make a big splash. He and his wife are dedicated to children and education. They are big contributors to the new Alberta Children's Hospital in Calgary. His major commitment is to education: to the University of Calgary, and his alma mater, the University of Saskatchewan.

At this stage in life, it is Murray Edwards' wish to be a player at the table of policy and ideas. He is a rarity in the Calgary oil industry, a Liberal in a Tory city where his fellow Liberal, headhunter Tim Hamilton, says "I am protected by the game laws." Edwards says his political instincts are complex: he is a fiscal conservative and a social liberal, which sounds like a centrist Paul Martin kind of Liberal. He finds that the major two political parties are closer together in views than at any time in history.

He has, for example, been picked by a Conservative government to be part of a federal panel studying Canada's competition landscape, including the debate over the alleged hollowing out of corporate Canada. The final report carries the unmistakable imprint of Edwards' economic views: a call for a more competitive economy, with higher productivity, an end to internal trade barriers, and a more aggressive business culture. It is constructive and intelligent but hardly revolutionary. The report even contains a trademark Edwards hockey analogy: "We must skate harder, shoot harder and keep our elbows up in the corners."

Yet Edwards is a man of nuanced and sometimes unpredictable opinions, most notably expressed when he broke from the energy pack in Calgary by agreeing with the thrust of the federal Conservative government's crackdown on income trusts, even though he had a fair bit of his wealth tied up in one major trust, Penn West. It was a highly divisive moment among the denizens of the oil patch, when their own party—their own Harper government—kicked them in the teeth by slapping a tax on hitherto untaxed income trusts, thus rendering them toothless and ultimately doomed. It effectively destroyed the bonanza in trust conversions, wiping out tens of billions of dollars in market value. It came after the Conservatives had promised in the previous election not to touch the trusts, even though it was clear these instruments were distorting capital markets and the economy.

It was clear to Ewards, a major investor and backer of trusts, there could not continue to be a gap between the tax rates of trusts and corporations. It would be the end of the taxable corporation and it would be bad for Canada's productivity. "For some time, I've advocated that there had to be a levelling of the field of tax rates between trusts and corporations," he had told Deborah Yedlin, then writing for the *Globe and Mail*. "Ideally, that would have been achieved by lowering tax rates on corporations . . . but that just wasn't doable politically or economically, from the point of funding our social programs. I think the government made the best decision in a tough situation."

Edwards got an easier ride from the energy community than Gwyn Morgan, a highly partisan social conservative whose public support for the income trust decision was treated as utter betrayal in Calgary. "I've got great respect for Murray," says Morgan, the former CEO of energy giant EnCana and a confidant of Stephen Harper. Morgan liked the fact that Edwards opposed the income trusts even though he was an investor and backer of one of the biggest trusts. "And he's a Liberal by God—but just a tremendous person and he just stands for principle," Morgan asserts.

Edwards is also a capitalist, a believer in wealth creation and he can be a tiger on the things he does not like. When I met up with him in early 2008, he was savage in his denunciation of the provincial government's energy royalty policies, which he argued were driving capital and investment out of Alberta. It had tipped over the balance in wealth creation, and betrayed a fundamental lack of understanding. Public policy, in Murray Edwards' mind, must not willfully destroy wealth.

As a native Saskatchewanian, he had seen his home province struggle through the 1970s and '80s, when a lot of university graduates like himself left the province because they couldn't see a future at home. Now the tables have turned and Saskatchewan is finally starting to see some serious wealth creation. He noted the province is a lot more cautious about major policy changes that would jeopardize that economic growth. Saskatchewan has seen the other side, he said, where you slide down a slippery slope of chasing away capital and investment. Now he believed Alberta was doing just that by raising royalties excessively. "You've got to have economic activity. You create far more value by having people working in good-paying jobs than you do by having too-high royalties."

For an exasperated Edwards, it is another example of flawed policy by people who don't take a broad view of the link between taxation and wealth creation. "I think that people saw the level of economic activity in Alberta and they assumed it would continue forever. And it's not a given right and the process of royalty review was a flawed result. I'm the first one to say there are opportunities to have royalties adjusted upwards. You could make changes but you had to make sure those changes are not so extreme they will imperil investment."

It is a show of pique that reminds me of another aspect of Murray—he is not a good guy to cross. Canadian Natural Resources had announced it was moving much of its natural gas drilling activity out of Alberta because of the royalty squeeze, although it was still committed to the nearly completed first phase of its Horizon project in the oil sands.

When Edwards is asked if he is an Albertan first or a Canadian, he says he would consider himself a Saskatchewanian first. This is where a lot of his values evolved. They are similar to the values in Alberta—pioneering and entrepreneurial, but he talks a lot about being well grounded, and not going to extremes in personality or moods. "I think part of my approach is not to get too high on the successes or too down on the challenges, because if you do you will drive yourself crazy. And as you get too high on the successes, you will forget about the value system that got you there."

Murray traces that balance back to hometown Regina, where he was born into a family that was not "poor," as some accounts suggest, but not well off either. His father, Bill, was a chartered accountant and his mother, Noreen, a schoolteacher. His parents are said to have nurtured a love of education and hard work in their children. Murray has a brother who is an oral surgeon in Calgary, and a sister who is an optometrist in Regina.

With that kind of background, it is no wonder the family is sometimes amazed by what one of their sons has accomplished. Many years later, when Murray was worth a lot of money, he wanted to give his mother $15,000 for a Christmas present. She said no thanks, commenting that Murray couldn't really afford it. Murray tried to be gentle: "Mom, do you read what the newspapers write about me?" His mother thought about it and said she didn't believe what they write. Murray finally explained to his mother that if half of what the media wrote about him was true, he could quite easily afford the gift.

Edwards has said his father was not a capitalist type—he had a healthy skepticism of investments and entrepreneurialism. Murray became a rebel in pinstripes by defying expectations and pursuing a commerce degree from the University of Saskatchewan. Even then he was interested in politics and represented the college of commerce in the student government, where for a time he was vice-president, finance.

Westerners are not known for being old-school types who

wallow in nostalgia for their university years. But Murray's time at the University of Saskatchewan produced friendships that endure to this very day. In fact, at university, he began to assemble the tight web of personal relationships that now constitutes "the friends of Murray."

Brett Wilson remembers meeting Murray in student politics, where Wilson represented engineering and Edwards was the commerce delegate. "By about the third week, we were both sitting in the corner so we could talk about the stock market and life and girls. We just stayed in touch." After his commerce degree, Edwards journeyed east to the University of Toronto to get a law degree and then headed out to Calgary to join Burnet Duckworth & Palmer, the law firm co-founded by Jim Palmer, an elegantly congenial force in the Calgary legal scene. The bow-tied Palmer grew up in the Maritimes and is the great-grandson of a Father of Confederation from Prince Edward Island. He graduated from Dalhousie Law School in Halifax in 1952, and hitched a ride with a friend who was heading home to Calgary. At that time, Calgary was a cowtown of 120,000 people, not today's metropolis of a million. Palmer, who was somewhat disillusioned with the stagnant East Coast economy and the Maritime sense of entitlement, fell in love with the rough-and-ready place. He became a confirmed westerner and now carries the ultimate Alberta badge of honour: "When I came here, everybody had a chip on his shoulder toward the East and now I have a chip on my shoulder," he laughs.

He has carried the Liberal torch in the city for years, even when being a Liberal was treated like an incurable disease. He even ran for the Liberals federally in 1979, the standard-bearer for the very unpopular Pierre Trudeau. Trudeau would make his trademark comments insulting to the West and Palmer would call up Trudeau aides to complain: "For Christ's sake, I'm running out here."

He was fated, of course, never to become an MP, but his law

firm was scrappy and was known for taking smaller entrepreneurial clients to pay the bills, rather than the big oil companies.
It had some rough years in the 1980s in the wake of the energy
meltdown, but it survived to catch the next wave and did well
from the income trust boom. It is now one of the four elite firms
of Calgary, which also include Bennett Jones, Fraser Milner Casgrain, and Macleod Dixon.

Murray Edwards was mentored by Palmer and made partner within three years, the youngest to obtain that designation
in the history of the firm. But he was always interested in investing, and one of his principal clients was the start-up investment
boutique Peters & Co., founded by a hotshot broker named Rob
Peters and populated by young phenoms whom Peters had attracted to the business.

The turning point for Edwards came during a Stampede
party in 1987 when a twenty-six-year-old friend suddenly became sick and was diagnosed with brain cancer. He would die
fifteen months later. Edwards once told the *National Post*:
"The whole time he was sick I'd visit him a lot. He was a broker and a Liberal activist. I used to tell him, 'Why don't you
smell the roses? Why don't you go walk in the grass and just
read a book?'

"Instead he spent his time on the phone, talking to his
clients, or selling Liberal Party memberships to anyone who
walked into his hospital room.

"Watching somebody so young struggle with cancer taught
me how precious life is. I was twenty-eight and I said to myself:
'I want to do exactly what I enjoy.' So I decided to go out and
try my skills as a businessman."

He joined forces with two men who would change his life,
Ron Mathison, a tightly wound chartered accountant from Winnipeg, and Jim Grenon, also Winnipeg born and a smart financing guy. Both were rising stars at Peters and they joined up
with Edwards and their own firm to form a joint venture, Peters

& Co. Capital, a merchant bank that would take stakes in companies, recapitalize them, turn them around, and make them grow.

It was a golden moment in the modern evolution of Calgary because it brought together such an all-star cast—Mathison was brilliant at structuring deals, Grenon was a financing whiz, and Edwards a shrewd strategist, always thinking several steps ahead of the pack. And Peters & Co. had other rising performers who were close to the magical three—people like Mike Tims, the grandson of a Calgary bricklayer who had worked on building the Banff Springs Hotel, and Wilf Gobert, who hailed from a Belgian-Canadian farming family in western Ontario and became Calgary's top energy analyst—probably the best in Canada.

But it was Edwards, Mathison, and Grenon who set themselves apart from the rest. They would sit around the table and make things happen. They invested, for example, in a company called Canadian Natural Resources, a kind of grab bag for mining and other resource interests, and they focused it entirely on oil and gas. When they took it over it had a capitalization of $10 million. Recently, the market capitalization was more than $35 billion, and it is building the next oil sands mining project, joining Syncrude, Suncor, and Shell. A similar formula worked for Penn West and Rio Alto, as well as services player Ensign. All became powerhouses as the team performed its magic. Edwards loved being part of that team and making a difference, which he could not do in law.

Mathison is a handsome, finely boned man, a proud person who clearly cares about his legacy, but if anything, he is even more private than Murray. His name rarely appears in the press, even though he is among Calgary's wealthiest people. The two are friends, and remain partners in some ventures, but it was perhaps inevitable they were to part company. "You don't need to have two drivers on the same bus," says one business leader who knows them both well.

Mathison's bootstrap biography is fairly typical of the new guard. His background is rural and if not poor, at least undistinguished. His father grew up in Gleichen, a small town east of Calgary, which has developed a legend as a hothouse for business leaders. One of the central gathering spots in Gleichen was a butcher shop run by Dick Haskayne's family.

Ron was born in Calgary, but the family moved to Winnipeg where he attended the University of Manitoba. He came out with a Bachelor of Commerce degree and later a chartered accountant designation. He went back to Calgary as a senior tax manager at Peat Marwick, but he started doing a bunch of work for Peters & Co. through Jim Grenon, and he met Murray Edwards. "Murray was our counsel, we were doing deals and he was at Burnet Duckworth & Palmer, and he was the lawyer of choice for stuff we did," Mathison recalls. "He and Jim had always talked about forming some kind of enterprise and we ended up getting through a complicated series of transactions."

Working at a time of low oil and gas prices, Edwards, Mathison, and Grenon made big, smart bets on the future of commodities, but really their ability was to wring operational leverage out of these ragtag companies. They would make the companies run better, become more efficient. Thus, when the commodity prices started to move up, the bottom-line leverage was dramatic.

Eventually, after making a lot of money together, the partners began to drift away to their personal projects. Edwards and Mathison remained investors together in the big legacy vehicles, such as CNRL. They both hold on to assets for long periods. At one point, Matheson liked to joke that he has only sold enough CNRL shares to redo the kitchen in his house. As for Edwards, he likes to say that "I'm a terrible seller."

One of Mathison's major vehicles is Calfrac, a true Canadian innovator in a method of drilling called hydraulic fracturing, a technology that Canada's energy industry has taken to the world. It has been one of the sterling examples of how the oil patch can stimulate innovation, that extraction is not the simple-minded process so stigmatized by the Dutch disease crowd. Mathison has collected a brain trust of expertise around the offices of his holding company Matco—he can quickly call on geologists, surveyors, drilling specialists in a kind of dynamic cluster of technical people. He does not own all these companies, but they are part of Mathison's vast sounding board, allowing him to pull some geologist into a meeting to get a point of view. This speed is valuable because the city's business community is still intimate enough that deals can be done with a handshake.

Mathison is also changing Calgary's skyline. He and some partners have been constructing a forty-nine-storey office tower called Eighth Avenue Place on the site of what was once a Calgary landmark—a retail mall called Penny Lane, assembled from buildings that date back a century. The building has its detractors who say they would have expected more than the box-like structure going up on such an historic site—a site that also contained the legendary nightclub Cowboys.

Yet Mathison, like Edwards, is concerned about the fabric of downtown Calgary, particularly the social stresses that are reflected in the panhandlers and drug dealers arrayed along the eastern blocks of Stephen Avenue, a pedestrian mall. Mathison is not noisy about it. He worries people will accuse him of naked self-interest and, obviously, it is in his interest to keep the streets clean. But he is alarmed that the old, safe Calgary is going, replaced by a grittier, grimier, more violent place, where drug deals and drive-by shootings will become more frequent. The city is going through a loss of innocence, and he is not happy about that. Calgary is becoming a world-class city; with that come world-class problems.

Murray Edwards always takes pains to indicate he was not actually part of Peters & Co.—he was just a joint venture partner with Peters in a merchant banking concern. So in the early 1990s, he reunited with his old university friend, Brett Wilson, and two other financiers, to form a rival boutique investment firm called FirstEnergy Capital.

Murray's leaving the Peters partnership to set up a competing firm is still a touchy point. But he has not burned bridges and remains close to many of his old Peters colleagues.

Peters in fact has a reputation for launching impressive careers, and then watching its graduates cash in after leaving the firm. It has been a kind of finishing school for some of the best business minds in Calgary, including Mathison, Edwards, Grenon, and George Gosbee. One problem in the early years was that Rob Peters, the charismatic founder, dominated the firm's profile and its surplus income pool. It was only when Peters left daily operations and began to sell off his equity in the mid 1990s that junior employees felt they could make serious money. But in some cases, that wasn't enough—there was more money to be made by investing on their own outside Peters & Co.

Mike Tims agrees the company has bred more than its share of tycoons, and the Peters culture is one reason. "There is a terrific pipeline of information here. There is a style of doing deals and thinking about deals. People who come here find that the learning by osmosis is really dramatic. We bring young people in and after a year or two it's shocking how much they know. A lot of it is because there is a great idea exchange and different points of view discussed."

The stockily built Tims is widely admired in Calgary for his straight-shooting honesty and likeability. Asked why he didn't go off on his own, he lapses into what sounds like the usual clichés about loyalty. In his case, it rings sincere. He is the institutional memory at Peters, he acknowledges. "I'm not an out-there kind of person. I'm trying to have a level of humility in my life. I would say that's a good way to describe it—I'm a lot of the memory and glue and part of a lot of the relationships."

Murray Edwards' new firm, FirstEnergy, did well by catching the boom in oil and gas financings through the 1990s and the early years of the twenty-first century. Along the way, it has gone through some transitions. It struck a partnership with the French bank Société Générale, which became a 20 per cent owner of the Calgary operation.

In the late 1990s, Brett Wilson, its co-founder and driving force in marketing the investment bank, suffered a number of personal crises. He went through a divorce in 1999 and he had to rebuild his relationship with his three children. Then in 2001, he was diagnosed with prostate cancer, which has caused him to re-evaluate his life. He slowed down his client work, switched from president to chairman of FirstEnergy, and turned his considerable charm and enthusiasm to becoming a highly public philanthropist with a sense of mission. A roguishly handsome man, Wilson has a disarming candour. He is a salesman at heart, and you just want to buy from him, whether it is an equity deal or some charity pitch. And he is astonishingly frank. On meeting him for the first time, you know all about his kids, his passions, his sicknesses.

When I met him in March 2007, he had recently been through some rough times. "I had some health issues this fall that were worse than the cancer," he told me. "My pumping system shut down and there was bleeding." He admits he went through three and a half months of hell and, during that time, working with spiritualists and other untraditional support, he decided to pull back even further from FirstEnergy.

He was building up his personal merchant banking business, and was easing himself out of the day-to-day grind. But he was just as engaged in a cascade of volunteer projects. He told me he doesn't plan to give his fortune to his children, except to fund their education. His money will go to his charity projects, whether domestic-abuse issues, native problems, building projects in underdeveloped countries, or cancer research. Asked how his two daughters and son will be able to cope, Wilson says: "None of them can live through the inheritance because basically there will not be one. Both my ex-wife and I hope the children will develop passion in their own right." He is pleased they seem to be doing just that.

Wilson knows a lot of people in the West, and he was planning a big event to fight prostate cancer, a fiftieth birthday party in June 2007 at Calgary's Jubilee Auditorium for himself and thirteen other energy executives. By invitation only, it raised $3 million for cancer research and signalled the definitive changing of the guard in Calgary philanthropy. Peter Noone of Herman's Hermits performed, as did Randy Bachman and Burton Cummings of The Guess Who. The birthday boys were the middle-aged boomers of the oil patch, including lawyer John Brussa, veteran energy executive Keith McPhail, and Wilson's FirstEnergy partner Jim Davidson.

Oil-patch veterans have at times questioned whether the new guard would step up to the charity plate. That suggestion has rankled Wilson who had poured his heart into charity work. "The older guys are hogging the profile, but there is a lot of work being done in the trenches," he says. His philanthropy also focuses increasingly on his home province, including his birthplace of North Battleford, and the University of Saskatchewan in Saskatoon, where he has supported the new Wilson Centre of Entrepreneurship and Innovation. "I'm doing a lot of charity work there because the dollar for value equation is outstanding. I want to knock the whining down a bit—about Alberta always doing so well."

His father was the sales manager at a Ford dealership in North Battleford. "I understood sales, and understood the car business, and my mom was a social worker with an interest in child welfare. My roots are capitalism with a heart."

Meanwhile, he remains close to Murray Edwards, whose insight he admires. He notes that as a major shareholder, Edwards still attends FirstEnergy partner retreats, as well as the odd meeting where there is a fair bit of controversy. "He can come in as a kind of not-so-gentle arbitrator because he is willing to take anyone to task," Wilson says delicately.

Wilson admits that he and Murray had a disagreement four or five years ago that ended in them not speaking to each other. "Then someone put us both in a room and slapped us. I think he sort of apologized and I think I sort of accepted it. Those words weren't used but we rekindled the friendship. For a while we were communicating through our staffs."

Bring up Brett Wilson's very public conversion to high-profile philanthropy, and Murray Edwards suggests that is not his way. To each his own, and he would never comment on a friend's style of giving. Yet Edwards is going through a less intense version of Wilson's transformation. Murray, the workaholic, admits he is searching for more balance in his life, as part of his new role as husband and father.

In 2003, he took himself off the list of Calgary's most eligible bachelors by marrying Heather Bala, a former spokeswoman for Herb Dhaliwal, a Liberal cabinet minister who served as minister of natural resources. It was a typical low-key Murray production—just seventy of his close friends and family members. He had met Bala while Dhaliwal was pushing for ratification of the Kyoto Accord, which Edwards, like many oil titans, did not find workable. He had joked at an investment conference that the wedding "is the only good thing to come out of Kyoto."

There is no doubt that, besides giving birth to their child, she is good for him in helping attain balance. When he started out in business, he liked to paraphrase a line from Professor Henry Higgins in *My Fair Lady*: "Happiness is the man whose vocation is also his hobby." It was an appropriate credo because Murray had little life except work. He loved what he did, not just the making of money but the making of companies. As he got older, moving into his late forties, the Henry Higgins line still largely applied, but he was trying to get a life outside his work.

When he first got involved in Canadian Natural, Rio Alto, and Penn West, those companies were producing small amounts of oil. But they ultimately grew to be 100,000- to 500,000-barrel giants—including CNRL, which would be one of the champions of the oil sands. "I naively thought as these companies got bigger they would take less of my time. And although my role changed they still took a lot of time. I've been trying to simplify my life and focus on fewer rather than more."

Edwards is a captive of his management style. He believes in flat organizations, where every senior manager has responsibility not only for his or her area, whether finance or marketing or operations, but also for understanding what is happening in every area of the company. He does not believe in the all-knowing CEO who can make decisions on every aspect of the organization. He says companies are more capable and happier places to work when everyone is involved in charting the company's course.

But to listen to Edwards, that lack of hierarchy—the collegial decision making—puts tremendous pressure on the guy who is the glue for the organization and, in the Edco circle of companies, that guy is Murray Edwards. He is not an executive in any of the companies in which he is an investor, but he is often a director or even a vice-chairman. His leverage is at the board level and it is highly personal. He must keep on top of decision making at companies across diverse sectors—energy, energy services, tourism, manufacturing, aerospace and aviation, mining and hockey. "People tell me, gee, Murray, you're a lucky guy, you don't have any boss, you just do what you do," he says, laughing. "And I say, no—in fact I have more bosses than anybody I know. That's because I'm involved in a number of different activities and because I like to have organizations that are fairly flat."

At the same time, at under fifty he is clearly not ready to retire, and spend all his time giving his money away. He is one of the happiest men in Calgary because he loves what he does. "I really believe people go to work for more than financial reward. They go to work to be part of something. That's what motivates me. I like to be part of building something and having success." It sounds easy to say if you are only forty-eight and worth more than $2 billion, but he clearly believes it.

He agrees that in recent years, he has stepped forward as more of a philanthropist. The University of Saskatchewan donation, which bestowed the Edwards name on the school of business, was particularly important to him because the institution gave him so many of his tools. "If you give enough money to anything, they'll name it after you," he says, groaning a bit.

While Edwards has diversified his giving, he is also ranging wider in where he puts his investment capital. In 2007, he made a small—for him—$40 million investment in a Toronto wealth management company called Jovian Capital. For Murray it was recognition that he had a lots of exposure to the resource sector and that sector has enjoyed a good run. But with the higher royalties and a tougher conventional energy market, he figures there are headwinds coming and he is simply transferring some capital away from resources to financial services. And wealth management looks increasingly attractive as the boomer generation prepares to retire.

His golden touch has not been apparent with another part of his portfolio, the Ontario-based aircraft-parts maker called

Magellan, which like many players in the manufacturing industry has been hit hard by the soaring Canadian dollar. Brent Jang, the *Globe*'s transportation reporter, figures Edwards lost $164 million from his investment portfolio over the decade leading to early 2008 because of the collapsing value of his Magellan shares. Jang also reported that he was trying his best to keep Magellan afloat by providing loans totalling $65 million to the aircraft manufacturer, as well as backstopping the company's operating line of credit of $90 million (U.S.) and $75 million (Canadian). He had pledged his own collateral to the lenders—Canadian Imperial Bank of Commerce, Bank of Nova Scotia, Royal Bank of Canada, and Pennsylvania-based Sovereign Bank, according to a credit agreement filed with regulators. This commitment is not critical in a fortune that is worth more than $2 billion, according to Jang's calculations, and is heavily committed to the oil sands, but it shows the depth of Magellan's and manufacturing's woes if they confound the man who in some other sectors seems invincible. Edwards was getting much more involved in Magellan than he wanted to be at this stage in his career.

When I talked to Edwards in early 2008, it was clear that the Magellan situation was vexing him. The dollar was the major irritant because the currency had just in the past year moved up by 25 per cent—and this in a company where gross profits were only 15 per cent. "I don't care who you are—there is going to be pain adjusting. It's been a real challenging sector for us, but as I tell the guys, we've been knocked off our horses, let's get right back up and go at it."

He was also critical of an Ontario government whose policies had at times militated against the competitiveness of its manufacturers. The province had failed to harmonize its sales tax with the GST and it had, until recently, imposed capital taxes that actively discouraged investment. Indeed, Magellan was increasingly investing abroad, mainly in Great Britain, because the tax situation was more coherent there. In Edwards' view, it was another example of the lack of good public policy.

Alberta, despite the royalty irritant, was a more pleasing topic of conversation. There will be some ups and downs but Murray is convinced Alberta will be a rich economy for decades to come. It will be a resource economy, not a highly diversified industrial powerhouse. He is not convinced that forced diversification is a good idea. Like many Albertans, he sees the province diversifying within resources, rather than looking for silver bullets elsewhere.

He reaches for one of his reliable hockey metaphors: "I would argue that you always play to your strength," he says, and if you have a Sidney Crosby on your team, you don't work on how to play without your star player. "You've got to play Sidney Crosby on the power play, on penalty kills, at full strength; you play him the last minute of the game; you play to your strengths."

To Edwards, resources are the Sidney Crosbys of the Canadian economy and so you go with resources. "In Canada and Alberta, we are somewhat of a resource-based economy, we can't get around it. We shouldn't deny we have that . . . People say we have to diversify the economy. I argue that no, we have to make sure first that the resource sector is a very resourceful sector. Over time Canada has become a world leader in technology for mining and oil and gas—in horizontal drilling, fracking methods, in manufacturing methods in Nisku for building rigs—and equipment being taken around the world."

The way to build a sustainable economy, he says, is to develop technologies and expertise that spin off from what you do well. He is confident the resource sector is going to be a major part of the Alberta and the Canadian economy for the foreseeable future. "I remember a senior member of the government telling me when Nortel was $110 that this was the future of Canada, and that Nortel was going to be what would lead

Canada to the next generation. I said, 'I love Nortel, great company, but be careful we don't forget our strengths in the resources.'" Of course today Nortel is a shadow of its old self and all the action is in resources.

Edwards sees himself as Mr. In Between, a kind of bridge from the old Calgary of wildcat drillers and explorers to the new world of investment banking, finance, and oil sands chemists and engineers. He's been in Calgary for twenty-five years and he has seen it change—and not change. However much of a modernizer, he is still a willing captive of the old myths of Calgary as a community with heart.

Edwards, a man known more for the poetry of the balance sheet than of the spoken word, gets positively mystical when he talks about how these values are formed from the geography of the place. "The mountains ground you," he says looking out his window at the peaks in the horizon. "Mountains keep things in perspective; the mountains are there; they've been there for generations. The permanence of that granite rock, I think it creates a grounding in Alberta that I don't see elsewhere."

CHAPTER 12

THE HOUSE THAT GWYN BUILT

EnCana's construction

IF YOU LOOK FOR THE PHYSICAL things that define Calgary, you might think about the mountain vistas, the Calgary Tower, Nose Hill Park, or the Saddledome arena. But for about a year in the first decade of the twenty-first century, it was the big crater in the eastern end of downtown that blocked a whole major artery on Sixth Avenue SE, frustrated drivers and pedestrians, and dominated the centre of the city. It was the building site of the Bow, a fifty-eight-storey skyscraper whose construction was stopping traffic and starting dreams of a more powerful, confident city.

When finished, it will be the tallest building west of Toronto, a twisting eccentric masterpiece that is the conception of the superstar British architect Sir Norman Foster. Just as the Bow defines the new Calgary, it is also a perfect representation of EnCana, the company that will occupy the building for its head office—an unconventional building based on unconventional resources whose exploration and production were spearheaded by an unconventional personality.

The Bow is the House that Gwyn built, but Gwyn Morgan was not around to see its construction. In fact, he had become as much of a lightning rod as the building that will emerge from that construction site. He built EnCana to be the biggest company in the West, the biggest company in Canada by market capitalization, the world's largest producer of natural gas, a true Canadian champion—but he then retired suddenly at sixty for a brace of directorships and bully pulpits for his brand of ideological conservatism.

He did not go gently into the night. As a confidant of Stephen Harper, in the period after the 2006 federal election he was to become a kind of appointments czar for the new prime minister but was beaten up by a parliamentary committee that seized upon his right-wing agenda and controversial views on immigration. Then he quit the EnCana board in the middle of a dispute over energy trusts, whose termination he had endorsed— just as EnCana was contemplating its own conversion to a trust. So he became the most incendiary business figure in Alberta, in Canada, even as he moved to a new house he and wife Pat Trottier had built near Victoria. There are parts of Calgary where people spit his name, but in another breath insist that he was crucified by eastern ideologues and leftist slimeballs. Like the Bow building, Gwyn Morgan unleashes polarized views in Calgary, ranging from "Gwyn Morgan was lynched" to "Gwyn Morgan is the reincarnation of Benedict Arnold."

Gwyn is thus the true Alberta maverick and his exit, physically and emotionally, from the city he helped mould is a sign of how badly the province deals with real renegade behaviour. He is the ultimate Albertan of legend and myth. They should already be sizing his plaque for the wall of the mavericks exhibition at the Glenbow Museum. He is a rags-to-riches story, courageous, patriotic, and even heroic in having created a true Canadian champion, but also strident, self-righteous, and out of touch with the lives of ordinary people, people who are not fit, not healthy, and not conservative, like him. He is the kind of guy you'd want to lead you into battle, but would not necessarily want running the peace that follows. What might be viewed as courage is viewed in some circles as just excessive rigidity.

Not that he cares much. "If someone says to me I'm rigid, I

say no, I'm principled," Gwyn says to me one morning in Montreal where he is attending a board meeting at one of his directorships, that of engineering giant SNC-Lavalin. With hardly an ounce of fat on his body, he is a lean, taut whippet of a man in crisp white shirt and tie, and bright eyes that flash out at you behind spectacles. "If people want to accuse me of being rigid around principles and values, then I'll stand up for that."

It is this courage, this contrariness, that made him an effective business leader in leading Alberta's transition from a producer of conventional energy—the easy-to-harvest oil and gas, which is declining—to unconventional oil and gas, which is the future. When oil and gas were in huge supply in the Western Canadian Sedimentary Basin, it was a game of finding the stuff, drilling it, and moving on. But decades of extraction had taken their toll on the basin to the extent that every barrel being harvested was not being replaced in newly found reserves. The smart money determined that the future lay in unconventional sources—that is, in the oil sands, heavy oil, gas that could be found in shale, in deep and narrow pools, in sources that were hard to find, hard to extract, and hard to refine. With the oil price rising, and gas following its own volatile path, and with new technologies beating down operating costs, out-of-favour energy sources became the hot tickets.

Gwyn Morgan was a visionary of this unconventional wisdom, as were Murray Edwards and his friends at Canadian Natural Resources, and Rick George, the CEO of Suncor, the other Canadian giant of the oil sands. A strikingly handsome man, George turned around the once-tattered Suncor, a Canadian remnant of Sun Oil Co., of Philadelphia. Sun Oil's owners, the Pew family, were early converts to the oil sands and, often against conventional wisdom, drove the creation of the Great Canadian Oil Sands project of the 1960s. Long after Sun Oil (later Sunoco) divested its Canadian arm, Rich George is carrying out the Pews' vision in Fort McMurray.

While Morgan can be a bit of a loose cannon, Rick George brings a cool, corporate style to his job. He simply looks like a CEO: solid, athletic, with a face that creases into deep lines when he smiles. He is a U.S.–born engineer but he has become a Canadian citizen and he insists he is absolutely devoted to Canada. While Gwyn Morgan is a Canadian who often respouses American values, Rick George is an American who sounds uncommonly Canadian. "I love this country and all my family is Canadian, my wife and children," he says. "I think it is a good culture, a caring culture. It's a country that does care about all of its citizens." George also loves Alberta, a province where everything seems so accessible, particularly for a guy who is devoted to the outdoors. Yet he keeps his weekend home in Montana, south of Alberta, where he is a downhill and cross-country skier, a golfer, and a fly fisherman.

George's great breakthrough was building the big Millennium expansion to Suncor's oil sands project, at a time when the price of oil was far below $20 a barrel. He was aggressive in using forward contracts to limit Suncor's exposure to fluctuating prices, but was caught unawares by the startling rise in global prices. His road has never been an easy one. Suncor has always grappled with capital and operating costs that rose above expectations. But George has remained the picture of calm in the midst of crisis— and there have been crises. In January 2005, the Fort McMurray upgrader was hit by a devastating fire that sharply reduced production for nine months and sucked away a great deal of management focus at a time when the oil price was soaring past $50 a barrel. In early 2007, Suncor sued a group of engineering firms, including giant Bechtel Group, for $630 million, alleging substandard piping contributed to the fire's outbreak. Suncor was suing on behalf of its insurers, from whom it has already collected almost a billion dollars in business-interruption payments. It is one of Canada's largest business-interruption settlements and another example of the scale of investment and risk in the oil sands.

Born in Brush, Colorado, George had literally grown up in the energy business and worked as a labourer in oil camps to finance his way through engineering school. He came up in the Sun family of companies, moved to Britain as a Sun manager, and came to Suncor in the early 1990s, when it was still a neglected Sun subsidiary. Basically, he rebuilt it, but he had help. It was a Suncor oil sands executive named Dee Parkinson, a Queen's University–trained engineer, who carried the torch for Fort McMurray. A rare female executive in the oil patch of the 1980s and 1990s, she was central to the decision to switch from the unwieldy drag lines to the truck-and-shovel mining technology. But she left the company in 1996, and George has continued the unconventional legacy, not only in the oil sands but also as a pioneer in ethanol production and in moving his company into wind power.

"I often talk about the oil patch as kind of moving in a herd," he said in an interview with the *Globe and Mail*. "There are three or four hundred oil companies in this town who move together. Part of it is because if commodity prices drop and our costs get too high it impacts everybody. But I often say if you see that whole herd move in one direction, you'd better look somewhere else because the money usually is being made in a different direction."

That has been Suncor's credo, just as it has been EnCana's, and it very much reflects the strong personalities of the two CEOs who led these companies through most of the past decade. Gwyn Morgan first developed this sense of purpose early in life on a grain and cattle farm near Carstairs, Alberta, an hour north of Calgary. His father was born in Wales, the son of a baker, and his grandparents moved the family out to homestead in Alberta. They were not ready for that life. "It was godawful, hardscrabble bush country west of Carstairs," Morgan says. "My father didn't have a farm the first winter, it was minus forty and he lived on shooting rabbits."

Morgan was formed by the discipline of farm life with its early rising, its physical demands, and its hard work. Chores occupied two hours of every day. "I was a tough little farm kid," he says in an interview with the *Report on Business Magazine*. It was fitness and discipline that became his guiding principles for the rest of his life.

He got off the farm by pursuing a degree in engineering from the University of Alberta. When he graduated in 1967, Morgan planned to continue his studies and become a biomedical engineer, but he lacked the money. "I was broke; my credit cards maxed out. You go where life takes you," he once said. He had worked summers in college as a field operator for Imperial Oil and could see there were opportunities in the oil patch for a bright young engineer. The year he graduated, he joined an oil and gas regulatory agency in Alberta as a rig inspector. Three years later, he became manager of operations and engineering for the Canadian upstream subsidiary of Northern Natural Gas, a Nebraska utility.

In 1975, he landed a new job as a petroleum engineer at Alberta Energy Co., an organization created by Alberta premier Peter Lougheed as a repository for the province's strategic interests in energy, mining, and other areas. Interestingly, for a man who is an arch conservative, his formative years would be spent in a partly government-owned creation, which at that point was becoming a company traded on the Toronto Stock Exchange. For Morgan, it was an opportunity to get in on the ground floor of a new company that was a rarity in those days— a Canadian-owned independent that was developing oil and gas in the Western Canadian Sedimentary Basin. "This company, which had virtually no production at the time, had a vision of becoming one of the biggest independents. That was compelling," he said in an interview with *Oil and Gas Investor*.

During the next twenty-five years, as the company shed its forest product, coal, steel, and petrochemical assets and focused

more on growing its oil and gas base, it became not just one of
the biggest independent producers in Canada, but one of the
biggest in North America. Gwyn rose through the ranks and, in
1994, took the top job as president of Alberta Energy.

The late 1990s to early 2000s were a period of upheaval,
when a number of Canadian firms were being taken over by
buyers from the south. Foreign firms had departed Canada in
the wake of the National Energy Program, but they were back
with a vengeance, and the then-low Canadian dollar made Canadian firms available at cut-rate prices. Anderson Energy, founded
by a Nebraska-born engineer, J.C. Anderson, had been acquired
by a U.S. buyer; Canadian Hunter, Jim Gray's company, was sold
to Burlington Resources. Rumours were buzzing around that the
next targets might be both Alberta Energy and another domestic behemoth, PanCanadian, a spinoff from the breakup of the
Canadian Pacific conglomerate, now run by a lawyer from Montreal named David O'Brien.

The prospect loomed of losing the entire Canadian-owned
contingent of major energy companies, but O'Brien and Morgan had another idea. Secret negotiations began between this
odd couple, the strong-willed Morgan with his black-and-white
views, moulded in a rural upbringing, and the more worldly and
relaxed O'Brien, with his urban roots and sensibilities.

The idea was to achieve a merger of equals to create a Canadian champion. When they announced the blockbuster merger in
2002, they had to sell the idea to investors. It was a different age
then, and they could pull it off because they had a loyal contingent of long-term investors, not the cut-and-run types who dominated stock markets over the next half decade. It was a
crowning achievement of both their careers. Morgan and his
wife came up with the name EnCana—a combination of Energy
and Canada—while cross-country skiing in the Rockies.

In later years, the two men would marvel over what they
achieved despite such differing world views. They had a common

purpose: to create a true Northern Tiger in the parlance of Dick Haskayne, a friend of both men. O'Brien later explained the different perspectives: "I came from the big city and I saw the issues in big cities and so I am politically not as right wing as Gwyn. It doesn't make me correct but I believe in capitalism and the market economy as a great engine of wealth creation, but I also believe in reasonable redistribution coming out of that. Mine wouldn't be a pure survival of the fittest; we should help everyone along the way."

Morgan feels the differences between the two men were not a reflection of his background or his rigidity, but simply the difference between being a Liberal and a Conservative today. "I just think it is a view about how big a government we should have. That's what he is talking about." The distinction, Morgan says, is that he feels that decades of state activism have taken away Canadians' personal sense of responsibility, which is reflected in a host of social problems, from the economic crisis in the Maritimes fishery to the coddling of corporate basket cases. There is no room for weakness in the world of Gwyn Morgan.

Morgan says his wife often says that "Gwyn never has any problems—he only has opportunities." He sees himself on a personal mission to make the country work and to make people's lives better. "At the end of the day, what I'm most proud of is whatever I did to make people's lives better—the communities I worked in, the shareholders and pension holders." In his view, he created a Canadian company "that has an impact across the country, including supporting more social programs than all of those socialists are supporting."

Morgan is famous for being a fitness fanatic, a runner, a hiker, a skier, who skips rope almost every day. He sees it as a form of therapy and told *Report on Business Magazine* that he composed eulogies for both his parents' funerals while running. The interview also contained his admission that he can be overly judgmental when it comes to physical fitness. "My wife says I judge people too quickly, especially people who don't take care of themselves," he said. "It doesn't necessarily affect how I behave toward them, but it's there."

He certainly did not shy away from making tough decisions as the CEO first of Alberta Energy and then EnCana. In 1998, Morgan gave the RCMP permission to blow up an Alberta Energy maintenance shed in a bizarre operation that was intended to flush out vandals who had been sabotaging installations in the Alberta oil fields. It was, in essence, a sting operation aimed at boosting an informant's credibility in a bid to convict Wiebo Ludwig, a notorious oil-field terrorist who had targeted Alberta Energy. Ludwig later went to jail for blowing up oil wells.

In Morgan's view, it was another example of sticking by his principles no matter how painful it might be. He saw the vandalism as a physical threat to his employees and he was standing up to it. He himself was put under personal protection during the incident, but he never flinched from his duty. "The point is, unless you stand up for principle, where do you go? What is it all about?" At one point, after raising about $300,000 for the Canadian Olympic Association, he quit his post as the Alberta head of the Canadian Olympic Federation, criticizing the Olympic movement for conflicts of interest and lapses in integrity.

Morgan also spearheaded an effort to guide his employees' personal values through a document that EnCana calls its Corporate Constitution. The constitution contains the usual boilerplate stuff about creating a great company and a vision—to be "the world's High Performance Benchmark independent oil and gas company." But it also demonstrates more than the usual corporate compulsion to channel human behaviour.

"To excel, to achieve our goals, we must have a shared set of moral principles—an inner compass—that guides our behaviour," the constitution says, "and we must have business principles that clearly show the path we will travel. We need to define what we should expect of ourselves and what we can expect of each other."

There is nothing wrong with building companies with high ideals, that are principled organizations, but Morgan's charter for EnCana is unusually detailed in what it expects in terms of the behaviour of the people who work for it. In many ways, the charter tells as much about Gwyn Morgan as it does about his former employees. The charter declares that EnCanans are, among other things, positive: "We have a positive attitude that is both realistic and progressive. We strive to keep a sense of humour and care about each other." Even more telling is what EnCanans are not: They are not egotistical, arrogant, or cynical; unwilling to adapt or change; or players of internal politics or games.

For many in the oil patch, this is remarkable hubris, because Gwyn Morgan earned the reputation, deserved or not, for being one of the most arrogant people in his industry. He is also courageous and confounding—in other words, the true maverick. His greatest accomplishment was how he built this company in his mould, not so much in channelling the behaviour of employees but in guiding an independent strategy. It starts out with the premise that the Western Canadian Sedimentary Basin is a declining region. The future lies not in the big fields and big finds, but in unconventional locations. EnCana understood this well in advance of others, and accumulated a huge land base and active drilling programs to find gas in these otherwise marginal assets. It said this was a strategy of "resource plays." It also pulled back from global initiatives and pursued North America entirely. The strategy was scorned by many but it has paid off in spades.

"The kind of strategy EnCana developed was a bit of a maverick strategy," Randy Eresman, the current EnCana president, told me in an interview for the *Globe and Mail*. "We went away from the conventional oil and gas exploration business and became 100 per cent focused on unconventional assets in onshore North America. That was pretty much the opposite of what a lot of similar companies our size believed they needed to do. And it is continuing to prove to be the only long-term strategy for the exploration and development of oil and natural gas in North America."

While Morgan is widely praised for the strategy, it is as much the product of Eresman, who also came from an Alberta Energy background and had been the solid operating mastermind standing behind the more charismatic Morgan. Erseman, shy, publicly awkward—the polar opposite of Gwyn Morgan—was born in Medicine Hat and worked in the oil fields as a kid. But he travelled one of the most unlikely paths to the executive suite. He went to the local college in Medicine Hat and tried some university transfer courses, but he dropped out. He was determined that he was going to come home with a piece of paper of some kind and stuck around to get a diploma at Northern Alberta Institute of Technology in a geology-based program.

After working for a couple of years, he faced the reality that the NEP had basically shut down the oil patch by 1982. So he took advantage of the depressed conditions to go to the University of Wyoming for two years, where he got his degree. When he got out, there were virtually no jobs. He had worked for Alberta Energy in the summers and so he had an opportunity to get a contract position and he was able to stay. "Then I seemed to take on projects that had a lot of scope and weren't very sexy. I was able to put teams together." One of the most critical teams was the one he formed with another rising star named Gwyn Morgan. As Gwyn rose to CEO, Randy came up in the ranks to be his No. 2.

I asked Eresman how EnCana had developed its out-of-the-box thinking in resource strategy. "First, we believe that companies that are very successful have a very simple strategy, and they have a core competence," he said. "We searched internally for that competence in EnCana and it really was the ability to search for unconventional assets. In everything else, when we looked at what we were doing in a competitive way, we were no better than anyone else."

EnCana also understood how the world had changed in the wake of the terrorist attacks on the World Trade Center and the Pentagon in September 2001. "We saw the 9/11 event as a point in time when energy security in North America was going to become much, much more important. It took a while before it really played out and the way it played out was in the tensions around the world. We also saw a change in the tipping point for natural gas in North America, with conventional gas going to run out. All of that became the framework for a vision. We had something we were good at and had an understanding of what the future might look like."

The result was an aggressive campaign of land acquisition in North America that turned EnCana into the continent's largest natural gas producer. The company, at one point, controlled almost 11 million hectares of land in North America. "Nobody else has anything close to that, and it is in the right places," Eresman says.

Morgan comments that "we have the best landowning in North America and people thought we were nuts." Then on top of that, EnCana acquired a position in the oil sands to develop an in situ project, creating a two-headed company—one very strong in natural gas, the other an emerging force in the oil sands.

So Gwyn and Randy had saved EnCana, had secured its place in the energy future, and now Gwyn was ready to save the world. The role of the CEO, he once told me, is not to sit quietly while the world was changing. "I think that to be silent on issues that are fundamentally important is not in the interests of the country or your company." While CEOs have different comfort levels with public policy statements, "I very strongly believe that the success of a country only comes through engagement of its leaders."

The fullest expression of this political activism came in a speech in Calgary given to the Fraser Institute, an organization that Gwyn had come to support, and which shares his free-market orientation. Morgan gave a meandering talk that touched many of the hot buttons for conservatives—anti-union, anti-bureaucracy, pro–private health care as an option. It was classic Gwyn—oblivious to political correctness, straight from the heart.

Then he waded into uncharted territory when he brought up immigration. Canada had benefited greatly from immigrants, he allowed, but "immigration has a social side as well as an economic one. The social side is all too evident with the runaway violence driven mainly by Jamaican immigrants in Toronto, or the all-too-frequent violence between Asian and other ethnic gangs right here in Calgary.

"Politicians talk of the need for more police to protect the public. Immigration groups blame 'poverty' or 'police discrimination' or 'lack of opportunity.' Once again, these are symptoms, but not the root cause.

"Here is the root cause they all know but don't talk about: the vast majority of violent, lawless immigrants come from countries where the culture is dominated by violence and lawlessness. Jamaica has one of the world's highest crime rates driven mainly by the violence between gangs competing for dominance in the Caribbean drug trade. Why do we expect different behaviour in Toronto, Ontario, than in Kingston, Jamaica?

"Similarly, a portion of our Indo-Chinese immigrants have lived in situations where violence is necessary to survive. Again, the violent behaviour continues in Canada."

He went on to say most immigrants who abuse our society have come in as refugee claimants rather than economic immigrants, which means they not only are more likely to have violent tendencies, "but also much less likely to have the skills, training and attitude necessary to contribute to our society . . ."

His speech urged a concentration on economic migrants, and the targeting of skills that Canada really needs. He cited EnCana's success in recruiting immigrants, in whom "we identify the skills we need, the value system that we live by and then go out and aggressively recruit people who can contribute and succeed in our company."

The speech raised a storm for its attack on entire communities, and many of Morgan's friends were embarrassed by the tirade. But the controversy seemed to have largely faded into the background when he suddenly retired in late 2006, handing over the CEO job to Eresman, his second-in-command. He said it was time to walk away, but it was clear he was itching for a broader canvas on which to sketch out his social and political ideas.

Then came the announcement that he was being put forward as a dollar-a-year appointments boss for the new prime minister, Stephen Harper. It turned out to be a bumpy initiation to party politics and minority government. Using the Fraser Institute speech as a stick, the Liberal and NDP members on the government operations committee beat up on Morgan. His appointment was rejected and, in fact, Harper suspended the proposal for an appointments coordinator. In the view of many in Calgary—even people who don't share Morgan's politics—the cost of the committee's actions would be more cynicism and a reduction in public participation in civil life.

Yet this reaction seems strange, given the tone of the speech that had turned Morgan into a sitting duck. It was within his rights to give that speech, but to tar entire communities with that violence brush was shallow and foolish. And for someone considering stepping onto the public stage, it was political suicide. Perhaps Gwyn just loves the tumult too much. Or you might speculate that the government that appointed him, which is led by a shrewd political strategist, was actually anticipating what would happen, and may have welcomed the furor.

Almost overnight, Gwyn's persona descended from martyr to pariah—and it was all the fault of John Brussa. Brussa is a middle-aged lawyer at Burnet Duckworth & Palmer who in the

1980s capitalized on a tax loophole to create the non-taxable energy trust. It found a way into the market, and it bred hundreds of imitators in all kinds of industries. But its most important role was to answer an important question: How do small junior energy operators with a nice but mature cash flow turn that income into funding to start all over again? It turns out they could sell their income stream to a non-taxable trust that would market the securities to a public looking for a steady stream of income.

It may have been the most important innovation in the oil patch since Karl Clark's discovery of the process for separating sand from bitumen. But it was a feat of financial engineering, not chemical engineering. It signalled that the conventional energy industry had become a gold mine for financial people, not geologists. While it was no longer possible to find a lot of oil in the basin, it was possible to aggregate a lot of mature production in an energy trust.

Brussa was the son of poor Italian immigrants who were so destitute in Italy that they lost one of their children to malnutrition. There was little hope of making a good living on the small family landholding, so they moved to Windsor, Ontario, where John's father worked in construction for forty years. Brussa is a gawky, amiable guy with a shock of unruly hair, who would not be out of place in a comedy troupe like, say, the Three Stooges, who happen to be his heroes. Growing up in a unilingual Italian household, he learned to speak English watching the Stooges, and his first words were apparently "nyuk, nyuk, nyuk," according to a report in the *Globe and Mail*.

His father wanted him to stay in Windsor and become a doctor, but John was drawn to law—and he was not impressed with his hometown as a place to make a living. Windsor had the feel of a zero-sum society where "if a guy gets a piece of the pie and keeps it, the guys without it never get it." Leaving law school in 1981, he came out to Calgary, a city he liked for its informality and upward mobility.

In 1981, Calgary was in terrible shape from the NEP, but Brussa saw it only as a land of opportunity. In the mid 1980s he started working on the concept of a non-taxable energy trust and, in 1987, the first one was launched in collaboration with an innovative chartered accountant named Marcel Tremblay. In the next twenty years, the trust phenomenon mushroomed.

In Brussa's view, the energy trust served an important economic function in a conventional industry that was not growing and needed vehicles for extracting value for its maturing assets. And it met the need for investors who wanted a reliable high-yield income earner. It created good times for investment bankers, for small oil and gas entrepreneurs, and for John Brussa, who became a director in twenty-five companies, mainly oil and gas trusts.

If Brussa's innovation had been confined to the energy industry, it might have survived. But by 2006, it threatened to turn the entire Canadian economy into one big income trust whose main priority was to feed the distribution hunger of unitholders. CEOs had little choice but to convert to trust status because being a non-taxable entity was so appealing. Bleach companies, water-heater businesses, small oil and gas suppliers, and real estate landlords were making the transition. It triggered big severance compensation for CEOs, such as Hank Swartout, who took home $43 million simply because his Precision Drilling was converting to trust status. Swartout's improbable bonanza tended to overshadow all the good things he had done as a hard-nosed businessman building Canada's major energy services company. It left a bad taste in the mouths of some shareholders—but Swartout's millions symbolized the excesses of the age.

Then all of Canada's major industrial companies discovered the joys of conversion, and there were even rumours that EnCana was contemplating such a shift. The last straw was the announcements that two of Canada's biggest companies, BCE and

Telus, would convert to trusts. It would have meant hundreds of millions of dollar of lost annual tax revenues but even more seriously, would have been a threat to national productivity. Companies would be directing their free cash flow to income distributions, instead of investing in technology and growth. Over the entire economy, it was a looming disaster—the end of the tax-paying corporation and a crash in already lagging productivity.

The Conservative government of Stephen Harper eventually came around to that view—despite its election promise to keep its hands off trusts. That triggered the Halloween massacre in 2006, when the government said it would equalize the tax burden of trusts and corporations. It was the end of the great trust game, and it triggered the loss of $25 billion of stock market value in a couple of days. In Calgary, particularly, there followed fierce anger and charges of betrayal. The Conservatives had simply used up a little of their political capital to make a tough decision. Where would Alberta turn now—to the hated Liberals? The Greens? Not likely. It was masterful, cynical, bare-knuckle politics.

A couple of weeks before the massacre, Gwyn Morgan had quit the board of EnCana. He had opposed the trust conversion, but, according to the company, Morgan's leaving was part of his planned exit. Morgan has never been one to leave it at mere actions when a little rhetoric was available. After Ottawa lowered the boom, he went very public in defending Harper and the income trust crackdown and it was widely believed Morgan had had a strong influence on the government.

Morgan says he knew the government was going to get a lot of flack because of the decision but he could see no alternative. If Ottawa did not move, it would be the end of the corporation as an entity, and it would be a greater threat to the country than foreign companies taking over our national champions. It would have meant that because of the typically high distributions in income trusts, companies would have no cash to reinvest in buying equipment or replacing energy reserves. "Here you have a country where investment in capital equipment is gone and people are running out on the street paying out cash—and there are no international champions. So why did Gwyn Morgan come out with these points of his? I've got people in Calgary who are very upset with me, and people who think, 'Thank God, somebody said this.'"

John Brussa was not one of those saying "Thank God." He argued that the annual cost in tax leakage from the trusts, estimated by Ottawa at about $600 million, was insignificant alongside the value destruction in the stock market and the taxes that might have been paid on that added investment value. Clay Riddell didn't applaud either. The oilman lost a quarter of a billion dollars in the market value of trusts he controlled in the two days of trading after the Halloween announcement. Neither did thousands of people, many retired, who saw their savings hammered. The transition rules were considered short and difficult. No wonder that people in Alberta would step to the other side of the street when they saw Morgan coming.

Brussa said he had built up a structure that allowed mom-and-pop oil companies to cash out. The trusts were not tax driven but economically driven, he said, and now that they were gone, there would be the need for some alternative mechanism. Morgan snorts at that statement, arguing that it assumes that all the small oil and gas companies didn't have a viable business. In fact, they didn't need income trusts to cash out, not when oil is $80 to $100 or more a barrel.

"At the very end of the day, it is simple: what they are talking about is moving assets from being taxable to being nontaxable. Of course, that is a nice thing to do—you'd be really dumb not to do it. The problem is that at the end of the day, you just have to get rid of the corporate sector because no CEO could justify paying taxes. How could you justify paying a billion or more if you don't have to?"

You might think that the government's about-face would offend Morgan's principles, but he argues that politicians say a lot of things when they are in opposition that they regret when they get into office. "You might say I'm never going to send troops but a bomb goes off and you change—and a bomb went off and that bomb was Telus, BCE, and potentially EnCana."

Meanwhile, Brussa was taking it all well despite some flashes of anger. Any day he gets grumpy with his life, he just thinks of his father, an Italian immigrant who didn't drive, didn't speak English, and rode his bicycle to a construction site where he was a terrazzo grinder. "I don't care what happens to me, it is like 5 per cent as bad as that. Life is pretty good actually."

Of all Gwyn Morgan's triumphs, his greatest accomplishment was handing over a great company to his capable second-in-command, Randy Eresman. The torch was passed from Gwyn, charismatic and strident, to Randy, humble and a bit shy. EnCana was ready for a bit of a break, a respite from Sir Gwyn the Brave, who increasingly saw his CEO job as a podium for his arch-conservative views.

An interview with Randy Eresman is a different kind of experience. For one thing, he's not happy to talk about himself because, frankly, interviews that go beyond simple financial statements and reserve numbers are about as welcome as a migraine headache. Gwyn, on the other hand, never met a microphone he didn't like. After Gwyn's bristling energy, Randy's humility is a radical change. I asked if the company run by Randy Eresman is different than a company run by Gwyn Morgan? It was clear Eresman didn't want to answer, but he did allow that he is more of a hands-on manager. "I have a pretty good understanding of every play in the company, and what is the activity level in each of them."

Morgan, on the other hand, was more about high-level strategy. He also gave a lot of attention to public policy matters. Will that continue? "To the extent that it directly affects our company, I will be very involved and our people will be very involved in the issues of the day," Eresman said. In other words, don't expect a big pronouncement on Jamaican immigrants soon.

For Eresman, the Bow building is not so much a monument to his achievements but simply a structure big enough to contain all of EnCana's business units that have been scattered around Calgary. "Every year, because of our evolution, we have averaged about 2,000 moves between one office space and another." Asked if the Bow says something about how EnCana sees itself, he says: "It says that's how big the building needs to be in order to house us. We took every effort to make sure that building wasn't any taller than it needed to be." In fact, the builders had to knock off a floor because it violated an unwritten rule that no building should cast a shadow on the Bow River.

Randy Eresman is no Patton, but more of a good soldier. In advance of taking the job, he hired a coach to work with him on dealing with the public and the media and being on centre stage. "The coaching helped me a great deal in recognizing my impact on others, which is something you don't think of as you are coming up in the organization. For the most part I kept my mouth shut the first year." The most revealing insight was that Randy Eresman, like many of us, battles a weight problem. In fact, he has a slight paunch. Before Eresman took the job, he lost ten to twelve kilos, which has helped increase his stamina. It's an admission Gwyn Morgan would never have made.

Randy Eresman should not be underestimated, for he was about to put his own stamp on EnCana. Eresman was on top of a colossus, the biggest gas producer in North America and one of Canada's most highly valued companies, with a stock market capitalization of more than $65 billion. It had actually become two companies, one a natural gas behemoth and the other, a substantial player in the oil sands, a status that Eresman had cemented through a deal with U.S. giant ConocoPhillips. With its huge resources, including a stake in the oil sands, with energy prices likely to stay high, EnCana would be very difficult to take over, even for a global multinational such as Shell (long rumoured to be a suitor) or Exxon Mobil. Essentially, Gwyn was gone but his legacy was to succeed in making EnCana so big, it was probably too big to buy—and certainly, too strategic for Canada to surrender without a fight. In Gwyn's eyes, it was proof the market system, with all its short-term considerations, could allow the building of a national champion.

But Eresman and O'Brien, now EnCana's chairman, had one more card up their sleeves, a card that gambled with Gwyn's vision. They felt the market valuations of EnCana's two arms—gas and oil sands—were being diminished because they were locked up in the same organization. Even at $65 billion in capitalization, the company was not realizing the true value of its underlying assets. There was a model to emulate in O'Brien's breakup of Canadian Pacific in 2001, which unlocked tremendous value for its five spinoff public companies and made a lot of money for investors. So they shocked the market in May 2008, with the announcement that they would break EnCana in two, creating a natural gas company headed by Eresman and an oil sands operation run by chief financial officer Brian Ferguson.

The company that had been too big to buy suddenly would become very buyable in two parts, when the deal was to close in early 2009. Eresman, a more humble man than Morgan, had chosen to run a company that was much smaller, but, in his view, more reflective of its true value. Gwyn, the visionary, the maverick, had given way to Randy, the pragmatist. In a sense, that had been their respective roles for twenty-five years, and it continued.

There is tremendous irony around the breakup of EnCana. The deal was announced on the same weekend that workers laid the concrete for the $1 billion Bow building that would serve as the head office of EnCana. It was, according to the engineers, the largest continuous pour of concrete in Canadian history and the third largest in the world to date. There had never been a building base in Canada that was so big. It would transform the eastern edge of downtown, helping light a fire under plans for redevelopment in the East Village. Suddenly, there were all kinds of questions about the future of the two companies that would rise above that base.

O'Brien was clearly hoping and betting that the two EnCana offshoots would be big enough—and well capitalized enough—to be global champions on their own. At the same time, he had effectively put them in play as potential takeover targets. He had once said: "I guess if a BP or Shell decided to make a big bid, one of the disadvantages for Canadian companies is that while they can be very significant within the Canadian context, they are usually smaller than our big international rivals." At that point in 2007, he said, "BP and Shell would be four times the size of EnCana although EnCana is perhaps the biggest oil company in Canada. Its market cap is huge but not relative to others. So when the consolidating starts, we're more likely to be the dinner than the diner."

By creating these two smaller public companies, O'Brien had effectively sent out invitations to the feast. In the constant tug-of-war between short-term investors and long-term national interests, the short-termers had trumped the country once more. That's the way the market works. The same fate could be in store for Suncor, as well. Rick George conceded there have been rumours about Suncor being taken over for almost every year since 1991, when he became the CEO. The ability to remain independent is directly tied to the company's performance. If it can execute, and keep costs in line, it should have a high stock price—"and that will be our best protection." He adds that: "I would also tell you Suncor is not for sale. Somebody would have to come in hostile and it would not be an easy task." But not impossible, not when the company is widely held and possesses one of the richest pieces of energy real estate in creation. It would be very expensive to take out Suncor as it would the two EnCana offshoots, but hardly insurmountable for one of the world's energy titans, or for a sovereign investment fund from China, India, or Russia.

It is inevitable that Canada will face this critical dilemma—to lose its energy champions to outside buyers, or stand firmly for our future interests as a country. It will be one of those defining moments, and it will come, because Canada has assets the world covets. We had better be prepared in our public policy arsenal. We had better have subtle, diplomatically shrewd political leaders. If, indeed, EnCana does become someone's prospective dinner, you would want someone stubborn, brave, cocky, and a little messianic at the helm—someone who could rally troops to save a Canadian champion. In short, you would want someone like Gwyn Morgan. But he is off slaying new dragons, the ones with dangerous socialist ideas.

CHAPTER 13

....

INDIRA'S DREAM

Revolution on the river valley

EVERY MORNING AT 6 A.M., I wake up cursing Indira Sama-rasekera. I start mumbling expletives in the name of the University of Alberta's president as the trucks roll in and the jackhammers start pounding on the construction site of the Mazankowski Alberta Heart Institute, a massive building that is rising across the road from my tiny Edmonton apartment.

On this November day in 2006, I am living in a converted office building across the road from half a billion dollars' worth of construction, in the health-care complex taking shape on the southern edge of the university. On a leave of absence from the *Globe and Mail*, I am watching the Alberta economic miracle take shape, brick by brick, girder by clanging girder. Within these blocks, there will be a heart research institute, a new diabetes education and research centre, a new hospital for women, and soon, the ground will be broken nearby for a massive billion-dollar outpatient clinic, dubbed "Mayo North" after the renowned Mayo Clinic—and all this includes the existing university hospital and children's hospital.

This is part of Alberta's grand plan—not to drive me crazy, as I have assumed on mornings like this—but to build institutions that benefit the rest of the country, the rest of the world, that make Alberta not just the target of envy but of respect and appreciation, even gratitude, from other Canadians. And to win a little respect from Ontario, which, after all, is what Albertans really want.

There are other people to blame for my early risings—it's Peter Lougheed's fault, for setting up the Heritage Trust Fund, and its offshoot in medical research, which have helped spawn this torrent of funding. There is Don Mazankowski, a car dealer from Vegreville, east of Edmonton, who became a powerful cabinet minister in the Mulroney years and whose name graces the heart institute. There is Capital Health, the body that runs the city's hospital system. But the most convenient target of my wrath is Indira Samarasekera, the ubiquitous University of Alberta president who is changing the university, changing the province, and quite possibly changing the country.

Alberta cannot achieve the greatness to which it aspires, unless it boasts a great university. The University of Alberta has flirted with greatness and comes close in a number of areas. Now this medical science complex, and assorted other building projects underway on campus, aim to do just that. All this building started before Indira arrived, but she is the juggler who keeps all the balls in the air, whether it is the new, federally funded National Centre for Nanotechnology, an engineering department that goes from strength to strength, or a new pharmacy school. She is a force of nature, pushing her dream for this hundred-year-old institution to be among the top twenty public universities in the world by 2020.

She blew into town in 2004, and she is still greeted with a mixture of bemusement and pride on the south slope of the North Saskatchewan River valley. She is a different kind of player in this resource economy that historically has been dominated by fifty-something white men—she is female, dark skinned, born in Sri Lanka. In one important way, she totally belongs. In a beautiful twist of fate, she is an engineer, a metallurgical expert, in a university, a town, and a province that love engineers.

"There is more of an engineering culture here in Alberta—engineers are celebrated in this province," enthuses Indira, a woman in her early fifties who came from the University of British Columbia where she had been vice-president of research. "Look who is running all the big oil companies. It's good for Canada as a whole if engineering gains prominence. It's a very attractive career option now and I look at that and say bravo!"

That's the way Indira talks, very clearly, very succinctly, but scattered with enthusiastic interjections, such as "bravo." It is the voice of the well-educated South Asian who wears her enthusiasms on her sleeve. She has raw ambition. Her aim is to build a global university in this tough, blue-collar, refinery and hard-hat town. "A university is the most powerful institution to connect a country to the rest of the world," she says.

In building Alberta into more than just a place to make money, Indira's mandate is as important as that of Rick George, Neil Camarta, or Murray Edwards, the giants of the oil sands. It is to show Canada that Alberta is putting together infrastructure that will pay off for the rest of the country. To be blunt, Alberta needs to persuade the rest of Canada that it doesn't need to do a money grab like the National Energy Program to spread the benefits around—that the resource wealth is recycling through Canada, saving lives, enriching culture, that it is being put to work in hospitals in Hamilton, Ontario, engineering shops in Cape Breton, or artists' studios on Toronto's Queen Street. Building a great university is part of that.

A great university can be the genesis of a sustainable industrial cluster of the kind that has grown up around the University of Waterloo in the Kitchener-Waterloo area, an hour west of Toronto. The university has the largest mathematics department in the world and has spawned a computer science expertise that ranks Waterloo with the best schools anywhere. This aptitude, combined with a liberal university royalty policy that offers strong incentives for researcher-entrepreneurs, has helped create an assembly line of technology companies, including such names as Open Text, Sandvine, and Descartes. The most prominent by far is Research in Motion (RIM), the most successful Canadian company in the past fifty years, whose ubiquitous BlackBerry was based on the work of a Waterloo undergraduate named Mike Laziridis (who, incidentally, headed out to commercialize his wireless product without ever getting his undergraduate degree).

The University of Alberta could use its own RIM, a technology gorilla that generates huge industrial benefits, creates massive stock market value, and breeds wealthy entrepreneurs who recycle their money back into the community and university— in the way that Laziridis and his co-CEO, Jim Balsillie, are doing in Waterloo through institutes in international studies and pure physics. There are some promising contenders, such as BioMS, the developer of a multiple sclerosis drug that initially came out of research on the U of A campus. One of the users in an early trial was Robin Giese, an MS sufferer whose life improved by using the drug. Her husband and brother-in-law, both veteran entrepreneurs, were so impressed they formed BioMS, a company to help researchers further refine the drug. BioMS went public and, late in 2007, signed a blockbuster deal with giant Eli Lilly to develop and market the treatment. The deal included a $87 million upfront payment and the potential for hundreds of million more. The university still owns a chunk of BioMS. Could this be U of A's RIM?

Meanwhile, Indira talks about getting the missing pieces that will allow the U of A to compare favourably with the top public universities in the United States, her competitors in getting graduate students and foreign applicants. It is not easy. She faces a demographic crunch that has left her with an aging teaching staff, and the university is still rebuilding from the Klein-induced downsizing of the public sector in the 1990s. That has left it painfully short of teachers in some areas, particularly the arts and humanities. "I need five hundred new professors hired over the next five years and I'll get U of A to be top-of-mind within the next eight years," she pledges in a matter-of-fact way.

But her stretch goal is to recruit thirty to forty academic superstars, the kind of people who would win Nobel Prizes or at least turn heads, people like the U of A's own David Schindler, one of the country's leading environmental scientists, and Raymond Lemieux, the late scientist who first synthesized sucrose thus leading to breakthroughs in medicine and chemistry. She talks excitedly about the Polaris awards set up by the Heritage fund in medical research that give her a bit of a hunting licence to recruit health scientists. The awards provide $1 million of funding each year for three years for one of these bright stars.

So Indira has the money and the drive, but does the province have the will to create a great university on the banks of the North Saskatchewan? It will be an intimidating challenge because universities get caught up in the politics of Alberta, where the underpopulated and often anti-intellectual countryside has extraordinary political pull—so much so that academics often speak despairingly of the democratic deficit in the province.

Yet this is a province that, in population, is overwhelmingly urban, and where two-thirds of the people live in Calgary and Edmonton. Then there is that weird Calgary-Edmonton dynamic at work. The universities in the two cities battle in an unseemly manner for money, students, faculty, and prestige in much the same way that the two cities battle over everything else. The feeling is that the U of A gets the lion's share of government research largesse while the U of C gets the billionaires' oil patch money. It's a generalization that carries some truth, but each institution roams freely on the other's turf.

And Indira's U of C counterpart is no pushover on the fundraising side. Harvey Weingarten is a voluble science academic from Montreal who was recruited away from McMaster University in 2001 to head Alberta's junior university, although hardly junior in the mind of Weingarten. He is in the midst of a

$1.5 billion capital spending program that will add another 7,000 student spaces. On the day I speak to him, he is looking at building projects at various stages of completion that add up to a whopping $900 million in investment. And U of C can draw on the seventh-largest university endowment in the country at $430 million even though it is only forty-five years old, while the top six schools are much older.

Weingarten tries to position himself in a different way than Indira's much-publicized Top-20-by-2020 goal. "I don't put it in terms of 2020. I don't want to be like a lot of other universities," he claims. His mantra is that public universities in Canada aren't changing fast enough to accommodate an evolving society, new demographics, or student expectations. In a typical burst of words, he says "Our job is to provide the most contemporary, relevant, useful educational experience for our students so that when they graduate from there, they are creative thinkers, innovative thinkers. That they're prepared to take on and solve challenges, some of which we know now and some we cannot anticipate."

He says the U of C is heavily committed to experiential learning, which means students are regularly put in the position of dealing with real-life problems. That means engaging more with Calgary's downtown and issues such as homelessness, poverty, and urban life. Like the College of Art's Lance Carlson, he is committed to moving parts of the university from its soulless suburban site. Weingarten says the university is committed to a campus in Calgary's East Village, and has already moved some programs downtown, including nursing and a graduate program in dance that operates out of the local Y.

He says Alberta should look at its four universities—Lethbridge and Athabasca are the two others—not as a bunch of independent institutions but as entities that serve a system. "It would be smart to have a bunch of differentiated institutions, each doing what it can to contribute in the best possible way." He is encouraged that government seems to favour that direction, but in reality he is dreaming in Technicolor. Will the U of A cede its space as a business school and allow the U of C to be the dominant player? Will Calgary surrender its engineering programs so the U of A has full sway? Try explaining that to a roomful of alumni.

What's more, Weingarten vows that his university will be going after more stars in the style of top economist Jack Mintz. He says the recipe for success in the academic business is to decide what you want, hire a couple of outstanding academics in that area, and the rest will want to join them. So you build up clusters of academic excellence. He believes this approach has worked well in the development of a new Institute for Sustainable Energy, Environment and Economy, anchored by people like David Keith, a superstar climate scientist.

Ralph Klein once joked that it was easy to rule in the years of deficit fighting because you could just say no to everyone. Now, in an age of affluence, the choices are much broader, the demands more insistent. Weingarten sees the university, like the province, moving through a wrenching transition from deficit reduction to growth mode. The University of Calgary has some big hold-over issues from the deficit period, including a $300 million gap in deferred building maintenance. But the new wealth raises unbelievable expectations. Salaries are rising 7 per cent every year, and the university has to rely increasingly on enterprise revenue—from business deals, fundraising, and private programs—to fill the gap. In the end, the new affluence is clearly welcome. "Lord knows, no complaints," Weingarten chuckles.

This increasing reliance on enterprise means tapping all those people who became rich in the oil booms. The U of C has done well from donors like Dick Haskayne, Jim Palmer, Murray Edwards, and Al Markin. But, unlike Calgary, Edmonton as a city does not possess the big-name public companies, the EnCanas, Enbridges, Suncors, or Imperial Oils—although many of these companies' bosses are U of A engineering grads and support the university.

That means Indira has to rely heavily on the quiet money that made fortunes in prosaic areas like liquor stores, construction, pipefitting, and real estate. While there is the occasional oilman like Stanley Milner, who sold his company Chieftain for $600 million in 2001, there is also John Ferguson, a savvy low-key real estate developer who is on the board of Royal Bank of Canada (and a former university chancellor); Fred Singer, a men's-clothing retailer; Irv Kipnes, a liquor store baron; Bob Stollery, the late boss of giant PCL Construction, the country's largest contractor; and Daryl Katz, head of the Rexall pharmacy empire. Katz breaks from the norm by the fact he is truly mega-wealthy, with a fortune of $2.1 billion. Indira loves to rub shoulders with these hard-nosed entrepreneurs, including the combative Katz, whom she managed to persuade to give $7 million for the new school of pharmacy.

Now she tells me the push is on to build reputation. The U of A is respected and admired. However, Indira wonders what people think it stands for. What does the U of A brand mean? The university can win all kinds of research grants but can the man on the street tell you what it brings to the game? She went searching for that rare commodity—someone who specialized in building a university brand. After looking high and low in Canada, she turned to marketer Sandra Conn from Michigan State University, who is now the U of A's vice-president, external relations.

She also faces formidable challenges in rebuilding the university's arts and humanities capabilities, which in this very practical province often get lost in the funding wars. There is a concern that in building all those things that matter in medicine and science, she may miss the most important ingredient—providing Alberta with wide-ranging, thoughtful leaders, and for that, you need the balance that comes from the humanities and social sciences. Martha Piper, the former president of the University of British Columbia—herself an illustrious ex-vice-president at the U of A—has advocated the establishment of the Alberta Creativity Fund to focus on the humanities, social sciences, and the arts—in the same way the Heritage Foundation for Medical Research and the Alberta Ingenuity Fund have generated innovation in engineering and science.

The university's tradition is steeped in science, ever since Edmontonian A.C. Rutherford became the first premier of the province in 1905. Rutherford's city became the capital of the new province, thus fomenting the century-long feud with Calgary that still hobbles Alberta. He exacerbated matters when Edmonton became the site of the provincial university. He invited Henry Marshall Tory, a mathematics professor from McGill, to become the first president of the university.

Tory was born poor in Guysboro, Nova Scotia, one of three upwardly mobile brothers who went out in the world to improve their lot. Brother James became a Liberal MP and lieutenant-governor; brother John ran Sun Life Insurance's operations in Ontario. This John Tory of Sun Life had a son John S.D. Tory, who became a lawyer and founder of a venerable Bay Street law firm that still bears his name: Torys. The lawyer John Tory's twin sons, John and James, became powerful advisers to Ontario's great family fortunes, and John's son, also named John—the fourth John Tory in the line—is the leader of the Ontario Conservatives.

If anything, Henry had an even more illustrious career than his brothers. He taught in rural schools before heading off to take a degree in mathematics and physics at McGill. A fervent Methodist, he left math to study theology, was ordained, and preached for two years before returning to his study of mathematics and becoming a McGill professor. He served as a kind of roving ambassador for McGill, scouting out locations for branch junior colleges. On one of these scouting trips, Tory ran into Rutherford, then premier of a new province, who invited him to come to Edmonton. Along with providing the new institution with its strong research base, Tory enhanced its reputation through his work to establish the Alberta Research Council and later as the head of the National Research Council. He was also one of the godfathers of the oil sands, having initiated research in upgrading the molasses-like substance into oil and inviting Karl Clark to teach at the university.

Besides his work at the U of A, Henry founded Carleton University in Ottawa and one of his junior colleges evolved into the University of British Columbia. The oil sands and three universities! Not a bad legacy for a math teacher from rural Nova Scotia. In fact, there were four universities in his legacy if you count the University of Calgary, which was created in 1960 as a U of A branch campus, before breaking off entirely in 1966.

The University of Alberta may be the most distinguished of Henry's offspring, but for any would-be Nobel Prize winner getting off the plane at the Edmonton airport, the trip northward to the university might seem a bit grim, with its endless stream of strip malls and fast-food joints. The payoff comes at the university itself, set atop the ravine overlooking the river and across the valley from the downtown. It is a splendid sight, particularly on winter nights from the faculty club, when the snow and lights dazzle the eyes, making Edmonton's inhospitable inner core seem, from far away across the valley, like an urban wonderland.

The school's ace in the hole is the same thing that drives Edmonton's economy. It sits on the edge of the North, and it is the access point to the oil sands, the diamond mines, the forests, and other resource treasures. In a sense, the university was founded on this premise, that the North would prosper and Edmonton would be the staging point for the North. With that location, in Indira's mind, comes responsibility to be a truth-sayer about the environmental risks of resource development.

I talked to Indira shortly after fall graduation in 2006, when she had stepped into the global warming debate. She had given a speech indicating that climate change is no longer a matter of conjecture; it is a fact of life and we all have to start working together to combat it. "The evidence is overwhelming—we are irreparably harming our planet and irrevocably diminishing the quality of life for future generations," she proclaimed. The speech would be hardly revolutionary at most campuses, but in an institution that practically invented the oil sands and prospers from them in many ways, where the chancellor is a former oil sands executive, it was an impressive, perhaps even a courageous stand.

"I want this province to get out in front of the debate, because we will have the most to lose if we are not out in front," she said later. "Elsewhere in this country and the world, they are not even arguing about the importance of moving ahead, but we're still having a debate about whether there is global warming."

She described her role as "a quiet influencer—or a not-so-quiet influencer, perhaps." She talked about the need to walk a thin line—to be engaged in the discussion of global warming without costing the institution support from key stakeholders. "I have to be bold enough to position the school—not so I am seen as one of those heretic types or a crazy president—but as a thoughtful citizen who is leading a university and saying what is true, and now let's decide what to do about this scientific truth."

She was delighted that people called her environmental speech bold. "This was not gloss on my part; I believe the balance has tipped. As a scientist, I absolutely believe that university presidents need to be public intellectuals, and I don't know if enough of us are doing that. "A number of people came up after the speech and said: "Are you sure your chancellor is still talking to you, because he is from Syncrude?" In fact, Eric Newell, a former Syncrude president, is the kind of thoughtful energy executive who would welcome this kind of discussion.

She asked how the oil sands were any different from the great nickel slag heap at Sudbury in Ontario. "In some ways it is no different, you dig up soil and I'm a metallurgical engineer and I can tell you the operations are absolutely similar." While making this point, she did concede the oil sands' voracious consumption of extremely important resources—including the mass conversion of a clean fuel, natural gas, into dirty oil—and then there is all that water. But it was a politely delivered reminder that the oil sands are not the only degradation of nature in Canada. It is in fact part of a long tradition in this country.

This is actually Samarasekera's second stop in Edmonton. Born in Sri Lanka, she earned an honour's bachelor of science in mechanical engineering from the University of Ceylon and, as a Fulbright Scholar, received a master's degree in mechanical engineering from the University of California in 1976. Then she went north to Canada to get her PhD in metallurgical engineering from the University of British Columbia in 1980.

As part of her doctoral research she was posted to Edmonton to conduct experiments at a mini-mill run by Alta Steel, then part of Stelco and, typical of Canada's steel industry, now owned by a South African steelmaker. The idea was to test the application of mathematical models to large-scale industrial processes. Dressed in hard hat and workboots, she would stand out in the mill from midnight to 2 a.m. in minus-fifteen-degree temperatures doing her experiments. She says she can't even remember today where the mill was located—she was so focused on her research. It was part of the knowledge transfer, she explains, from the university lab to a mostly male Grade 12–educated workforce. It is a microcosm of what she intends to do at the U of A. "You had to earn people's trust and confidence," she says.

At the time, she was studying under a giant in the steel research field, Keith Brimacombe, a distinguished professor at the University of British Columbia. Brimacombe loomed large in her life, a man who had deep intellectual ability and sensitivity to her needs as a young mother. (She is married and now has a grown son and daughter.) She speaks of him with deep respect as a mentor and scholar. Brimacombe died of a heart attack in 1997 at only fifty-four.

She never intended to be a university president. "My best and highest focus was to improve the materials business," she likes to say. But she ended up as vice-president for research at UBC under its charismatic president Martha Piper. Indira learned the university game under a good model. Piper had been a powerful force in putting the U of A on the map in the 1990s, and then turned around UBC's reputation and finances in her eight years as president. When Indira was offered the U of A job, she joked that she was the player to be named later in the trade for Martha Piper.

She saw the appointment as a great opportunity to transform the university and, as she sees it, the province. Early in her presidency, she sat down with the *Globe and Mail*'s political columnist Jeffrey Simpson and, from that conversation, came up with the idea of reaching for the Top 20 by 2020. It was the kind of thing that focused everyone's attention on what Alberta could become. It may never happen—in fact, the concept still evokes arched eyebrows among some in the faculty—but no one is betting against her either.

There is not yet a culture of international leadership at the university. She also faces the practical barrier of a long winter and a cold climate in a remote city, a hard-to-sell environment in a global academic marketplace. Yet that also reflects the university's competitive advantage. With its northern location and demanding climate, it is the most Canadian of all campuses. The U of A has to embrace its geography, the fact that it sits on the edge of the North, with its resource wealth, and its biological, ethnic, and linguistic diversity. This is the aspect of Canada that fascinates much of the world. So what if winter sets in about Halloween and finally departs around May Day! So what if the architecture is utilitarian and the downtown cries for revitalization! Where do you think you are? Vancouver?

When I talked to her in late 2006, Indira had just returned from a sorrowful trip home to Sri Lanka. It was a different kind of Indira, not the dynamic whirlwind of a university administrator but a daughter who had just lost her father at age eighty-two. "It's an inexplicable kind of feeling," she said, displaying characteristic candour. "On the rational side, he's not going to live forever, but the child in me says, 'He's my daddy and I've lost him.'"

It is a crisp winter night and the best and the brightest of Alberta's capital city have gathered at the Hotel Macdonald, the dignified old hostelry on the edge of the river valley. They are there to honour Irv Kipnes, one of Edmonton's quiet millionaires, and his wife, Dianne, who are giving $3 million to set up a new chair of the University of Alberta business school.

Indira Samarasekera is there; it's another late night for her, following on the previous evening with Jean Chrétien, who was the focus of the first of the U of A's centenary conversation series with Canada's prime ministers. Also attending is Stephen Mendel, the droll, laid-back mayor, and a couple of provincial legislative members. Business school dean Mike Percy gets up and pays his tribute. When Irv Kipnes rises to the podium to explain his reasoning in funding a chair in finance and international development, he is remarkably humble. He admits that he was never a student of development studies, he never paid a lot of attention—except he did notice a lot of poor countries lack a respect for personal property rights.

He also made it clear that a certain Professor Morck helped guide him in how he directed his money. He is referring to Randall Morck, global finance expert, academic rainmaker, the intellectual imp of the West—a man with an apparent blank cheque to travel the world in pursuit of his myriad interests. No individual in finance academe in Canada has a broader academic wingspan. He is an economist, the Jarislowsky Professor of Finance at the University of Alberta, as well as a research associate at the National Bureau of Economic Research in Cambridge, Massachusetts, at Harvard, and at the European Corporate Governance Institute in Brussels. He has negotiated an enviable deal with the university that reflects his special status and provides money and time for him to indulge his interests.

A lot of ink is devoted to the University of Calgary and its intellectual provocateurs in the political science department—the people who helped construct the world view of Stephen Harper, an economics graduate of the university. But Morck is one of the smartest business minds in Canada, in a league with stars such as Henry Mintzberg, the strategy guru at McGill University, and Roger Martin, the hyperactive dean of the Rotman School at the University of Toronto. He is the fundamental building block of the University of Alberta's business school, which is right up there with the University of British Columbia for bragging rights to supremacy in the entire West. Dean Mike Percy is an economist and policy wonk who is well connected in the power corridors of Calgary and Edmonton, but Morck is an academic superstar. At times, at the business school, events and people seem to radiate around him like planets around the sun.

If Morck is not a household name, it may say something about the U of A, which tends to have a wonderful reputation as a research school but doesn't really have a strong enough brand on the streets. Morck is a hugely respected academic, but has not risen to the level of prominent public intellectual. At one point Indira told me that "we need to bring a top philanthropist to name the business school." With money from a large donation, the school could do all kinds of new and exciting things, she said. One of those things would be to promote luminaries such as Randall Morck. The problem is that the school already has a brand—"The Alberta School of Business" and it is loath to give up the Alberta tag. Yet the world at large has not embraced the "Alberta" label as distinct from, say, the University of Calgary. The school would no doubt take money and a name from a major donor, if the payoff was rich enough. The Mannix School of Business has a nice ring, but Alberta's richest, most secretive family may not appreciate the public profile.

It seems incongruous that the University of Calgary has not eclipsed its Edmonton rival as a business school, since Calgary has all the head offices, and its naming donor, Dick Haskayne, is a business icon. Yet the Haskayne School of Business has been hampered by a rotating door of business deans, with three different appointments in the past seven years, and two periods of long temporary assignments—in all, five deanships in seven years, hardly a track record that inspires greatness. The school has a reputation for being difficult to run, although it is hard to conclude whether that unruliness caused the dean turnover or is the result of that turnover. At one point, Michael Grandin, a veteran financial executive, tried to run the business school at the same time he was CEO of Fording Coal. Needless to say, it did not work, and after two years he reverted to full-time at Fording, leaving the business school once again without a leader.

In 2007, Weingarten recruited a new dean, Len Waverman, a respected Canadian academic who was at the London School of Business. Waverman has intellectual depth and he is a student of global communications trends and energy economics, which is a great plus in a town like Calgary. There are questions about whether, in his mid-sixties, he has the energy and staying power to rebuild a demoralized program and take it to new heights. For many in business academic ranks across Canada, it seemed an odd appointment, but Weingarten is confident that Waverman has the strategic insight to rebuild the faculty. One of his challenges is managing a steady relationship with the U of A, which is the Haskayne School's partner in an executive MBA program that is well regarded internationally. The partnership almost fell apart. The schools are, after all, rivals for provincial supremacy, but the two deans patched up their differences. The University of Calgary gains extra academic heft from the U of A, and the U of A desperately needs access to that great pool of MBA candidates in the office towers of Calgary.

At the University of Alberta, the business school possesses one compellingly strong advantage in its location close to the corridors of power in the Alberta government. Walk around the business school and you're apt to run into the province's minister of finance or a senior public servant. The U of A, and particularly the business school, operate almost like a second government. It's an easy drive to the university from the legislature across the hectic High Level Bridge over the valley.

The business school has some outstanding academics—people like Joseph Doucet in energy economics, and Lloyd Steier, who has put the school on the map for family business research. But Randall Morck carries a special cachet, not only for his academic prowess, but also because he likes to toss intellectual grenades into a crowd of professors, students, or business people and watch them explode. That's not just for causing trouble, but to guide discussion along more interesting lines, says Morck, who although fifty years old, has the boyish appearance of a very bright, very precocious, very brash graduate student.

I met with him one day for coffee and he wanted to talk about the West. On this subject, he can become unacademic and passionate. He explained he is the son of Danish immigrants who came to Olds, Alberta, where his father was a carpenter. The Morcks, as immigrants, grew up outside the French-English dichotomy that so dominates the dynamics of central and eastern Canada. In fact, he admits that as a child growing up in Olds, he felt naturally suspicious of new arrivals from eastern Anglo-Canada, who seemed to have uppity airs and lorded it over first- and second-generation immigrants.

"Maybe there was a bit of a sense that some of them thought they were better," he says. "I kind of cringe when I think about that sort of thing because it really was nasty and insulting."

Then the conversation turns to global warming and Morck is the natural provocateur. As long as the relationship between greenhouse gas emissions and climate change is still unproven, he says, perhaps the best thing to do is construct the best possible emergency measures in case New York, for example, is submerged in water. He watches my reaction and then he smiles that enigmatic smile as if to say: "You can't really tell if I'm kidding or not, can you?" In fact, he is totally serious, citing the disaster in New Orleans as compelling evidence that the world's urban areas are woefully unprepared for natural disasters, no matter what the origins of global warming might be.

Morck brings that intellectual playfulness, combined with research depth, to a mind-numbing host of issues: corporate governance; efficient markets; China and India; the Danish stock market; psychology and economics. "I feel academics have become too specialized and I am sort of flailing against that," he says. He often works in tandem with long-time collaborator Bernard Yeung, who left the U of A to become a professor at New York University. On two occasions, Morck was ready to leave but negotiated richer deals at the U of A that gave him more salary and research funding. Every year he gets at least two offers from other schools, but, so far, he is staying put. It is hard to move, he says, so any offer would have to be considerably superior to what he gets now. And in return for the income and status, he is expected to act as a kind of roving ambassador for the school. "The big problem with Alberta is geographic isolation," he says.

His most high-profile work is in the area of family dynasties and corporate control. Research conducted with Yeung and another colleague shows that countries in which the wealth of billionaire heirs is large relative to gross domestic product grow more slowly than areas where established wealth plays a smaller role. Indeed, family-dominated economies spend less on innovation than other countries at similar levels of development. Morck's team also found that, by contrast, countries in which self-made entrepreneur billionaire wealth is large relative to GDP grow more rapidly. The natural conclusion is that it's better to have a country full of self-made Bill Gateses, than an economy dominated by, say, a gaggle of inheritors like Paris Hilton or South American oligarchs.

The paper says these findings are consistent with the view that wealthy entrenched families often have objectives other than creating public shareholder value. They are more interested in perpetuating lifestyles, and they do it through intricate financial controls and political influence. Even more than that, Morck says, it shows any economy should operate like a kind of tournament "where you pick the very best, the most highly qualified people, put them in charge of your people's savings and let them run great corporations—and if they screw up, you dispose of them unmercifully."

He says that happens in all kinds of successful growth economies, such as the United States, Singapore, Hong Kong, and even Great Britain. But it tends not to happen in Canada. "These family-owned businesses tend to be very forgiving with family members who screw up," he says. In their research, Morck and his team relied on data for Canadian companies, and found that heir-controlled Canadian firms are relative underperformers in financial results, the use of capital, and R&D spending. The team called this condition "the Canadian disease."

"It's the idea that you don't go to the same lengths as in other countries to make sure that the very best people are in charge of your national wealth," Morck says, adding that it is a simple matter of mathematics: "If you are choosing the best person from among six members of a family versus among 35 million Canadians, the maximum quality you get is very different."

This creates an interesting intellectual tension in the school, which has a strong family business unit. It is also consistent with how Alberta views itself: a land of no baggage no ingrained interests, where fortunes are made and sometimes lost, in a single generation, and there is little sense of generational entitlement. This is clearly not the East, where established family wealth—see the Desmarais, Thomsons, Molsons, and Irvings—still holds sway. Morck concedes that it might be a simple matter of time. The West may be too young to have acquired family empires. "It's hard to find western Canadian firms who can be more than a generation or two old," he says. "Before they feel superior, they have to wait and see how they screw up over the next century."

There will be opportunities to test this thesis because Alberta is now breeding some huge pools of family wealth in this age of the oil sands, and it is a big challenge how it will get reinvested in the economy. That is becoming, increasingly, the focus of family business study in the school and its affiliated Alberta Business Family Institute: how wealth is redeployed through generations for sustained economic growth. It means wealth management will be a huge business in Alberta over the next twenty years as the riches from the oil sands, conventional energy, and oil services get recycled over and over. This business of managing money is attracting a wave of investors from Murray Edwards to Winnipeg's Richardson family. That is also why Indira's great goal has to be taken seriously. Along with her rival-partner Harvey Weingarten, she can count on a growing army of private donors who share her passion and who can take inspiration from a wise and wily property developer named Sandy Mactaggart.

When you pass behind the great wall, through the gates, and into the elegant rooms of Chinese tapestries, books, and Buddhas, it's like you are shutting yourself away from Edmonton, its smoke-spewing refineries and its tacky mega-mall. In this secluded riverfront estate, you are entering the world of Sandy Mactaggart, adventurer, world traveller and philosopher-king of the Alberta business class.

He is an elegant man who looks like an aging sea captain, with trim beard, turtleneck, and double-breasted blazer. He is also the dean of Edmonton's private entrepreneurs, as the co-founder of a fifty-year-old property company, Maclab, which is the largest private company in the property rental business in Alberta.

He is deeply involved in the university that engages his agile mind as he enters his eighties. Education is his primary philanthropic cause. He gives money to his old prep school at Lakefield, Ontario, and to his alma mater Harvard, where he helps striving young Albertans pay for their tuition. (One of my former bosses at the *Globe*, an Albertan named Chrystia Freeland, had her Harvard training subsidized by Sandy Mactaggart's generosity.) But the U of A occupies a key part of this life. He recently made a $37 million donation of Chinese art to form the foundation of a new institute aimed at building bridges to China, a country he first visited in 1971 and has made his life work to understand. It is the largest single gift ever made to the university, and is to be matched by a cash donation from the province.

Sandy is quintessential private Edmonton money, little known in the rest of Canada but hugely important to Alberta and its destiny. Although he is a house builder and apartment owner, he is also very dependent on oil for his wealth. It's the same with anyone in business in Alberta—you may be a retailer or a developer or a trucker, but it is energy that ultimately underlies your fortune.

Yet in many other ways, Sandy is not your classic Edmontonian. He was born rich in Scotland, the son of Glasgow's biggest house builder before the Second World War. In a way, he is the last of that old Alberta tradition, the remittance men who were sons of well-off families who fled to the Canadian West and were kept alive by occasional transfers of money from back home.

"I owe my prosperity to Hitler," Sandy likes to say. It was because of Hitler he was evacuated as a teenager during the Second World War and spent time at Lakefield College in Ontario. After the war, he landed at Harvard Business School, where his roommate was a California used car salesman. The two got along okay but their neighbouring roommates did not—one was a Boston Catholic and the other a French Huguenot named Jean de la Bruyère. Mactaggart and de la Bruyère were thrown together by the tense circumstances and they had a lot in common. They became friends and later roommates.

On graduation, Sandy had no thought of going back to Scotland to work for his older brother. He wanted to go into business with his new friend, Jean. The two men asked themselves, "Where could we go that, no that matter how stupid we were, we would do alright?" They looked at oil-rich Venezuela and at Edmonton. "We were more likely not to get hung in Edmonton so we came here," Sandy quips.

The two young men set off across the continent, arriving on the banks of the North Saskatchewan in the middle of an ice fog. When it cleared away they found an inelegant city of 100,000, where the hotel bars still admitted "men" in one room and "ladies and escorts" in another, and where people were still wounded by the Depression. They thought about opening a restaurant, but that was too risky. They knew nothing about the oil business, so that wouldn't work. "But we decided no matter who provides the oil, they've got to live somewhere—and so we went into the housing business."

They created the name Maclab from the first three letters of each of their last names and purchased some building lots. To help with the financing, Sandy borrowed from his British family company. In the first year, 1954, he says they built forty homes and lost $300. They were inexperienced and haphazard in their subdivision planning. At one point, they discovered they had built a house on a lot they did not actually own. They went to the owner, who did not know about the already constructed house, and told him they had a great idea—they would pay him twice the going rate for his land. He accepted, and they breathed a sigh of relief.

They were a great team because of contrasting personalities. "Jean was very good at leaping off cliffs without looking to see if there were any jagged rocks down below," Mactaggart said. "I was the more conservative person; I would never have done half as much as we did because of Jean." They were notorious around Edmonton as jaunty young pilots, balloonists, and auto racers. The pair had a strange philosophy for this obsessively hard-working city. "Most people worked for the company," Sandy says. "We always believed the company should work for us."

That led to the decision that the owners should try to take three months off each year. They would travel the world and find out how other people did things. In addition, they built a strong team inside the company that could easily fill in. The partners were lucky in the 1980s because they had expanded into the United States, so they were not exposed to the full blast of the energy downturn in Edmonton. Pierre Trudeau's NEP changed Sandy's view of Canada. "I don't think anyone really grasped that the political power could alter the deal to that extent," he says. "While there wasn't strong separatism here, it grew after the NEP. I don't think you could get away with that again; I think there would be a really strong view to separate." He adds that, "a lot of us feel more Albertan within Canada than we ever did before. The province was never important to us then, but it is now."

The partners' bon vivant style paid off in unexpected ways. When they were still in business school, Jean had invited Sandy to Paris, where the plan was to visit Pigalle, the racy nightclub quarter. They needed to change some money, so they dropped into Jean's gambling club. They didn't get out of the club for three nights and they never got to Pigalle. Sandy, who was not a gambler, parlayed a $100 stake into $3,000, which was a lot of money in the early 1950s.

With the funds, he bought an elegant door, which now adorns his house; his first old car, a Bentley; and his first Chinese textile at a shop in London. "You need to do mad things occasionally in order to enjoy life," he says. "That was my first use of mad money, to take a slice of things I wouldn't have done if I hadn't done it in that weird way."

Today, the Maclab property business is into its second generation and is professionally managed. Jean de la Bruyère died in 1991 and his son Marc, also a Harvard graduate, manages his family's side of the business. He divides his time between Edmonton and New York, where he lives in midtown Manhattan with his wife, Pulitzer Prize–winning biographer Stacey Schiff. Sandy's son Alastair, also a Harvard Business School MBA grad and now a developer in San Francisco, commutes to Edmonton to help oversee the Mactaggart side of the partnership. Sandy, whose mobility is slowed by osteoarthritis, has little contact with the family business. He is into the business of leaving a legacy.

He was one of the early supporters of Edmonton's acclaimed Citadel Theatre, but he has no illusions about the role of culture in a frontier land. When he arrived, there wasn't much culture, and it has been slow progress. "Look around at the architecture of the place. You get what you deserve in terms of the arts. A few people fight for them, we tried very hard, but the normal person who is coming down from the tar sands is not really interested in that. So you have to wait for that to go and it normally happens in the generation after the money has been made."

His first investment in Chinese textiles, drawn from his gambling winnings, turned into an elaborate collection of Chinese art that Sandy and his U.S.–born wife, Cecile, built up through trips to the shops and auction houses of Europe. It fired an interest in China, which has only grown through many visits to the country since 1971. He was amazed at visiting Tiananmen Square in Beijing where a picture of a Canadian, Norman Bethune, held equal standing to Mao and Marx. Since that day, Sandy's passion for China has never diminished.

He and Cecille gave their entire 700-piece Chinese art collection to the university, with the idea of creating an institute that would foster understanding between the two countries. The donation also showed that Sandy and Cecile Mactaggart aren't your usual Edmonton "quiet money." The provincial matching money took some time to arrive and, at a reception to mark the launch of the institute, Cecile went public with her frustration that, nineteen months after the announced donation, the province had yet to cough up any cash. Some of the money was immediately advanced. A few months later, she went public again with the couple's concern about the Canadian government's increasingly hostile policies towards China.

Sandy agrees with his wife's views, that democracy will only come to China if capitalism is encouraged and supported by the West. "If we can create here a China institute which becomes the leading institute, that can foster exchanges in understanding between China and Canada, that will be the most valuable thing in our lives," he says. He then adds how strange it is that a hobby could become so influential. "I never realized collecting Chinese art would end up creating something very important."

Then again, much has surprised Sandy Mactaggart in the sixty years since he left the common rooms of Harvard Business School and headed out to the beverage rooms of the Canadian prairies. And now he is part of the vision of the great university that Indira Samarasekera aspires to build on the south bank of the river.

PART THREE

NEW DIRECTIONS

CHAPTER 14

·····························

WHEAT STALKS RISING
How I almost missed the big story

FOR THREE DECADES, the image of three lowly wheat stalks has graced auto licence plates in the province of Saskatchewan. The stalks, combined with the motto "Land of Living Skies," are an evocation of the province's prairie landscape and its rich agricultural history. But in the summer of 2006, economist Todd Hirsch felt emboldened to tear down this beloved symbol from its iconic stature.

The three wheat stalks are an antiquated logo for the province's economic fabric, he wrote in the *Globe and Mail*. Agriculture is no longer the industry around which Saskatchewan should be marketing itself. "It is the fashion equivalent of walking around with a piece of straw in your mouth, acid-washed jeans (no belt) and a baseball shirt with I Love Fishin' in vinyl letters," he wrote in his cheeky style, so unlike an economist.

Ditch the wheat stalks, he urged, and replace them with a symbol that is more relevant and forward looking—perhaps something with molecules or electrons, more befitting of the province's big stake in biosciences and other thrusting new technologies. And what happens to the motto "Land of Living Skies"? How about "Canada's Science Capital," he recommended.

Todd anticipated that some traditionalists would protest his proposals, arguing the stalks are a tribute to a glorious agricultural past. "But that's what museums are for," he opined mischievously. Predictably, his column evoked a storm of opinion, both pro and con.

Todd, who at the time was chief economist for the Canada West Foundation and now works for Alberta Treasury Branches, was being consciously provocative. However, he was making a serious point—agriculture was the past and science and knowledge were the future. Grain was a declining proportion of the provincial economy, while Saskatchewan had an impressive roster of growing technology companies, a number of them clustered around the University of Saskatchewan in Saskatoon. If Saskatchewan was to attract new business, it should sell its science future, not its farming past.

More than two years later, Todd should have been eating his words, along with his morning cereal. Suddenly, wheat was king, and so was corn, canola, soybeans, and a brace of other farm products. But he was also right in a way, because the province's growth was more than grain. It was being turbocharged by fertilizer, whose major input—potash—was being hailed as the new oil. Saskatchewan is the biggest supplier of potash and the leading producer of uranium globally—and uranium is booming because nuclear energy is back in people's good books in a time of expensive, dirty oil. "For just about everything it produces, Saskatchewan is getting a high price," marvelled Todd, now abashed by the seemingly appropriate nature of the wheat-stalk symbol.

Along with bountiful oil and gas, these hot resources have made Saskatchewan, in the words of Craig Wright, chief economist for the Royal Bank of Canada, the "It" province in Canada, along with Manitoba, another area rich with wheat fields. You could extend that same term to areas of rural agricultural Alberta, which are waking up again, after being sidelined in the oil sands bonanza.

I sympathize entirely with Todd because I almost missed this story. I was so caught up in the amazing run of Suncor, EnCana, and CNRL; of Murray Edwards, Rick George, and Randy Eresman, that I missed the story of Potash Corp. of Saskatchewan, which in early 2008 was sporting a stock market capitalization bigger than that of EnCana, RIM, and the big banks. And Agrium, a Calgary-based fertilizer and farm retail operation that had doubled its stock price in a year, was not far behind. The potash sands are trumping the oil sands. Not that the oil sands were in decline—far from it—but farm-related commodities had seized the spotlight.

In fact, oil and potash reflect two sides of the new reality—the renaissance of resources. It signifies a new and even disturbing trend back to human basics, the need to eat, drink and stay warm. The hot industries are not manufactured goods, not computer chips, not the Internet, but the stuff you need to just survive. And could it be that the vaunted computer technology has reached its peak? Does anyone get excited anymore about computing power, which has become a cheap, undifferentiated commodity? And the Internet? It is turning out a steady stream of nifty applications but there are no new, new things. Yes, we all feel that we need our BlackBerrys, and we all want games, sports scores, and videos on our handheld devices. But online applications are becoming ho-hum. They are expected and, frankly, what do they do to solve the survival challenges of most of the world's population: How to eat? How to keep warm?

Commodities have become the new source of instant added value. As Sir Terry Mathews says, if you stick a shovel in the ground, and it turns up $130-per-barrel oil, this is the biggest "value add" in the world. Stick another shovel in the ground and you get potash at $1,000 a tonne. The early years of the twenty-first century represent a revolution in how to look at value creation: We are seeing the commoditization of technology, and the decommoditization of commodities, such as oil, wheat, nickel, and potash. Global economics has been turned on its head. That is extremely good news for the Canadian West and not so good news for the consuming centre of the country.

In this new age, oil is the new Internet, and food is the new oil. In the future, there will be new substitutes for hydrocarbons, such as batteries, fuel cells, and wind power, but there is no substitute for food. If we are truly entering an age of severe climate change, when droughts will be more common and large populations will be trapped in Malthusian struggles to subsist, food will constitute the next great investment bubble and it may be a permanent one. The last bubble of all will be water and that presents a whole raft of other challenges.

Hence, with all the excitement about Saskatchewan's renaissance, there is also nervousness that the world is somehow spinning out of control, with food riots and predictions of $200 per barrel oil. It represents a reversion to the basic elements that farmers in Mesopotamia (ancient Iraq) grappled with 4,000 years ago: Who has fuel? Who can eat? Where can we get water?

I should have seen it coming. In 2005, I had travelled to China to report on how Canadian companies were faring in what had quickly become the hottest economy in the world. I had pinpointed a company called Hanfeng Evergreen, listed on the Toronto Stock Exchange with a Toronto head office, but run mainly out of Shanghai by a former Chinese bureaucrat named Xinduo Yu. He had left the public service with the idea of starting a landscaping business to create greenery in urban centres such as Dalian and Beijing. But along the way, he was convinced that after the new capitalist awakening would come another revolution in agriculture. After China built up its industrial bases along the east coast, in places like Shanghai, Guangzhou, and Shenzhen, the government would turn to extracting more productivity from the interior. An industrial society would have to feed itself, and the peasant culture, with its tiny plots and subsistence model, was not prepared to do that.

Thus, there would be demand for agricultural innovation, including huge injections of advanced fertilizers. Yu saw a burgeoning appetite for not just any fertilizer, but slow-release fertilizer with extended life and impact, stuff that Hanfeng was now manufacturing and distributing with a Canadian partner. I sat with Yu in his Shanghai factory, in his plain boardroom below the dormitory where many of his workers lived, and I listened to an interpreter outline his vision: after toys, cars, and cell phones, China would train its sights on food production, and Yu would be on the forefront of change.

The last time I looked, Hanfeng was doing fine as a niche player in a burgeoning field, and analysts indicated it will likely be one of the companies to prosper in this new era when food is king. It would perhaps not be a giant like Potash Corp. of Saskatchewan, but it would benefit mightily from the galloping increase in the Chinese middle class, which was now demanding meat in addition to its standard rice diet. The ripples from China's huge appetite extended beyond Shanghai to other Asian and African countries, where crop failures and high prices had unleashed angry protests. They emanated all the way to the potash mines of Saskatchewan, Manitoba, and New Brunswick, and to the wheat fields of the West.

The economics of China is a major catalyst in turning the world around. When China can graduate 300,000 high-tech technicians and engineers a year, it is not overwhelmed by the challenges of computer or telecom technology. If China is lagging in a specific technology, it can simply adapt what's out there in Europe, the United States, and Canada. It can buy it; it can steal it; it can engineer it. Computer technology is no big thing; it is a commodity just like all the other things the Chinese create in vast quantities at a cheaper cost than the old industrial world.

But food? That is another matter. It is not so readily available in the peasant acreages. The Chinese hunger for better, more diverse food, and a more secure supply. They need a productive agricultural industry in the same way that they need natural gas and oil, and they will naturally look abroad for both the commodities and the technology to make it happen. Those two commodities—food and fuel—are what Canada's West has in vast quantities and that is why this is its moment. As long as the Chinese boom continues and the Indian boom follows close behind, the West will prosper.

The West is also feeding off American paranoia, another great fount that keeps renewing itself. It was the fear of the Arab world, springing from 9/11 and the invasion of Iraq, that sent the price of oil soaring, making the oil sands not just economically viable but hugely profitable. U.S. concerns about the security of crude oil supply in the Middle East sparked massive government subsidies for alternative fuel, including ethanol, which relies on corn as a feedstock. The price took off and farmers shifted their acreage to the tasseled plant. As acreage became squeezed by corn mania, that lit a fire under global prices of other commodities, including wheat, canola, soybeans, and suddenly western farmers were feeling pretty good about themselves again. But the U.S. ethanol subsidies are the unstable aspect of the farm boom. They could be—and should be—taken away as quickly as they were introduced.

More substantial perhaps is another seminal food trend—toward healthy eating in the industrial world, particularly the move away from trans fats, which is sparking a technological revolution of its own. In fact, one week in 2008 highlighted the striking confluence of trends. First, McDonald's announced it has moved entirely away from trans fats in its North American markets, changing over from hydrogenated oils to using a blend of canola, corn, and soybean oils. A week later, Winnipeg's Richardson family announced it will go ahead with a new canola, crushing plant in Yorkton, Saskatchewan—the second major canola plant slated to open in Yorkton, for a total investment of over $300 million. Forget about West Texas Intermediate Crude—canola is the hot new oil and Yorkton is a canola capital.

Hartley Richardson, the head of his family's holding company, said the revolution in healthy eating was pushing the family to hike its investment in canola crushing. In fact, the Yorkton factory had been on the planning boards for more than two years, but soaring construction costs in the West had delayed any start to construction. Now, the Richardsons could actually get a handle on their costs, as the energy boom plateaued slightly, and the outlook for canola was so robust.

As I travelled the West, I found that my story was changing in remarkable ways. I started out by covering the surge in energy prices, and the terrific positioning of Alberta to reap the benefits of this change. As for farming, I initially felt a lot like Todd Hirsch did—it was the Old West and it was declining. I saw farmers as victims who were being left behind in the massive run-up in energy costs and the inability to hire people at the inflated wages available in the oil patch.

But I gradually began to sense things were changing as I visited an area of northeastern Alberta near the Saskatchewan border, about two hours east of Edmonton. It is a beautiful land, of rolling hills, small copses of trees, and clusters of deer. I have grown to love that land, and I had ties there, through my cousin Cathy and her husband, Marshall, who had retired to the community where they had first met and fallen in love as high school students. Marshall had worked for the federal government across Canada and they had raised three kids. Now, they were back farming in the rolling land north of Vermilion.

When I first visited them, farmers were having a tough time, and many depended on oil leases on their property to break even. Even Cathy proclaimed proudly to me one day that she had become an oilwoman. One of the heavy-oil companies was planning to put a well on her land. It was not big money— maybe a few thousand dollars a year—but it helped pay the soaring fertilizer and fuel bills.

But even as this was happening, some farmers in this area could see the tide turning, as wheat prices started to climb and then went through the roof. In late 2007, it was clear that life had changed for many producers. Tim Harvie, who grew grain and raised cattle near Calgary, felt caught in an odd paradox of the best wheat prices he had ever seen but with a beef market still suffering from the temporary shutdown of U.S. export markets in the mad cow disease scare of 2003. And nothing is simple. As the price of wheat soared, the cost of cattle feed experienced staggering increases.

There was a part of me that was relieved that the farming bonanza was not universal. I hail from a farm background and have come to expect the worst. This attitude has seeped into my work as a journalist. If I've had a good week with a bumper crop of good stories, I fully expect things to get worse next week when the inevitable drought sets in. I am naturally skeptical of all the good-news stories coming out the Canadian prairies. I expect bad weather, bad markets, a bubble of over-supply and crashing prices—and all these things will surely come to pass. And yet, another side of me says: "Isn't it great that, for one brief moment, it is the prairie farmer's time in the sun?"

It was a strange and fragile prosperity, created by an unstable world and by frenzied speculation in farm commodities. It is saddening to see our farmers prosper again while people are starving in sub-Saharan Africa. And making money is not easy, because costs are stunningly out of control. Still it is better than nothing for the people who live not in Calgary or Edmonton, but in Saskatchewan towns like Yorkton and Moosomin, and in Alberta's Wainwright or Acme.

In early 2006, I had written a story in the *Globe and Mail* about Canada's cities, built around the role model of Kitchener-Waterloo, Ontario, a region with the remarkable ability to keep renewing itself. Even as its auto parts plants faltered, Kitchener-Waterloo remained a healthy economy because it kept moving on to the next new thing. And the next new thing in Waterloo was Research in Motion and the BlackBerry. I made a point of saying that one city that had not kept up with economic change was Regina, still stuck in its agricultural past and hampered by its civil service mentality, with a stagnant population.

A Regina economic development official said his city was no different than others in the Great Plains that stretch from Saskatoon south to Fort Worth, Texas. It was a victim of a battered farm economy with little hope in sight.

Neither of us realized that even as he made those remarks, the seeds of a turnaround were being planted in China. Two years later Regina had one of the hottest real estate markets in Canada, and two years from now, it may be suffering a cyclical decline again. As a farmer, you don't get too low in the bad times, or too high in the good times. But I would still put my long-term money on food. When the world is driving cars powered by fuel cells and windmills are powering your home, people will still need to eat.

Todd Hirsch is stubbornly unrepentant about his remarks. Yes, he says, the world will need more wheat from the Prairies. But, more important, it will need better ways to grow wheat, corn, and canola—and that will mean innovation in plant and life sciences, which Saskatchewan still needs to foster. "It's the brain economy that will determine Saskatchewan's future," he insists.

Food may be the new oil, he says, but for how long? Is this a long-term seminal shift, or a short violent cycle? And what are the implications of climate change for the northern Great Plains, which at the moment can only yield just one crop a year, not the two crops that warmer climates can achieve? Will the crop cycles change irreparably? So many questions, so hard to answer—but Todd is no longer asking for a repeal of the wheat stalks.

CHAPTER 15

THE PRAIRIE IS FLAT
The boom that knows no borders

THE WAY YOU KNOW WHETHER you are in Alberta or Saskatchewan, people tell me, is the condition of the roads. In Alberta, the roads are paved, if not with gold, at least with asphalt. On the other side of the border, in poor, dysfunctional, socialistic Saskatchewan, the roads are unpaved and potholed, surely reflecting an economy that has been held back by state control, regulation, onerous taxes, and all kinds of bad leftist policy.

So I tried out this theory in Lloydminster, the busy oil town smack dab on the Alberta-Saskatchewan border. I searched hard to detect a difference in roads, but it wasn't readily apparent. They just seemed the same to me. And the homes were not shacks on the Saskatchewan side and huge mansions on the Alberta side. It was not Dogpatch vs. Daddy Warbucks, but more like *Corner Gas* on both sides of the line. The town they call "Lloyd" is "Lloyd" on either side. In fact, the Saskatchewan side has the big Husky Energy upgrader, the source of the economic vibrancy of the region, and one of the best little museums I've ever encountered, the Barr Colony Heritage Cultural Centre, complete with a real-life western town inside.

Lloydminster is perhaps not typical of every Saskatchewan town—the road inequality is more apparent off the beaten track, people tell me—but it is proof positive that resource wealth is not hemmed in by artificial boundaries. And in this resource-driven economic era, the world may be flat, as Thomas Friedman says, but the prairies are really, really, really flat—all the way from Longview, Alberta, to Steinbach, Manitoba. Any province, any region, in the twenty-first century can prosper if it has oil, gas, potash, uranium, and, astonishingly, wheat, which is finally coming back after the worst farming years since the 1930s. This is the age of the commodity, and the prairies are bursting with all the right ones.

The prairies are also a land where the patient money eventually wins—money that outlasts downturns, droughts, and plant diseases. It is about the team at Cameco, the world's largest uranium producer, which was buying assets in the trough of its economic cycle. Or it is the Richardson family of Winnipeg, which has 150 years of experience in managing ups and downs in energy, commodities, and real estate—and is poised to make some money from the best farm cycle in decades. Or it is the prairie wheat farmer who has hung in through the worst grain years since the Dirty Thirties and now is ready to reap this odd bonanza triggered by a suddenly hungry world and a mad U.S.–subsidized dash to ethanol fuel.

It's the way of economic cycles. As long as you can wait them out and manage your debt and cash flow through the lean years. Saskatchewan, Manitoba, and, for that matter, rural Alberta, couldn't stay down forever, no matter what stripe of government ran their provinces. Eventually the Alberta energy economy had to lose its glitter because of its high costs, labour and material shortages, and a new provincial Conservative premier who just didn't seem to appreciate the oil industry's easy ride on royalties. Capital is mobile, capital will take flight, and, in the last years of the first decade of the twenty-first century, it was moving next door to Saskatchewan, which was showing no signs of changing its energy royalties—in fact, it has been making them less onerous. So Saskatchewan is the new Alberta and Manitoba is the new Saskatchewan, on the verge of an economic break-through of its own.

It would be nice to say that Saskatchewan's prosperity was driven by clean coal (of which it is a pioneer), carbon capture technologies, or all those smart little biotech companies that have popped up around the University of Saskatchewan, or the massive synchrotron in Saskatoon, a device that emits ultra-bright light and can expose the structure and composition of all kinds of materials. But to a large extent, the "Saskaboom" was about dumb old resource extraction, including fossil fuels, and Saskatchewan's own smaller trove of oil sands. "The dinosaurs did not stop at the border," explains Cal Nichols, the Edmonton businessman who left Paradise Hill, Saskatchewan, thirty-eight years ago to become an energy entrepreneur in northern Alberta. In short, Saskatchewan's future lies with the House of Saud, as well as with the House of Sod. The same forces that are build-ing the oil sands are propelling an overheated farm commodity market.

Yet, in its supply of the most important resource, people, Saskatchewan has been a persistent loser. The population has been stuck at just shy of a million for more years than anyone can remember. Cal Nichols is typical of the sixty-year diaspora of Saskatchewanians to Alberta, drawn by visions of opportunity and prosperity. They have been labourers, engineers, and top execu-tives of some of the biggest and best Calgary and Edmonton com-panies. Over thirty-five years, from 1972 to 2007, more than 420,000 Saskatchewanians decamped to Alberta, the Canada West Foundation reports. That's enough to fill two cities almost the size of Saskatoon. On a net basis, 164,000 people departed to other provinces over twenty-two years and, sad to say, they were usually young, educated, and ambitious. They have made great careers in Toronto, Ottawa, Calgary, and Vancouver, but not in Moose Jaw or Swift Current. In fact, there is a little riddle that Saskatchewan-born Calgarians like to inflict on their friends:

Question: What do you call a Saskatchewan person living in Alberta?

Answer: Boss.

Even as Saskatchewan's economy perked up in the early 2000s, the outward flow of people continued unabated. "In broad measures like per capita income and unemployment rates and so on, Manitoba and Saskatchewan are humming along quite well, but the underlying reality is there are no more people there than in 1931," Todd Hirsch commented. He observed that there are labour shortages in both provinces, but they are more a function of people leaving than a heightened demand for labour. Manitoba too had suffered net outflows of people to other provinces for twenty-four straight years but, at least, it attracted large immigrant inflows from other countries. Saskatchewan couldn't even claim that distinction.

Finally, it seemed the boom was pulling people back to Saskatchewan. In 2007, for the first time in twenty years, the province experienced a net in-migration of people from other provinces, including an actual net gain from Alberta. One major source of the new inflow is the same people who led the exodus out of Saskatchewan. The province is teeming with returning sons and daughters who are buying land, investing in property, and laying claim to mineral resources. It is like the return of the émigrés after the French Revolution or the Czechs and Hungarians coming home after perestroika. It means a huge injection of money, but also a little condescension towards their stay-at-home brothers, sisters, and cousins as in, "we were the ones who had the gumption to leave, and look at how well we did."

In my travels through the West, I kept hearing about the apocryphal "Calgary middle manager," now on the verge of retirement, who was selling his Alberta house for about a million dollars—a house he had bought for a song fifteen years ago. He was able to pick up something for $200,000 or less back home in Moose Jaw and he would still have money in the bank to spend every winter in Phoenix. It is the perfect prairie life—family picnics and church socials in the summer and endless golf in a gated community in the winter.

Larry Pollock, the congenial president of Canadian Western Bank in Edmonton, gives a typical example of the new real estate economics. In 2007, he was in the process of selling his mother's house in Melville, Saskatchewan. It was a great house, a heritage property in a prairie town. It was fetching $59,000 from a guy coming in from High River, Alberta, just south of Calgary. Larry didn't know anything about the house the Albertan was selling, but the price tag might have been as much as $500,000. That was the trade-off—$500,000 vs. $59,000. No wonder people were moving back to the land of their birth.

And these émigrés are buying farms as well. Brett Wilson, the Calgary investment banker, who was born in North Battleford, has been snatching up agricultural land in Saskatchewan for a couple of years, taking advantage of new rules that lift landownership restrictions on people from outside the province. "We bought five ranches last week alone," Wilson told me at one point.

Proudly wearing his Roughrider jacket, surrounded by Roughrider football memorabilia, Paul Hill is clearly pumped as he sits in his hotel room in the shadow of Toronto's cavernous Rogers Centre—the venue where a few days hence, his beloved Riders would win the Grey Cup for the first time since 1989.

This is very big stuff in Regina where Hill's family has being doing business since the early years of the twentieth century, where it is now one of Saskatchewan's major business dynasties, as owner of a conglomerate of insurance, oil and gas, and broadcasting. In 1905, the Hills actually sold land in Regina to the new Saskatchewan government on which the province built its legislature building. Now, they own a bunch of companies under the name Harvard, because Harvard University in Cambridge, Massachusetts, is where Paul's father, Fred, got his MBA in the years after the Second World War. Cambridge is where Paul was born before Fred and his young family came home to Regina to run the Hill businesses. Underlying the Hill family ethos is a strong Jesuit adherence. Paul went to Georgetown University in Washington, a Jesuit school, and all of his five children have been educated at least in part by the Jesuits. In fact, it could be said that Paul Hill's religions are Jesuit Catholicism and Saskatchewan Roughrider football.

He is hardly unique in his worship at the altar of the green Riders. Nowhere else in North America is a pro football team so identified with a province or a state. The closest approximation can perhaps be found in Lambeau Field in Green Bay, where Wisconsin fans gather at the shrine of Lombardi, Hornung, Taylor, Favre, and other Packer gods. In Saskatchewan, the pantheon includes Ron Lancaster, George Reed, and Kerry Joseph, the latest quarterback hero (alas, destined to leave for Toronto in a much lamented trade).

"In Saskatchewan, the Roughriders are the biggest thing in the province, our heart and our soul," Hill explains amidst a clutter of green trinkets. "Not only that, we re-branded ourselves ten years ago as 'Canada's team,'" explains Hill, who has served on the board of the football team.

Why Canada's team? Surely the Riders do not boast a following comparable to the Dallas Cowboys, who carry the title "America's team." But Hill is talking about all the people who have left Saskatchewan. In every stadium that they play, it's like the Riders are the second home team. There are as many people cheering them as supporting the local team. It's a great lift, but a discouraging fact of life. Saskatchewan's greatest export over the past sixty years has been well-educated people—whether Bank of Canada governor Gerald Bouey, broadcaster Pamela

Wallin, or Calgary energy titans Murray Edwards and Hank Swartout.

Paul Hill and his family stayed and tried to stem the tide by investing in Saskatchewan, and trying to attract new business—such as Paul's big mission to bring the headquarters of Crown Life to Regina in the 1990s. But Hill admits many of his investments for the past thirty years have been outside the province, in Alberta and the U.S. Southwest, where his family saw better opportunity than in sluggish Saskatchewan.

The Alberta investments turned out very well, particularly when he caught the tail wind of the resources boom. He also had a wild ride on the Internet roller coaster in California where he invested $200,000 in a technology incubator called IdeaLab. The incubator attracted a billion dollars in investment capital from people like computer titan Michael Dell. Paul Hill's $200,000 stake rose in paper value to $36 million and the company was about to go public. Then the tech market crashed, the public issue was postponed, and valuations plummeted. Hill's paper millions fell back to $40,000. Yet IdeaLab was well funded and was able to stay in business, and Hill saw his investment climb back.

The experience left his head spinning. "The big story is I had a great net worth, I lost most of it in the decline, but not all of it," he said. Fortunately, he had invested heavily in the source of the next big bubble—the energy industry in Alberta. "I took advantage of that, I was able to leverage that up and I've done well over the last six or seven years."

Despite that one wild ride into the Internet, the Hills are patient money, and now it is the time to reap the rewards of hanging on in Saskatchewan. I asked Hill if he was going to pull more money back into his home province. He says he never really left Saskatchewan, but he is also alert to the lessons of history. Every twenty years or so, there is this unique opportunity to invest in Saskatchewan—and this is one of those times. "In the last year, when the tide is rising everywhere in the world, you have this one hole down here. Eventually, it starts spilling in to fill up the hole. Basically that's what's happened."

For a province that has been stuck in that no-growth hole through years of drought, low wheat prices, and out-migration, Saskatchewan has bred a nice little cluster of world-leading companies. It contains the world's largest producer of fertilizer called, appropriately enough, Potash Corp. of Saskatchewan. As fertilizer has gone through the roof, Potash Corp.'s market value at one point soared to $63 billion, which is 20 per cent higher than Saskatchewan's entire 2007 GDP. In other words, the stock market has put 20 per cent more value on the province's largest company than the market value of all the goods and services produced in the province. The province also boasts the world's leading uranium producer in Cameco, as well as agribusiness giant Viterra (the former Saskatchewan Wheat Pool), one of the emerging powerhouses of the booming farm commodity markets in North America.

Saskatchewan companies have learned how to manage the economic cycles, a hard-won talent in the viciously volatile commodity economies of the past thirty years. Potash and Cameco both built their dominant positions by being buyers and consolidators during long down periods—Potash Corp. during the horrible farm slumps and Cameco during periods when nuclear power was out of favour. Both companies have been careful not to buy at the peak of their cycles. Jerry Grandey, the CEO of Cameco, was royally roasted by analysts and media because he was not buying assets as uranium soared to $136 U.S. a pound in mid-2007, from $10 five years earlier. But when the market price eased back into the $70 to $80 range, he was starting to look around for acquisition candidates.

Sometimes it helps, he says, to be based in relatively quiet Saskatoon where you aren't meeting deal-hungry investment bankers for lunch every day. You don't get caught up in the fads that drive bad decisions. It also helps that Cameco is protected by federal legislation that prohibits a foreign shareholder from owning more than 15 per cent of the company's shares, and any single shareholder, foreign or otherwise, from owning more than 25 per cent of the former Crown corporation. That gives you the comfort of a long-term view and has been critical to the career continuity of Grandey, who has survived mishaps that would have cashiered other CEOs, including the two-year postponement of a major mining project because of site flooding. It has also left Cameco open to the allegation that it has been a sleepy giant, slow to take advantage of wealth-creation opportunities.

Perhaps there is a lesson in the story of IPSCO, the venerable steel company based in Regina, which also had a strong long-term business model to be the dominant supplier to the networks of steel pipe bringing oil and gas out of the Canadian and U.S. West. It even pulled its small executive team out of Regina and put it in a Chicago suburb. That gave CEO David Sutherland and his team of seventeen people a base to build a large U.S. business, with a continuing presence in Saskatchewan and Alberta. "It was unfortunate but we have to grow in the United States, and so we relocated a number of ourselves here," Sutherland explained at one point. "It may not have been a vast number compared to the 900 or so people in Regina at the moment, but it's a smaller province and these were all relatively high-profile, highly paid people." As a Saskatchewanian, Sutherland regretted the move, but it made sense for a company with a continental, north-south outlook.

In time, IPSCO's head office location became irrelevant. It could not survive in the wave of global steel consolidation, and it was taken over by SSAB, a Swedish steel company, in a block-buster $7.7 billion deal. Sutherland drove a hard bargain for IPSCO, did well for shareholders, but IPSCO was a widely held company, and was doomed to be acquired. There was no dominant shareholder, and no protective legislation.

The fact it was a Swedish company that did the acquiring was even more intriguing. How does a country with nine million people preserve and protect a steel champion, but Canada with 34 million people no longer boasts of a major steel company? David Sutherland had the right idea, a North American pipe powerhouse, but he lacked the firepower to play that game.

As a CEO, Sutherland was representative of another subtle strength of Saskatchewan business. In this province, they are very smart about north-south business trends. Why would a team of Saskatchewan executives locate itself in suburban Chicago? Because that's where the action is. Conversely, all three of Saskatchewan's major private companies are run by transplanted Americans: Cameco by California-born Grandey; Potash Corp. by Chicago native Bill Doyle; and Viterra, the grain handling and agribusiness giant, by former Kansas farm boy Mayo Schmidt.

In Saskatchewan, there is no sense of being hemmed in by national borders. It is a perspective that comes with having a long view of the Great Plains stretching from Saskatoon south to Dallas–Forth Worth. It also reflects the continental, even global vision of Canada's agribusiness sector. Even the Canadian Wheat Board based in Winnipeg hired an Australian to run it during a period when its very existence was under attack by many wheat farmers and by the federal Conservative government.

Potash Corp.'s Bill Doyle may be the best example of this classic itinerant U.S.–Canadian executive. He spends much of his time in Potash Corp.'s offices in suburban Chicago, and he keeps his primary residence in that city, as well as a home in Saskatoon. On the days when he resides in Saskatoon, he is the richest person in the province. His 2007 salary was a healthy $1 million, but his holdings of Potash Corp. shares and unexercised stock options lifted the value of his holdings to $600 million at one point in early 2008. The *Globe and Mail* columnist David Berman pointed out that "some of these options have strike prices as low as $10-and-change—miles below the current share price of $194.25, putting him well into the money." In lots of places, Doyle's wealth would be unexceptional. Put him in London or New York, or even his hometown of Chicago, and he is just a garden-variety multimillionaire. In Saskatchewan, that kind of money stands out like a maple tree in a wheat field. In fact, Doyle's stash is equivalent to more than 1 per cent of the province's gross domestic product. It is great to be alive and a resource executive in today's Saskatchewan.

Mayo Schmidt may be Saskatchewan's most fascinating executive because he took over the venerable farmer-owned co-operative that used to be called the Saskatchewan Wheat Pool, the operator of grain elevators that were once found in every prairie whistle stop. He turned it into a thrusting agribusiness force called Viterra, a company that is now the leading western Canadian grain handler, as well as a force in sales and processing. Schmidt, an American, is a U.S. former football player and iron-man triathlete who is a CEO in the hard-nosed Jack Welch mould. As a kid out of a Kansas college, he caught passes in training camp from Miami Dolphins' star quarterback Bob Griese, before he realized he was too small and too slow to ever be an NFL wide receiver. "I was six foot and a hundred and eighty pounds and playing in the NFL. That wouldn't have produced a long and prosperous career that would have achieved the kind of things I wanted," he told me.

So he channelled his hungry competitiveness into business and, for the past decade, has masterminded the transformation of a prairie co-operative, first rescuing it from near bankruptcy, and, more recently, turning it into a publicly traded acquisition machine. In 2007, he drove the SaskPool's $1.8 billion takeover of Winnipeg-based Agricore United, creating a powerhouse of elevators and terminals just in time to catch the farm commodity boom. It was a matter of cyclical management in the prairie style, but a lot of luck too.

As he has transformed the company, Schmidt has closed the chapter on a great name in Canadian agriculture—the Saskatchewan Wheat Pool—and replaced it with Viterra, something that sounds a bit like a product for erectile dysfunction. Schmidt is not prone to looking back. "It is a different business and as we evolve we will continue to change. We didn't want to create constraints in how we view ourselves and how the marketplace and customer view us."

He pointed out that Viterra is a combination of four western institutions: the Alberta Wheat Pool, the Manitoba Pool Elevators, the Saskatchewan Wheat Pool, and United Grain Growers. "It is the four companies that have between eighty and one hundred years of history each that have been combined. I wanted to create an environment where all the employees of those historic companies came together as one and not continue look at themselves as a legacy employee of a particular business."

He said employees have responded positively to the name change, particularly as the grain market has turned upward. "They want leadership in agriculture that gets it back to the front of the business section. For years and years, agriculture has largely been seen as a business that hasn't been recognized. Now we have economists saying that agriculture is leading—that if you look at a choice between energy and agriculture, their investment would be in agriculture."

Schmidt said the next challenge was to acquire businesses in the United States—to become a continental player. But he admits Viterra is somewhat handicapped by its location in Regina. "In travel, everything is a connection, and there is always several hours' delay," he told me. The biggest challenge in Regina is attracting top-quality people and keeping them. That is the great Saskatchewan dilemma. "There are other parts of the world that have a great draw for talent and if you are not playing at the top of the game, it is hard to keep people."

Three hours to the northwest of Regina, Saskatoon may seem even more remote, but it is actually better equipped to hire and retain private sector workers. It does not have Regina's reputation as a civil service town. Saskatoon has a solid core of private head offices, led by Cameco and Potash Corp., as well as research installations and high-tech start-ups spilling out of the university environment. Saskatoon is in many ways a mini-Edmonton, without the provincial capital. There is the South Saskatchewan River, a fine old railway hotel on the crest of the river valley, and a strong university on the south shore. The two cities share similar social challenges, stemming in part from a large aboriginal population—almost 10 per cent of the population in Saskatoon comprises aboriginals. They constitute a rich potential source of talent and skills—more than 2,000 aboriginal students attend the University of Saskatchewan—but the city harbours a malignant racism in some quarters that makes progress difficult.

In both Saskatchewan and Manitoba, native peoples make up about 15 per cent of the population and they present both opportunity and challenge. They tend to be a younger population amid an otherwise aging workforce. Cameco, in particular, has been effective in hiring workers from twenty-six aboriginal communities in the province's northern regions to work in its uranium mines. It has well over 1,000 aboriginal workers, making it the largest private industrial employer of native people in Canada. This is where the Saskatchewan edge might be found, in an aboriginal population that is yet to participate as a full partner in the provincial economy. In five decades, native people will make up almost a third of the population, which means that a closer convergence of aboriginal and non-aboriginal average incomes is critical if the province is to prosper.

In Saskatchewan's new spirit of optimism, a business-minded provincial government—the Saskatchewan Party led by Premier Brad Wall—is keen to make a mark. The previous NDP government under Lorne Calvert had also demonstrated a willingness to cut taxes and eliminate red tape. The Saskatchewan NDP has always been leavened by a streak of realism and many adherents believe that you need fiscal prudence if you are to accomplish sustainable social good. The 2007 budget, brought down by Brad Wall's team, signalled the fifteenth straight year of budget surpluses and the first fourteen of those were under NDP leadership.

Saskatchewan also got a boost from an Alberta government that has levelled the prairie playing field in many ways by introducing an energy royalty system that, from one perspective, claws back some of the massive giveaway to the oil companies— or from the energy point of view, bites the hand that feeds it. The irony is that while Alberta may have turned a little more socialistic, it is opening the way for a Saskatchewan that is a little less socialistic.

It's just a new twist in one of the great unfolding mysteries of Canadian public life: How can two provinces so close in geography and history be so different in political cultures? Saskatchewan has honking-big Crown corporations in telecommunications and power. Alberta will privatize anything that moves. Saskatchewan has had social democratic governments for forty-seven of the past sixty-three years. Alberta has had Conservative governments of varying intensity over that entire period.

Janice McKinnon, the former Saskatchewan NDP finance minister, says the two provinces experienced different immigration patterns, with Saskatchewan attracting large numbers of English working-class people who proudly carried the baggage of trade unionism. Alberta was heavily influenced by its U.S. imports, whether red-meat Texas oilmen or clean-living Utah Mormons. The two provinces came to reflect the separate strains of prairie populism arising from the farmers' movements of the 1920s and 1930s—ardently free enterprise on one side and collectivist on the other. Two charismatic preacher-premiers of the 1940s then put their stamps on their respective provinces—the Conservative evangelist William Aberhart in Alberta and the social democratic minister Tommy Douglas in Saskatchewan.

It was Douglas whom Paul Hill believes set the province on a pattern of depopulation and reduced aspirations that led to today's important turning point. Yes, that Tommy Douglas—the former Saskatchewan CCF premier and later NDP federal leader, who won the CBC's title of Greatest Canadian for introducing medicare in Canada. Could the Greatest Canadian also be one of the worst Saskatchewanians? That is the contention of some in the Saskatchewan business class.

There is some nervousness in taking on an icon like Douglas, but Paul Hill has no hesitation in blaming the NDP hero for sixty years of Saskatchewan decline. In 1944, the year of Douglas's election as premier, almost all the major Canadian oil companies had significant operations in Saskatchewan, Hill contends. "They had all of their budgets allocated to finding oil in Saskatchewan and then the socialistic Tommy Douglas got elected and they all left." Imperial Oil reallocated its capital budget to Alberta, and then struck it rich with the Leduc No. 1 strike of 1947. That set the pattern, Hill says, creating a powerful energy industry in Alberta, which the province nurtured by giving it a consistent positive environment, and the energy industry flourished in Alberta.

"Alberta has developed into a world centre for oil and gas. That opportunity existed for Saskatchewan and I believe with proper public policy initiatives that we would have been the head office centre of the oil industry for western Canada." But Saskatchewan, he argues, offered only inconsistent policy, heavy taxes and royalties, and actually confiscated private property in a binge of nationalization.

"Look I'm not saying Tommy Douglas didn't do some good things,' Hill said in a *Globe and Mail* interview. "But overall, when you are creating an unwelcoming environment for business, when you have a government that is confiscating and taking over industries, with an onerous tax system and a confiscatory regulatory and resources taxation system, you can't say that doesn't have a profoundly negative impact and it did."

Douglas remains a deeply polarizing figure. Larry Pollock, the CEO of Canadian Western Bank, questions whether, if the Saskatchewan formed by Tommy Douglas is so great, if its contributions to health care and social programs were so positive, where is Tommy Douglas's family now? They are not in Saskatchewan, he says, and neither are other enterprising people like Larry Pollock. They have voted with their feet and left the province. Pollock, incidentally, has been a fundraiser in Alberta for the Saskatchewan Party.

But Tommy Douglas has been dead for twenty years. It's like blaming all of Alberta's woes on Pierre Trudeau or all of Newfoundland's problems on the Upper Churchill fiasco. Canada's biggest handicap is memory, an obsession with past wrongs, past indignities. It may inspire political campaigns but it does not build a modern economy. Across the prairies, and across Canada, it is time for a bit less of the past and a bit more of the future.

※

There are some days when the intersection of Portage and Main in Winnipeg seems like the coldest place on earth. It is not just the winter months when the thermometer drops to thirty below and lower. Even in more agreeable seasons, there is a coldness that transcends the weather. The city blocks around Canada's most famous intersection are full of sad people, sad lives, and sad buildings that are closed and boarded up. Once the most vibrant corner in the Canadian West, the square is a monument to the shifting patterns of growth and development and how economic decline can hollow out a once-great city centre.

To remain committed to this city core requires great loyalty and patience, and an ability to overlook the crumbling detail and see the big picture. The thirty-four-storey Richardson Building still stands as a proud and haughty rebuke against those who would claim that downtown Winnipeg is doomed to endless decline. The Richardson family is now spread across the country, but this once-thriving street corner remains its cornerstone. This is where the eleven cousins who now own the family business still gather to make decisions, to strengthen their bonds, and renew their family spirit. The Richardson business empire is now 150 years old, having begun with a grain elevator in Kingston, Ontario, in 1857 and moved to Winnipeg to catch the wheat boom of the early twentieth century. It remains a force in this country—and no more so than on the prairies. And it is still, against all odds, a Winnipeg institution.

The Richardsons have always been the epitome of quiet money in Canada, so quiet that most Canadians know very little about them. They own businesses that span real estate, farm commodities, and wealth management and they are a rising force in private equity investment, having raised more than $1 billion to invest in Canada. In recent years they have started to make some noise, mainly by bidding to buy Agricore, a farm commodity company, whose complement of grain elevators would greatly expand the Richardson business in the handling of farm commodities.

The family ended up in a cliff-hanger battle with the Saskatchewan Wheat Pool (now Viterra), and in the end, the two companies split the assets and both went home happy. The transaction boosted the Richardsons' network of grain elevators and terminals by 60 per cent, just in time to catch the farm commodity boom that was sweeping across the prairies. It is proof that investors who look long term can do very well in the short term and anyone betting long term on Manitoba is finally seeing some major returns. The Richardsons' Canadian market share has risen to 25 per cent in grain handling, up from 15 per cent, although still behind the newly expanded Viterra, which controls about 40 per cent.

Hartley Richardson, the family's business leader and the fifth generation to run the holding company, likes where he is sitting. "The end result could not have worked out better, because we were able to secure a significant group of strategic assets, we were able to do this within our own resources and stay 100 per cent private in this our 150th year," Hartley said in an interview with the *Globe and Mail*.

The Richardsons celebrated their 150th anniversary party by giving 150 gifts of money to communities across Canada. Whether in charity or business, the family's investments and business interests know no boundaries. They are active in almost every province. They have been sharp investors in the oil sands, taking a stake in companies that are on the cutting edge of new technology, such as Columba Yeung's Value Creation. In addition, the Richardsons' private equity funds have taken a stake in Opti Canada, a company that is involved in a joint venture with Nexen to develop the Long Lake oil sands project at Fort Mc-Murray. Opti uses a unique technology to separate oil from the sands, one that also eliminates the wasteful use of gas. The process turns a certain grade of bitumen into hydrogen gas, which in turn is used to make enough steam, heat, and electric power for all of the Long Lake operations. The Alberta Energy Research Institute has called the technology "the future of Canadian oil sands expansion."

The Richardsons control a big part of the canola processing industry, bolstered by their plans for a new plant in Yorkton, and are investors in food science. "We think science will become more important and provide more value to the producer at the farm end and our ability to take it from the field to the table has a lot of opportunity for growth," Hartley says.

The Richardsons' investing rules are to always think long term, always aim to be a significant player in your field, and get out of any business where you are a minor contributor. Thus, the Richardsons got out of pipelines, and bulked up in grain handling and energy. While they are committed to commodity businesses— which is their heritage—they strive to differentiate themselves by investing in technology where they can make a difference. In their view, they are financing the decommoditization of Canada's commodities.

And they have never forsaken Winnipeg. Like the media-owning Asper family—who have their own head office across the windblown Portage-Main square from the Richardson Building—they are absolutely dedicated to retaining their headquarters in what has been their home for nearly a hundred years. Family members may drift away to Toronto or Calgary, but the head office stays. Hartley says it is simple: "Grain and grain business is our founding business and this is where you need to be if you are in the grain business in western Canada."

The family has also been an aggressive investor in the Williston oil basin in the southwest region of Manitoba—nothing like Alberta in scale but a solid income-earning oil deposit. All its real estate and many of its financial services operations are run from Winnipeg. Hartley Richardson says that from the Richardson Building, he can practically see all the way to Thunder Bay to the east and to Regina to the west. "This is a good place to come to from east and west. This is the centre of the country," he says. His cousin, Carolyn Hursh, the chair of the family company who lives in Calgary but travels to Winnipeg at least once a month, insists that, "we can attract talent, young people that want to come home to raise a family." She adds that "fundamentally this is our head office, this is our home and while the family has spread out, there is a strong affinity to Winnipeg."

Indeed, downtown Winnipeg is beginning to reward the Richardsons' patience. A new arena has restored some vibrancy to a stretch of Portage Avenue a few blocks from the Richardson Building, and Manitoba Hydro has been moving 2,000 workers into a new, ecologically progressive head office building. The Richardsons' attachment to the province is also paying off as the farm economy has flourished. Not only that, the region was benefiting from strong markets in nickel, copper, and zinc—all minerals with representation in Manitoba. What's more, the province is the beneficiary of some big public-spending projects, including an expanded Winnipeg airport, recently renamed the James A. Richardson Airport after Hartley and Caroline's grandfather. "All of the stars that can make Manitoba glow are lined up," said John McCallum, the veteran economist at the University of Manitoba who had seen the province weather a number of cycles. He points out the added advantage for Winnipeg: "It's not half bad being just 1,000 kilometres away from Alberta, and getting all that spillover."

The province has shown signs of shedding its status as the "middle province"—in the middle of the country and in the middle of the economic pack. In the past, it has grown but not too much; it prospered but not enough. It is a farming powerhouse, but it is still hit by some of the manufacturing woes. The worst knock against Manitoba is that it has been losing young people, mainly to Alberta and perhaps now to Saskatchewan. That is something even the Richardsons can't address on their own. In much of Canada, that is the most pressing challenge of the twenty-first century.

In downtown Edmonton, the side of an old retail building has been exposed, allowing passersby to see advertisements from around the turn of the twentieth century—the now-faded billboards of the time. The printed slogans extol the virtues of two very different companies—one is Cunard, an ocean-liner company still thriving but long gone from its original base in Halifax, Nova Scotia. The other is James Richardson & Sons, still prosperous and still based in Winnipeg—a reminder that a great merchant family can prosper and still remain loyal to the city that nurtured it. You can't help but wonder where the great Alberta fortunes will be in the next century. Will they be gone, like Cunard, or still fighting the good fight for their home city and province, like the Richardsons?

On the July 1 Canada Day weekend in 2007, just before the Calgary Stampede, Bonnie Dupont, the vice-president for corporate resources at pipeline giant Enbridge, drove east from her Calgary home into Saskatchewan. It was a familiar route to Swift Current, where she dropped in on her mother and stepfather and took a look over the farm she owns just north of the city. Then she drove her two elderly parents out to the little town where she grew up—a place called Herbert.

It's a ritual she has repeated for years, ever since she left Saskatchewan for a big job in the Calgary oil patch. "I just do it because it is good for my parents and good for me. We call it the crop inspection tour," says Dupont, who has survived a cancer scare and emerged as a gentle and humane powerhouse in the Calgary energy industry—and who rose to become the first female president of that former male bastion, the Petroleum Club of Calgary.

Dupont has kept her 800-hectare farm in Saskatchewan for thirty years and she rents it out. Her accountant keeps telling her that it is a drain on her finances and she should sell it. But she explains to him that it isn't a strictly financial venture. "Once you've farmed you can't get it out of your blood," she says. "I think I'm like a lot of folks in Saskatchewan and Alberta—you'll find it's hard to let it go."

In 2007, Dupont's investment in Saskatchewan land looked

like it would actually bear some fruit. The wheat economy was on fire and it appeared she would make some real money from her investment. Not only that, she was joined by a flood of Calgarians just like her: former Saskatchewan people who rediscovered the joys, and the thriving economy, of their home province. Some were speculators driving the price of Saskatchewan land to stratospheric heights—for Saskatchewan, that is. Not that Bonnie Dupont is ready to cash in. For her, the farm is not a matter of making a killing but of making a connection with her prairie roots.

Dupont is a pioneer in the energy industry, someone who has broken gender barriers at the dark wood-panelled halls of the Petroleum Club. It's a place that still reflects the old boys' club atmosphere of decades ago. There is a piece of folk art sculpture in the lobby portraying a group of men playing cards around the table. The tiny models are in fact representations of real people who constituted a regular poker table at the club. The artwork is called *The Choir Practice*—so named because when the wives would ask where the men had been, they would explain they were at choir practice. There are no women at the table. If Bonnie Dupont has her way, that will change.

Dupont is also unusual in her background. She started her career working in Crown corporations in Regina. Her early career is dominated by experience in government-owned organizations—because, in Regina, Crown corps are the biggest games in town. As a young woman, she was actually a union official for a while in Regina, which makes her not just a rarity, but an exotic creature, in the conservative oil patch. In fact, the Saskatchewan gang does bring a different vibe to the Calgary corporate scene, a liberalism that balances the sharp-edged U.S. style that the American multinationals bring north.

Charlie Fischer, the president of Nexen, the giant oil company, was born in Saskatoon, moved to Calgary with his family, and went back to school at the University of Saskatchewan. He has tried to inject Saskatchewan values into the oil patch and into Nexen's approach to global expansion in places like Yemen, where it is a major oil producer. "I call them just good old-fashioned Canadian values. You get engaged in the community. You don't go and tell people what they need to do, you listen to what they need, and you help them achieve their aspirations."

In Fischer's view, these are values that people have tradition-ally associated with being Canadian, but are now being lost as this country becomes more American in style and attitude. His-torically, Canada was a rural, underpopulated territory where people survived through personal initiative and by sharing and showing compassion to others. The result is a health-care and so-cial system where people do not fall between the cracks. In this society, community rights largely took precedence over individ-ual rights. "But I think we're getting far more egocentric, and in-dividual rights are starting to take precedence over community rights. I don't think that's right. I think that we ought to do things that not only benefit us but benefit others," Fischer says.

Fischer, who for many years has brandished a luxurious han-dlebar moustache, has a reputation for being "out there," maybe even a tad radical for the oil patch in his devotion to social justice. Yet he is also credited for giving back a lot of time and money to his city and province. He and his wife Joanne Cuthbertson are a power couple in the voluntary and not-for-profit sector— she has served as the chancellor of the University of Calgary.

Asked if his comments don't sound socialistic, he agrees he might be a bit leftist. He gets teased from time to time about being the company socialist. But this has a business purpose, as well. These community values are at the root of why Nexen has been so successful as a Canadian multinational. When it went to Yemen, for example, it sought to build relationships not only with the government but also with local communities.

Mind you, these socialist values did not stop Fischer from complaining vociferously and threatening to pull investment and philanthropy out of Alberta when the provincial government suddenly raised the level of energy royalties it collected. There are limits to his socialism, he admitted to me. He felt personally affronted by the new royalty regime, which suggested that Albertans did not really like or trust the energy industry that had been their benefactor for decades.

"The disappointment for me was the animosity people had for the sector and I found that really shocking," Fischer says. "It doesn't make you feel very proud of the sector because how did we get into the position where we contributed so much to the well-being of the province—and we're despised? I don't get that."

"As an individual engaged in the community, raising money, writing cheques, I sort of say 'what is this?' If we're going to be a social state let's be a social state; if we're going to become that great social society, government can pay for it all. I'll still be a philanthropist; I just won't be a philanthropist here. I'll take my money and give it to the developing world where they appreciate it."

So the love affair between the people of Alberta and the energy industry is a complex one of passionate embrace and hurt separation. It is now going through a period of disenchantment. As a result, the industry captains who once looked in disdain at Saskatchewan—or Manitoba, for that matter—are considering new options. From the big towers of Calgary you can look east and see a lot of land, a lot of opportunity, a lot of oil and gas, a lot of wheat, and, yes, a lot of people who have been patiently waiting for the turnaround. The prairie is truly flat and no province, no city, no company, can dare to be complacent.

CHAPTER 16

....

HOLLOW MEN

The gathering storm over foreign investment

IN 1835, URIAH SEYMOUR journeyed from upstate New York to the forests of Upper Canada. Seymour was a veteran ironmaster and smelter owner who had run out of ore and opportunities in his New York community of Wolcott, just east of Rochester. He knew of a large body of iron ore in a lightly populated territory just north of Lake Ontario, in Canada, and came north to exploit it. He would mine the ore in a big pit north of the settlement of Mackenzie Mills, and he would draw it down to his smelter in the settlement for processing. He was a technological innovator who experimented with different materials. When he ran out of charcoal for his blast furnace, he used local cordwood instead.

At its peak, the smelter produced two tons of pig iron a day. But the enterprise lasted only a few years before a partner absconded with some of the funds. More disastrously, the price of iron plummeted—a common occurrence in a commodity economy—and Uriah was running out of raw materials. Meanwhile, a small village, renamed Madoc, rose around the mill. Uriah's iron mine died, but he left a lot of legacies. His son Fred built the biggest house in the village, which still stands. His sister Cynthia's family came up from New York to work with Uriah, and his niece Maria married a local peddler and farmer named James Pitts and these two people were my great-grandmother and great-grandfather. Their descendants are scattered around Ontario. They are farmers, schoolteachers, civil servants, factory workers, salespeople, electricians, and the occasional journalist. In a sense, they are Uriah's most enduring gift to Canada.

Uriah was among the first of a long line of Yankee traders who have exploited Canada's natural resources. It is a line that extends down through the centuries, and their investments and their labour helped build this country. Uriah was not a major mine and smelter builder—his operation was pretty small, even for the times—but he played a small part in creating the Canadian iron and steel industry. He employed lawyers, geologists, ironmongers, and accountants. His legacy is why I am not inclined to condemn foreign investment but, in fact, to praise it. It has been this financial injection that has made Canada, whether the British and French adventurers who created the fur trade, the financiers whose investments laid the tracks of the transcontinental Canadian Pacific Railway, the U.S. capitalists who spun off Northern Telecom (now Nortel), or the investment funds that today finance the myriad neat things you can do on a wireless device called the BlackBerry. It is the money that is developing the oil sands, whether through foreign players such as Total and Royal Dutch Shell or through Canadian companies with large U.S. shareholding bases such as EnCana and Suncor. Our capital markets and financial institutions have been so small or undeveloped compared with the scale of our dreams, that we have always relied on foreign investment and that sometimes means surrendering ownership of our most strategic assets to foreign investors like Uriah Seymour.

If Uncle Uriah were alive today, I have no doubt that he would be aghast. The Canadian metals industry that he helped create—to which his tiny mine and blast furnace were minor but indisputable ingredients—no longer has Canadian ownership, at least for its large integrated producers. All major Canadian steel companies have been swallowed up by, if not just Yankee traders, by British, Swedish, and Indian traders. More seriously, not a single Canadian steel company had the guts, the gumption, or the energy to step up as one of the global consolidators. And base metals? They're gone too, with the sale of our two largest nickel and copper miners, Inco and Falconbridge—one sold to a Brazilian company, the other in the hands of a Swiss-British entity. The mines are still here, the steel plants are still standing, but the decisions are made elsewhere. The mining industry may soon be hardly worth a plug nickel in downtown Toronto.

If only, like Uriah Seymour, the new owners put down roots in Canada. If only they hired Canadians for their core legal, accounting, consulting, investment, or financing requirements. But they don't. They will perform some of these functions here but the foreign owners of our once-mighty steelmakers—Stelco, Dofasco, Algoma, and Ipsco—will look to their own countries for core services. For some reason, steel is clearly not considered one of our strategic industries—its divestiture was not considered a matter of this country's national security—and the industry's passage into foreign hands evoked hardly a whimper.

It was the same thing with all those industries whose ownership we surrendered in the early years of the twenty-first century. Alcan, our entry into the aluminum sweepstakes, was swept away by the British mining giant Rio Tinto. Control of our largest department store chain and a big part of our history, went with the Hudson's Bay Company to U.S. investors. Large swaths of our technology sector have slipped into foreign hands—strong niche players such as Cognos and ATI. In addition, we have lost the key players in industries as diverse as wine, ski lodges, and hotels. Hell, all our major breweries are owned by outsiders and nothing is more Canadian than beer.

In many cases, these foreign owners have maintained significant operations in this country and they have tried to mollify any concerns by investing large sums in Canadian operations. They would argue they are acting like Uriah Seymour, actually adding to the industrial fabric. They maintain mining towns in the Ontario North and steel cities in Hamilton, Sault Ste. Marie, and Regina. The mining towns provide good, high-paying jobs, but the best jobs in the mining industry are not in the small towns. They are in white-collar professional services, and they will surely decline in Canada. They will decline most precipitously in the head office cities like Montreal, Vancouver, and, above all, Toronto, where they are the lifeblood of commerce, the downtown office complex, and the funding of all kinds of good things like theatre, opera, and galleries.

It's called the hollowing-out effect, the loss of corporate head offices, and the tide of collateral damage that such losses can unleash. With the commodity boom, the rise of China, and the flood of cash washing around the world in the early 2000s, there has been an acquisition mania, and Canada has been not a net buyer but a net seller. In the short term the acquisitions have been good for Toronto, as the fees for mergers and acquisitions pad the bank accounts of lawyers and investment bankers. But the long-term effect will be disastrous because head offices are the brains of organizations. And it also means the growing marginalization of major accounting firms, large corporate law firms, the major stock exchange, the key investment dealers, financial analysts, the strategic consulting firms, and the power-lunch restaurants.

It is particularly damaging in the mining business because Canada had attained the status of the world's mining finance centre. It is what Toronto does well and it is now in peril. It is hard to believe that in the midst of the most bullish commodity market in history, in the centre of an amazing run on mining assets, at a time of a soaring Canadian dollar that makes foreign assets cheaper, an uncommonly wealthy Canada was actually removing itself from the list of mining superpowers. You may not care much for Toronto as a city, but it is Canada's financial centre and it is in decline and everybody loses.

At one point, there was the dream of merging Inco and Falconbridge into a Canadian champion in the nickel-copper business. It did not happen and both of these great companies were bought out by opportunistic foreign owners. It is easy to point fingers at a loss of will by corporate management, at gutless boards, and at a European regulatory process that ragged the puck, allowing investors to grow restive at the idea of a made-in-Canada merger. You can point fingers at short-term investors, who cared nothing about building long-term growth, and sold out to the quick buck. It is easy to direct blame at Scott Hand, the likeably bland American lawyer who ran Inco, but there was little he could do when the momentum turned against his Inco-Falconbridge union and left his own company prey to a Brazilian buyer.

It may have been a unique moment in history, when there was a remarkable wave of cash washing over the world, and a number of Canadian companies got swept away. That's the opinion of Lynton "Red" Wilson, the veteran business leader who headed a federal panel probing Canada's competition and investment policy. That moment came to a crashing halt with the U.S. credit crunch, which brought a respite to the takeover mania of the previous decade. Wilson argued that the evidence on hollowing out was inconclusive, but he allowed that many Canadians were deeply concerned about losing national champions.

The Wilson committee's report consists of a commendable shopping list of sixty-five measures aimed at bolstering Canada's competitive agility. But the panel's biggest contribution may have been underlining there is a problem. "Do we have what it takes to be the best or are we content with endlessly bickering over who gets what?" Red Wilson asked in a speech. If Canada doesn't get its act together, "we will have squandered a great legacy. No land on earth has ever been so well endowed by nature and as successfully developed by the efforts of our forefathers." But in fact, "we seem to be increasingly dysfunctional," he said.

In fact, the credit crunch gave Canadians a chance to take stock of their economy, its strengths and weaknesses. And there are many strengths in talent, creativity, and drive. Any country that produced powerhouses like Manulife, RIM, and EnCana can't be a total loser. But we can also see that the great sell-off of Canadian industry is in danger of reducing cities such as Toronto, Vancouver, Montreal, and even Calgary as financial and corporate centres. It won't happen immediately, but over the next few decades it will slowly eat away at the heart of Canada's commercial capital. Good jobs will disappear, students will look outside the country for opportunities, universities will suffer and public philanthropy, which is now in a kind of Golden Age, will not be as robust in the next generation. There will be fewer amateur hockey coaches, fewer church youth leaders, fewer volunteers for everything.

As Wilson's report indicated, all the numbers thrown around are not conclusive that the country is hollowing out. In fact, some people would suggest Canada is losing in the war to attract foreign direct investment, that it should be attracting more, not less, foreign capital. They base this assertion on the foreign direct investment figures over the past decade that show that, on balance, Canadians invest abroad more than foreigners spend in Canada. Of course, FDI is a broad figure that includes all kinds of investment flows, whether by mergers and acquisitions by corporations or individual minority investments in companies. And, yes, FDI has been a good thing for Canada.

The problem with using the FDI numbers is they are largely irrelevant to the issue at hand. It is not the net outflow of foreign direct investment that we should be worried about, but who is buying control of the world's major corporations. We aren't—and they are buying us. "People looking at FDI numbers and the relatively high levels of outbound investment, say there is no hollowing out. But they are actually counting apples to figure out how many oranges we have," says Ken Smith, the

Toronto managing director of the major Canadian strategy consulting firm Secor.

Smith has made a study of the hollowing-out phenomenon in the past decade and what he has found is alarming. In transactions involving the sale of corporate control—ownership control of real companies—Canadians have been huge sellers. "Canada has become the biggest net seller of corporate assets in the world, relative to market capitalization," says Secor in a report provided to the Wilson committee. Excluding the protected sectors—the arts, telecommunications, and financial services—Canada has sold a net amount of $80 billion in corporate assets in the three years leading up to 2008.

And it is ironic, given our history of paranoia about U.S. foreign ownership, that Americans are also big net sellers, right up there with Canadians. The buyers of both countries' assets are a varied lot: Swiss, Germans, Belgians, and French, certainly, but also the BRIC countries, Brazilians, Russians, Indians, and Chinese—in other words, people who in the past did not show up on the radar in concerns about foreign ownership. Now these countries are intent on global domination of targeted sectors, such as steel and energy. They have no compunction about using private markets to exercise their national will, using sovereign companies and sovereign funds.

We are living in a world where Canada is blithely handing over the keys to its stores, factories, and offices to foreign buyers, while we are failing to produce more than a handful of globally active major corporations. No one could sensibly advocate closing Canada's borders. That would be economic suicide. Inward investment, since the time of Uriah Seymour, has been key to building the country. In fact, we want more foreign investment, lots of it, but we also need to build true global powerhouses that can be leaders in their sectors. Not every sector, but the ones where we are knowledge leaders.

Ken Smith has found ways in which the playing field has

been tilted against Canada. We have in effect interfered with the ability of our own companies to survive in Canada and become international stars in their own right. He does not want to halt inflows but create the environment for a fair flow of capital both ways. "A combination of regulations, policies and practices make Canadian companies the easiest in the world to put into play," he says. "Canada's securities and governance policies are out of step internationally and offer little means to defend against takeovers."

The issue has sharply divided Canadian corporate leaders but most of them at least acknowledge the existence of a crisis. Roger Martin, the influential dean of the University of Toronto's Rotman management school, teamed up with Royal Bank CEO Gordon Nixon to highlight the challenge to Canada in a *Globe and Mail* article. Their conclusion was that Canada needed a major change in its taxation philosophy, a fine-tuning of Investment Canada's role as a watchdog for foreign takeovers, and improvements in the regulatory environment to allow our companies to become more rational entities. The aim: "To give our Canadian managers the best opportunity to build global leaders for the long term and succeed from a Canadian base."

Ken Smith and his consultants offer ten broad recommendations to level the field including empowering Canadian boards with more latitude to act in the long-term interests of a company. The government should have the right to review and block any deal that could threaten national security—as it recently did with the veto of the sale of the Radarsat satellite technology to the United States. There should be a drive to open up interprovincial trade, spreading the TILMA concept pioneered in B.C. and Alberta right across the country. Governments should ensure competitive fiscal arrangements for capital investment and R&D. Part of this is reducing taxes on capital—a process that is already well advanced in Canada, but needs to be forcefully completed.

There are also cultural factors, including a lack of national ambition among our large corporations and their leaders. This is the toughest nut to crack. How do you turn an unadventurous executive class into one that wants to conquer the world? How do you break the complacency of most of our leading corporations before it is too late and our corporate centres have been entirely hollowed out? How do you convince boards of directors that the long-term health of a company may actually lie in remaining an independent Canadian entity?

"It is arguable that Canadian managers have not been sufficiently aggressive in globalizing in the first half of this transformational age," Martin and Nixon argue, "and it is critical for them to step to the task in the latter half."

In fact, we once did have a national champion, a telecommunications giant called Nortel. It was the repository of many of our hopes and dreams to become a global technology superpower. But in the Internet bubble of the late 1990s, it got caught up in the orgy of inflated stock prices, takeovers, and delusions of grandeur by its top managers. Today, it is a shadow of its old self, a company that, at times, seemed to bounce from one crisis to another. The danger is it will either chug along on the margins or will end up as a takeover target that fills out some foreign company's complement of products. When it goes, will we even notice? Nortel shows the folly of excessive dependence on a single company, in a single industry, for our global aspirations. Meanwhile, RIM has emerged as the Nortel of our age, a company that has become the embodiment of all our hopes and dreams of becoming a technology power. It is a huge burden for a single company, especially one with a fairly narrow product line.

The more fundamental question is whether RIM survives as a Canadian company. Despite its vaulting market capitalization, its future may lie in being a product line for a foreign technology giant. It is hard to see RIM itself as an international acquirer, as its two middle-aged builders now immerse themselves in hockey teams and quantum physics. After RIM goes, what else is there? There is only energy.

※

Ken Smith points out that the hollowing-out phenomenon has enormous implications for the West and specifically Alberta. Unless there is some remarkable turnaround, the Toronto-based Golden Horseshoe has already lost its role of a corporate centre for several industries—steel, base metals, technology, and heavy manufacturing—a situation further exacerbated as the manufacturing industry appears to be lost to China and India. Toronto itself is taking most of its strength these days from financial services. This financial services base seems unlikely to be lost to foreign buyers because of legislated restrictions on bank ownership. But can it grow? Our banks are sliding down the world rankings because, with some exceptions, they are unaggressive in global business and, at home, are not allowed to merge to produce truly world-scale institutions. Of course, while Canada's limp status as a global banking player limits our upside potential, it actually protects us on the downside. Hence, our banks' relatively light imprint on international markets meant most of our financial institutions were not punished unduly by the U.S. subprime mortgage crisis with the exception of CIBC and Bank of Montreal. Our banks have generally lost global momentum—unlike our two world-class life insurance juggernauts, Manulife and Sun Life, which have used their ability to perform Canadian mergers as a base for building global scale.

There is however one area that holds some cachet as a rising corporate centre for a major industry. That, of course, is Alberta, which is one of the world headquarters for finance, consulting, accounting, geology, engineering, and analysis in the global energy field. This role should only expand as the oil sands rise in prominence as a world source of energy.

In the West, foreign investment undeniably has been a good thing. Powered to a large extent by Imperial Oil, the Canadian subsidiary of Exxon Mobil, foreign money has developed energy resources, and now it is about to tackle its most important and difficult mission—to develop the oil sands, the largest concentration of untapped hydrocarbon energy outside Saudi Arabia. Clearly, global companies, such as Exxon, Total, Shell, and BP will be a big part of this development. They already hold vast leases in the Athabasca Region, and are active buyers of more interests. Exxon has been a tiger in the oil sands as the pioneering investor and prime mover behind the Syncrude project, one of the two early movers in Fort McMurray.

As the price of a barrel of oil climbs to unforeseen heights, is Canada going to be a winner or loser in this oil sands game of global companies? "That's a real good question for the West," says Ken Smith, whose early career was spent with Exxon subsidiary Imperial Oil. "We want the investment. We aren't able to develop the oil sands at the pace we want without being welcoming to foreign investment. But will that investment come in the form of acquisitions of corporations? If it does, or if it is principally in that form, then we will have all the blue-collar jobs, but we won't have the benefits of the corporate centres."

He says people have tried too hard to paint a doom-and-gloom scenario around foreign takeovers. While that is not the case, he has seen Canada miss its opportunity to take its place as a head office centre, he says. Now there is new opportunity in the West, as it enters the age of the oil sands, with all the attendant spinoffs in research, engineering, and finance. As this new economy emerges, Calgary and, perhaps, Edmonton have the opportunity to become major financial centres, to fill the vacuum that Toronto has vacated. "If the corporate centres are there, there is going to be an investment banking community growing around them," Smith says. "And along with it comes a greater presence of the major banks, and downstream into accounting firms and law firms, and all the industries that support those."

If Alberta does not keep a critical mass of head offices, could it end up being a purely blue-collar West? That's not a condescending remark because blue-collar means innovation and expertise in the supply chain, upgrading, and refining. But if the West is going to be a superpower, it has to be a blue- *and* a white-collar region, with a fair degree of Canadian control of what is clearly an important global industry—the oil sands.

Some say that when companies are acquired, the money received by shareholders is recycled back into the economy as these individuals find new opportunities to invest. That has certainly been the model for the oil patch. An eager entrepreneur would start up a junior company, drill some wells, and succeed in striking pay dirt enough times to go into production. In time, he would sell off his maturing company, maybe to a foreign buyer or, recently, to an income trust, and reinvest in a new cycle of exploration and development. The oil patch is full of guys who cycled through several junior companies and trusts, and who made a lot of money for themselves, the industry, and their investors.

It's not going to happen quite like that anymore. Conventional industry has peaked and the future is the oil sands. They are completely different games. If you cash out your ownership of a junior company, you are not going to turn around and develop an oil sands project. These projects are massive, capital intensive, requiring big companies with large balance sheets, financing capabilities, and project management expertise. "I think it is going to increasingly be the world of large corporations," Smith says. "Do you want those large corporations to be all foreign? I would say there is a missed opportunity if we don't retain our fair share of those large corporations whose assets are Canadian."

The stakes get larger because gone too are the days when the Canadian oil patch is a minor player—the third or fourth region

in the world. It now has the potential to be the first or second region in the global energy industry. In that context, it would be a
missed opportunity of huge proportions if some of the major
corporations, if not a lot, were not Canadian. "Shame on us if
we fail to be the banks that capitalize," Smith asserts. "Shame on
us if we fail to be the corporate leaders who buy the asset next
door and, instead, wait for it to be sold."

Assume for a moment that the West produces some very
brave, very ambitious corporate leaders, people in the mould of
Gwyn Morgan and David O'Brien, the odd couple who created
EnCana, or Rick George, the bold builder of Suncor. With the
help of better securities rules, smarter regulation, and more reasonable tax policy—not necessarily rock-bottom corporate
taxes, but taxes that don't impede investment—they could actually retain a world-class corporate centre in the West, even while
the Toronto region has lost its edge in mining, technology, and
heavy manufacturing.

And if the West emerges as a strong financial centre for energy and all its ancillary services, why wouldn't the Canadian
banks move there too? Which will be the first bank to relocate
its corporate headquarters to Calgary or, perhaps, Vancouver? If
one goes, how many others will? That would be crushing for
Toronto but it is the way of Canada: the banks follow the
money. Just trace the history of the Royal Bank of Canada, as it
followed the money from Halifax to Montreal and then to
Toronto. The Royal has been the flighty flirt of the Canadian
financial system, tripping from one city to another. Why
wouldn't it move to Calgary if the dynamics in favour of the
West were so clear? Private wealth, corporate decision-making,
financial support services are all moving west. Even the tax rate
looks a lot better outside Ontario. It is not a good prognosis for
Toronto, but Toronto will survive. It just won't be as important
in Canada. And the movement of a major bank to Calgary
would be a powerful uniting factor in Canada, more nation-

building in its impact than a western-led majority government in Ottawa or a Liberal prime minister from Alberta.

Just for pure mischief, I would put forward another strong candidate to move its head office to Calgary—Toronto-Dominion Bank. The symbolism would be exquisite, because the name Toronto might have to be expunged from its name. Also, if you mention the name of TD's CEO Ed Clark on the streets of Calgary, you are like to encounter a blast of condemnation. Clark was one of the public-service architects of the National Energy Program and yet twenty-five years later he is the whip-smart architect of TD's aggressive expansion into the United States. Clark's journey, one of the most fascinating in Canadian business annals, has taken him from leftist federal bureaucrat to the superbly strategic CEO of one of the five major banks. It would be sweet irony if Ed Clark's bank became the first to move to Calgary from Toronto, just as the Bank of Montreal departed Montreal for Toronto. It would be a signal by Clark that the NEP is truly history, that the old Canada of the "eastern banks" is gone and we have entered a new age of the West not just as a junior partner, but the dominant partner in Confederation. (The one argument against the TD Bank moving to Calgary is the fact that it has focused its growth strategy in the eastern United States, which is close at hand for a Toronto-based institution.)

A more likely candidate to move might be one of the banks caught up in the subprime mortage crisis in the United States and its attendant difficulties. A plausible scenario might see Canadian Imperial Bank of Commerce, weakened and humbled by a series of financial scandals and strategic missteps, seeking to wipe the slate clean by moving its head office out of Toronto.

In any case, a westward move by a major bank is a scenario they talk a lot about in Calgary and Edmonton, where the banks are huge symbolic institutions. The eastern banks foreclosed on prairie ranches in the Dirty Thirties, and they financed the east-west trade that confirmed the domination of Toronto, Montreal, and the old families. Now, if only one or two would move West, it would cement Alberta's place in Confederation. Yet winning a Canadian bank might be a pyrrhic victory, for all of these financial institutions are in relative decline on a global scale. Canadian banks have not kept pace with their global competitors. The stifling of any merger possibilities by the federal government is a key factor. The banks are clearly slipping in the rankings of worldwide financial institutions. It is a severe threat to Toronto's status as a financial services centre. If the banks go West, then what is left in central Canada?

Whatever the banks' direction, Calgary's rise to global significance as a corporate centre would be compromised if no strong Canadian energy companies survived. The oil sands present a much more stable corporate environment than the industry of the past. There will not be as much short-term buying and selling of assets as in the past history of the western energy basin. The oil sands manufacturing process will spin off big investments in R&D, equipment manufacturing, head hunting, educational endeavours, consulting, and financing capability. These oil sands are just too important and too big to trade like hockey players. Will there be Canadian players and will they be in Alberta? Says Ken Smith: "The challenge to the West, if it wants to become a major centre, is that it has to have companies that are buyers, not sellers. You're not going to get banks moving to the West to serve a bunch of foreign subsidiaries." At the same time, he says, "Given the strengths our domestic oil patch would have, there is no reason some Canadian corporations should not emerge as the future Exxons. So unless it's mismanaged or sold off, it is a reasonable scenario."

At this stage the horse has already got halfway out the barn door. The majority of players in the oil sands are foreign owned with foreign head offices—but that is not a bad thing. It appears several companies are strong candidates to stand tall as Canadian champions—EnCana (as well as its proposed oil sands offshoot),

Suncor, and Canadian Natural Resources, but also Opti, Nexen, Talisman, and Petro-Canada, which is protected from foreign takeovers by limits on share ownership—a residue of its former status as a government holding.

They have high market capitalization and would be hard to take out, but not impossible for a company of the scale of Shell, BP, Total, or Exxon. The elimination of any of these companies by foreign takeover would be a grievous blow to Calgary's aspirations as a corporate and financial centre. In fact, it would be a blow to Canada, including Toronto, whose economy will only become more dependent on the West in the future. That means the stakes are high for governments to get their hands around this hollowing-out phenomenon. The goal should not be to stop foreign investment but to create the competitive conditions—and competitive drive—to allow our companies to be buyers, not sellers.

No one is more central to the hollowing-out controversy than Murray Edwards. He is a major shareholder in Canadian Natural Resources, one of the companies that ranks as a true Canadian champion. He owns part of Ensign, a services company that enhances our reputation as a global innovator. He is a nationalist and federalist and he sat on the Wilson committee that reviewed Canada's competitive landscape. He is also a capitalist who certainly would be a major actor in the future of Canada as a financial centre. He could be a buyer or a seller in the next stage of energy consolidation.

His perspective on hollowing out is surprisingly patriotic. It is a factor that is often overlooked in the battle of statistics. Canadians need world-class companies to feel better about their country and its prospects in an uncertain world economy. It feeds back into why we even exist as a country.

"I start with the premise that first and foremost I am a proud Canadian and I think that all Canadians want Canadian teams to win the Stanley Cup," Edwards says. "When a Canadian team wins over an American team, we are proud as Canadians. The same thing goes in business—that if we can have Canadian-based, Canadian-controlled, Canadian-owned companies, and be globally successful, the vast majority of Canadians would believe that is a good thing."

He says what is needed is good public policy that allows Canadians to compete globally with companies in other countries. "If you look at Falconbridge and Inco, I think if there had been other policies in Canada, those companies would still be around today. I think you are talking about fiscal policy, competition policy, governance policy, securities and regulatory policy, government policy." Like many corporate leaders, he believes Canadians are the Boy Scouts of the business world. "We want to be the good guys, but sometimes in doing that, we let ourselves be taken advantage of, or we lie down for other countries and companies who do not play by the same rules that we play by. Let's make sure our rules are fair, transparent, and ethical, but they are clear and they allow Canadians and Canadian companies to succeed."

In truth, the loss of Canadian competitiveness, reflected in the erosion of our major companies, is a national crisis, and there needs to be crisis management of a high order. The odds are very high that the next hollowing-out angst will involve the oil sands, our most important strategic asset. Already there is high foreign ownership—by France's Total, Norway's Statoil, the U.S.'s Exxon Mobil, and the British-Dutch behemoth Shell, which has signalled the future by buying out its Canadian minority shareholders and concentrating control of its Canadian operations in Houston. But we ain't seen nothing yet. The Chinese are the looming "elephant in the room," poised to take a major position in the biggest, safest energy play in the world. So far, their investments have been small, strategic, look-and-see forays, but it is just a matter of time before they make a big multibillion-dollar move on a major player in Fort McMurray.

The Chinese have been inhibited by the negative reaction in Ottawa when their state-controlled mining operation, Min-metals, pondered a takeover of the Canadian mining giant Noranda, which was later folded into Falconbridge (and bought by a Swiss metals giant). For national security reasons, the Harper government has been opposed to potential purchases by "sovereign buyers," government-owned companies or state funds, and any Chinese acquisition would be as a sovereign buyer. And yet there is a fair amount of double talk on this; CVRD, the Brazilian giant that bought our mining champion Inco, was deemed acceptable even though the Brazilian government owns "golden shares" in the company, giving it effective veto over corporate decisions. Also, there is already a state-owned presence in the oil sands, the Norwegian Statoil, and there are others that are privately owned, but operate as national champions, such as Total. Apparently, some sovereign buyers are okay and others aren't.

If the Chinese try to buy an oil sands player—either directly or through a proxy—it would be a humdinger of a battle, rattling the corridors of power in Edmonton, Ottawa, and Washington. The Americans assume, after all, that they "own" the oil sands because of their traditional primacy in Canada's resource industries. We are considered part of the home-field advantage for the United States. If the Chinese move to establish a beachhead, Fort McMurray will become a diplomatic and strategic hot spot, the centre of a firestorm of controversy. It will force the Canadian government to make a major decision: Whose face to slap, the Americans or the Chinese?

And the Chinese will certainly move on the oil sands because they yearn for energy security. They do not have enough of their own oil and gas supply, and they are on the move throughout the world to secure more of it. Hence, they are making deals with generally unpalatable regimes in Africa. It is not enough for Beijing just to nail down supply contracts. There is something in the Chinese culture, the Chinese psyche that needs to own the molecules in the ground, observes Pat Daniel, the savvy president of pipeline company Enbridge—or at least to own the leases to extract that supply.

There is also a huge potential for the Chinese to do some interesting things in research and innovation. They are already studying how to develop cheaper, more efficient ways of turning inky bitumen into something closer to sweet crude. As minority partners in the proposed Northern Lights project in Fort McMurray, the Chinese bring some interesting ideas to the table. The Northern Lights consortium has proposed an entire oil sands plant made not in Alberta but at fabrication yards in Korea, China, and Malaysia. The upgrading plant would consist of thirty massive modules, that would weigh 2,000 tonnes each and would be shipped across the Pacific, through the Arctic Ocean and then by barge up the Mackenzie River to Great Slave Lake, the Slave River, Lake Athabasca, and finally by the Athabasca River into the oil sands. The massive plan, if implemented, would reduce the labour by 55 per cent and the cost of the mine by 21 per cent, said Synenco, the Canadian partner in the project—a company that itself was being taken over by the French giant Total. It is a jaw-droppingly massive undertaking that would undercut the high-cost Alberta workforce. It would also sidestep the potential for the oil sands supply chain to source much of its production in the shell-shocked manufacturing industry of Ontario and Quebec. This proposal may be the most dangerous implication of a strong Chinese presence in the oil sands—less fabrication in Canada and more in low-cost Asia.

It shows the hand of the 40 per cent owner of the Northern Lights project, SinoCanada Petroleum, a subsidiary of the Chinese state oil company Sinopec. If Sinopec were to expand its reach, it would make Alberta the queen in the global commodity chess game—the prize to be taken. If the Chinese make a dramatic move in the oil sands, Albertans will gain terrific leverage in the national power game, but they will also be torn between their free-market instincts and their loyalties to the United States; between their inherent independent spirit and the geopolitical machinations of a national government in Ottawa. It would raise the spectre of another National Energy Program–like initiative that would be aimed at nailing down Canadian or, possibly, even American, control of the oil sands. It would demand more strategic corporate and political leadership than has ever been required in the province and in the global energy industry. And it would put to Albertans, for once and for all, the compelling question: Are you Canadian?

The Chinese would not have to make a move directly. Instead, they could count on a reliable proxy such as Li Ka-shing, the billionaire Hong Kong conglomerate-builder who is an honorary Albertan by dint of his long-time ownership of Husky Energy. "KS," as his friends know him, is a shrewd, very patient investor whose assets span energy, telecom, financial services. He is very close to the Beijing elite and has fronted the Communist leadership's efforts to understand the oil industry in North America. He has also been a major investor in the Canadian energy industry, taking a big bet on the heavy oil upgrader in Lloydminster—a factory that converts heavy oil into a more pristine crude suitable for refining.

KS made his investment when heavy oil was in disfavour, when there were many cheaper ways to find crude. He has held on while others have departed and now, with oil at an unthinkably high price, he is finally reaping the benefits. It has not been an easy ride for Li, but he has prevailed, and the upgrader is making money. Now he is a potential candidate to guide his Beijing friends into this new world where he is already a significant player.

Whatever happens, the Chinese will likely become part of the configuration of the oil sands, and the old image of the Alberta energy cowboy will undergo a startling transformation. It will be the Beijing cowboys who will be riding herd. More critically, Canada should brace itself for a showdown between the United States and China over the spoils of the Athabasca. As energy supplies weaken globally, as Mideast politics become more volatile, and as prices soar, the world's two major economic powers will want to secure their access to the last, best source of crude, before the world starts turning en masse to alternative energy. Who will win the battle of the oil sands? Even more important, who will stand up for Canada? And will we see an oil sands version of the Inco-Falconbridge mining retreat?

CHAPTER 17

THE VIEW FROM 12TH STREET

The West is on top. Now what?

IT IS 5:30 P.M. on a cool March afternoon and there is a man in a tuxedo *hitchhiking* on busy 12th Street in the northwest quadrant of Calgary. He looks as forlorn and out of place as a peacock in a henhouse.

I am that man. Let me explain.

The cab that was supposed to transport me from my friends' home to a black-tie dinner at the downtown Hyatt Hotel did not show up. I waited for twenty minutes and pondered what to do. My hosts were in Portugal on a holiday. As a stranger, an intermittent guest from Toronto, I had not met the neighbours. I kept phoning like mad but the taxi line was busy. After about 4 p.m., it seems, you cannot get hold of a cab company in overstressed, underserved Calgary.

I faced the prospect of having flown all the way from Toronto for this black-tie event, and I would miss it entirely. Desperate times demand desperate measures. I decided to hitchhike. Within five minutes on 12th Street, a major north-south artery, a black BMW pulled over to the curb, and a guy with a goatee beckoned me over. It turned out to be a bemused Rob Adamson, a Calgary architect, who happened to be heading downtown himself to meet a business colleague at a hotel. He took me straight to the Hyatt, and I made my dinner on time—although I had to cut short my libations at the cocktail hour.

Welcome to Calgary in the twenty-first century. That was the nadir of my experiences with the travails of the Alberta service industry. The mere act of calling a cab had become a nightmare for anyone used to the smooth flexibility of transportation in Toronto, Halifax, or Montreal. Alberta was clearly a province out of control, with too many demands, too few people chasing too many dollars, as it tried to cope with an overheated energy-mad economy. Beth Diamond, a Calgary public relations consultant, says the city had become like the movie *Running with Scissors*, and we were all feeling the sharp edges.

And it helps explain why many Albertans almost welcomed a slowdown as energy exploration activity shifted to Saskatchewan and B.C. and environmental impacts tempered the oil sands boom. The province had become an ordeal for anyone who wanted service promptly or efficiently—a cab on time or a cab at all; a waitress who could actually open a wine bottle without shredding the cork; a fast-food worker who did not snarl at you; or a car rental clerk who had been in town from Mexico long enough to know the best route out of downtown Calgary. It was like Alberta was trying to act all grown-up at the table but still hadn't learned the basic rudiments of using a knife and fork.

Yet my hitchhiking in Calgary was also indicative of the best of Alberta. Even when things don't work, the experience was salvaged by the kindness of strangers—people like Rob Adamson. Albertans are open, friendly, co-operative and have generally remained so through the indignities of the latest energy boom. Even at its worst, Calgary is usually a much more welcoming place than Toronto and its suburbs. It would be only natural for Albertans to stop and pick up a hitchhiker in distress. All that may change as the province "grows up," but I hope not.

The shortage of cabs also has an upside. It simply reflects the reality of a province that ripples with energy and ambition. Alberta possesses a heartbeat of optimism that Ontario and Quebec used to boast of, but now sadly lack. The reason I was wearing my tuxedo was that I was attending a gala dinner at the Alberta College of Art & Design, featuring a speech by U.S. innovation thinker Daniel Pink. My dinner jacket and my evening in Calgary symbolized the other side of Alberta—and the entire prairies—the yearning to be taken seriously, to be forward-thinking about how their cities and their provinces need to evolve. It is a West that has accumulated great wealth, entrepreneurial spirit, legions of millionaires, but is now working on the other side of the equation—how to bridge the reality from the stranded hitchhiker on 12th Street to a region that is smart, sophisticated, and engaged with the rest of Canada.

Canada will be a different place with Alberta on top. Over the next twenty years, the country might become more entrepreneurial, less social class–ridden, more deregulated, and taxes, particularly business taxes, will fall as all provinces tumble towards the Alberta model. Health care may be increasingly available as a private service. Not all of the changes will be welcome or positive to all Canadians, and the rest of Canada will not become a carbon-copy version of today's Alberta. But Alberta will change too, as a result of the influx of hundreds of thousands of Canadians and new immigrants. It will become more urban, more diverse ethnically and politically, less conservative, and less monolithically Christian in its faith. Its economy will be increasingly built around services and technology, as new businesses spin off the oil sands and the conventional energy industry.

Those are thoughts that have stayed with me as I travelled the province, indeed the country, over the past two years. From those travels, I have drawn some proposals, some modest, some grand—some relating to Alberta, some to the West, and some to Canada as a whole:

1. Re-brand Alberta.

The Alberta brand is in deep trouble. Alberta to the world is dirty oil, which means foot-dragging on emissions and defiance of global public opinion. Like it or not, branding is important. It is the global consumer, particularly the U.S. consumer, who will decide the market for Alberta's resources, for its bitumen and coal methane and gas. Consumers in some areas of the United States are turning green in a big way. If they don't like what they see and hear, they will vote thumbs-down on Alberta. There are other countries that will buy our bitumen-based oil but they are not as close, as rich, or as demanding.

At the moment, many Albertans say this scenario cannot come to pass, that Americans are not about to suddenly discard their SUVs entirely and turn down the opportunity to tap a secure supply of fossil fuels that lies right on their doorstep. True. The oil sands will thrive, no matter how green Canada and Alberta become. Yet an environmentally inspired slowdown, and a clamp-down on carbon pollution and water use, would actually extend the Alberta boom for a decade or two. It could be only beneficial in the long run.

Alberta should be building its brand for another era, after the oil sands, when it will have to live and die by its wits—indeed, its reputation—not by stuff in the ground. The bitumen era will pass, just as the conventional oil and gas industry has settled into gradual decline. The Alberta brand will remain and that is how the province will be judged. Will it want to be known for dead ducks on toxic pools or the pristine mountain air of Kananaskis Country? It is time for Alberta to think in terms of the next hundred years, not just the next energy strike. That is a wrenching cultural change because Alberta is, at heart, a short-term society.

Alberta and Saskatchewan have the chance to be the first great energy-producing region that is also an energy-smart region. In a decade, the area between the Rockies and the Saskatchewan-Manitoba border will be one of the world's two great hydrocarbon regions. Saudi Arabia is the other. That presents an opportunity to be a leader in the world of scarce $200-

a-barrel oil—the best in emissions control, the best in sensible development. It is time to make carbon capture the Alberta industry of the future: to ensure a future for coal, oil sands, and heavy oil. The company, the organization, that economically solves how to capture carbon from oil sands development and pipe it away to a central underground storage location—to return it to the earth—will be the twenty-first-century equivalent of TransCanada Pipelines, a transmission powerhouse and an economic titan.

My *Globe and Mail* colleague Shawn McCarthy has written about the work being done on carbon capture in the Alberta Research Council. He also wrote that, "ultimately, the driver behind carbon capture in Canada is likely to be Big Oil's fear of losing its $100 billion bet on the oil sands. There is a growing worry that climate concerns—notably the growing call for climate change action in the United States—will trump economic ones, and force companies to rein in emissions, notes David Keith, director at the Institute for Sustainable Energy, Environment and Economy at the University of Calgary." The article then quotes Keith, who is one of Alberta's rising intellectual stars: "You're just not going to be able to grow the oil sands without managing this problem. And you are not going to manage it without moving aggressively on carbon capture and storage."

2. Create the Heritage Fund for the Arts, Culture, and Social Sciences.

Alberta has done well taking its engineering smarts, its horizontal drilling, and hydraulic fracturing to the world. It is a global technology and skills leader, which is why Alberta engineers and tradespeople can be found on the job in Algeria, Venezuela, and Kazakhstan.

The next stage for Alberta is to emerge as an international thought leader. The engineers and scientists will come, attracted by the research money and the challenges of the oil sands. But it is time to think about how to develop the great novelists and short-story writers, political scientists, and social thinkers. Alberta needs more Tom Flanagans, more Andrew Nikiforuks, more Randall Morcks, more Aritha van Herks. This should be Alberta's next diversification push—intellectual diversification, a major industrial project that should absorb Alberta for the years to come. From the industry of the oil sands comes the industry of thought.

3. Run a bullet train between Calgary and Edmonton.

One of my enduring images of Alberta is riding the Red Arrow, a terrific bus service, from Calgary to Edmonton, on a winter day. As the bus approached Edmonton, I would begin to see the parade of cars that have slid into the median, and streams of yellow incident tape, from some previous night's snowstorm. It was practically a ritual that the strand of Highway 2 north of Red Deer would be littered with abandoned vehicles that have slid off into the median at the height of the storm. What a waste of time, insurance premiums, and productivity—and, above all, a waste of scarce energy resources.

Why not unite the two cities to create the Edgary of the future—two cities that operate as one? A train would be a signal of Alberta's embrace of a future less dependent on the car and jet plane. It would be a dramatic vote for sustainability. Imagine the pitch to Calgary travellers: "We can give you Edmonton in ninety minutes flat." This could be the Ed Stelmach government's defining project, something for the ages, for a post–oil sands society.

4. Establish a task force on the oil sands.

It doesn't sound sexy, but remember that a government-industry task force created the modern oil sands as a vibrant economic entity. Now the oil sands have reached a critical stage when they need some heavy thinking about what they are going to become. This new task force would take into consideration the factors of environmental degradation, infrastructure development, health effects, social decay, drug addiction, labour mobility, materials shortages, Native issues—the list of urgent priorities is endless. And it would be a government-private initiative that would engage Canadians in an open discussion of these issues.

Let's not indulge in foolish fantasies that the oil sands can or will be stopped. There is too much momentum already. The global market wants the energy from Fort McMurray, needs it, in fact, as we bridge the gap between the fossil fuel age and the age of alternative energy, wind and solar. How do we channel this resource into healthy, sustainable development that will allow the oil sands to achieve its full potential? It is not too late because its development, its costs, its economic distortions, will dominate Canada for the next twenty years.

5. Move a major bank to Calgary.

It will happen eventually so why not now? It is a move that would be heavy with symbolism but also a realistic response to a new economic dynamic in Canada, as Ontario moves to have-not status and Alberta leaps ahead of the pack. It would not be the end of Toronto as a financial services centre, just a shift of emphasis. It would be thrilling for Canadian unity and pride to see a CIBC building in downtown Calgary or a new TD tower in Edmonton.

6. End provincial trade barriers.

Okay, it sounds like motherhood but, in fact, the first steps have already been taken with the landmark trade and labour mobility pact between Alberta and B.C. The next steps should be an Alberta–B.C.–Ontario agreement, and ultimately the critical Quebec–Alberta pact. Central Canada would benefit hugely from such a move, just as the world enters a period of increased economic instability. The credit crunch of 2007 left scars in the U.S. economy that can't be quickly healed. Protectionism is bound to flourish once more. If a Democrat were to enter the White House and join forces with a Democratic Congress, you could start to see more barriers put up in front of north-south trade, although it will certainly not mean a return to a protectionist era. It is time to start preparing for that eventuality by reviving East-West links in Canada. The absurdity of provincial protectionism becomes more glaring every day.

7. Build universities of excellence.

There has been enough me-tooism in Canada, as universities have competed for the same programs, the same students, the same faculty members. Let's build excellent universities that are global thought leaders in their specialties. There is a chance to start the trend in Alberta with its small but economically rich network of colleges and universities. This would not impede a student from getting an engineering degree in Calgary, if he or she wished, or a political science degree in Edmonton. But it would determine where the big money goes. Alberta after the oil sands will live and die by its talent. The province is investing in those knowledge assets, but it needs to focus its efforts. It's time to get rid of the Calgary-Edmonton, north-south duplication of effort and to simply back winners.

8. Develop a national talent strategy.

My hitchhiking on 12th Street underlines the single-biggest challenge facing this country—where will we find enough working people in a time of aging demographics and huge talent demands. We need a national policy that embraces immigration, training and skills, relocation and mobility, housing and social services. Alberta is just the laboratory for the rest of the country. All the things that are going wrong—and right—in that province will be repeated in countless other markets.

How do we get people from inside Canada, as well as from abroad, to live in off-the-beaten-path resource towns like Fort

Nelson, B.C., and Wabush, Labrador. How do you get fifty-year-old laid-off manufacturing workers from Kitchener to move to the new boom towns of Saskatchewan? And it's not a regional migration issue. We just need more people, people to do everything—not just engineers and doctors, but to wait on tables and drive cabs that can pick up visitors when they expect to be picked up.

9. It's no more Mr. Nice Guy.

We need securities and tax laws that give Canadian companies the strength and flexibility to protect themselves and to grow by making international acquisitions. Put an end to the Boy Scout era, the lopsided equation that forced Canada to surrender big parts of its birthright and its economic future. It may happen just in time to save the oil sands from total foreign control, particularly as the United States and China gear up for a major geopolitical confrontation about who gets to control the supply of valuable bitumen. Canada should control the bitumen, of course, and our companies should also be major actors on the extraction, upgrading, and refining. We need to be the knowledge leaders in the emerging energy field, and we need smart companies that can do oil sands, heavy oil, wind, solar, hydro, and carbon capture. That can only happen if we give our own executives a decent fighting chance and the motivation and will to push out into the world.

10. Make over the zero-sum mentality.

Canada needs a psychological transformation away from regional myopia. When one province thrives, we all thrive. When one city wins the Stanley Cup, it is good for all of Canada, not just for the noisy Red Mile of downtown Calgary, the boisterous Whyte Avenue in Edmonton, or the riotous Rue Ste-Catherine in Montreal. So what's good for Alberta is good for Canada. Indeed, within Alberta, what is good for Calgary is generally good for the entire province.

Similarly, when one province declines, it is a loss for all regions of the country—particularly when, as in the case of Ontario, it is home to nearly 40 per cent of the country's population, the core of its manufacturing capability, its financial services might. Ontario's plight, which might be applauded in some hopelessly unthinking regions of the West and East, is a problem for us all, for it means the country as a whole is hurting.

As TD Bank economists have pointed out, Ontario's decline in relative prosperity has occurred in lockstep with a rising loonie, surging energy costs, and the emergence of China, which has created a perfect storm for manufacturers. "However, a closer look reveals that the relative decline is not so much a story of Ontario weakness," the economists say, "but it is of booming economic strength in Canada's commodity-based economies." So while Ontario is relatively hurting, Alberta, Saskatchewan, and Newfoundland are thriving—and it is that counter-cyclical imbalance that protects Canada economically. But it also threatens the union. The years ahead will be a huge challenge for Confederation, and why? Because one group of Canadians is doing much better than another and, in Canada, that seems to spell envy and trouble.

Instead of kicking Ontario and Quebec when they're down, instead of trying to detract from Alberta's and Saskatchewan's strength, Canadians should be thinking of ways to support all these provinces as they confront their particular demons—slow growth and, at times, hyper-growth. A rescue package for Ontario should not mean simultaneously attacking Alberta's wealth and industrial potential. We do not want another NEP, but Alberta needs a strong Ontario and Quebec as a rich market, as a dependable supplier, as partners in the Canadian economy.

Some things in Alberta are still underdeveloped: venture capital, the service mentality, intercity travel, and gentrification and architecture. In parts of Alberta industry, there is still the sense of being a good place to make money, but not to make a real life. That has to change. So it's time to put the great minds and entrepreneurial talent of Canada to work in making Alberta a global destination for industry, culture, and talent. We spend more time thinking about how to affect the transformation of Shanghai than of assisting in the great flowering of Calgary or Edmonton that should be taking place right now.

11. Learn to love resources.

We are a nation of hewers and drawers, but we are also energy processors and resource scientists. It is the one competitive edge we have, the edge that comes from our geography, and also from the resource-savvy brainpower that has flowered from this geography. We are a resource people and it has made Canada into the economic titan of the twenty-first century. Yet resource wealth is often dismissed as somewhat degrading, as an inferior form of wealth. It is not perceived as a sector that spins off great companies, great minds, or great technology. But, as Alberta has shown, it is possible to leverage your resources into brain-power, just as Toronto has shown how you can build an investment and finance infrastructure on mining and mining capital.

This has to continue. The oil sands are an energy resource like none other before because they are so capital intensive, manufacturing intensive, technology intensive, R&D intensive, and they have huge industrial and environmental spinoffs. There are applications for oil sands upgrading and pollution-control technology all around the world, for instance, in Venezuela, the United States, and the former Soviet Union. And the demand for oil sands technology could just help save parts of rust-belt Ontario. Canada should be the leader in carbon capture, the industry that could save Alberta and the world. Resources are not a curse, but they can be a window. It is time not to dismiss the Dutch disease—a serious threat to our manufacturing prowess—but to mitigate and perhaps cure ourselves of it. Our future still lies in manufacturing but also in making things for a resources customer, a moiler of food, energy, and mining.

I sat with economist Doug May in the restaurant of The Rooms, Newfoundland's magisterial new museum high above old St. John's with commanding views of the Narrows, the tiny passage between St. John's harbour and the Atlantic. It is one of the most magnificent urban views in Canada. We watched the hive of construction activity along the harbour—equipment being assembled for Fort McMurray, fishing boats from Norway and Iceland, and tankers from Halifax. We talked about Canada's options in a world of a dominant China and dirty, but hugely in-demand, oil sands. May, who taught for years at Memorial University of Newfoundland before retiring, suggested Canadians are in denial of their true selves. They want to be Americans or Europeans, but not Canadians. After all the laments about the death of manufacturing, why don't we accept that we are a resources-based economy, but a smart resources-based economy? "Technology does apply to the natural resources sector as much as to the computer industry," he observed. Resources is a knowledge industry, in fact. "Yet we deny our national competitive advantage. In Newfoundland, iron is important, oil is important, crab is important." And being in resources, being a skilled tradesperson, does not mean you're a second-rate citizen, he pointed out. That is the great lesson of Alberta—the way to succeed is not just through a university degree. People are getting very rich because they are pipefitters and welders, and not necessarily MBAS.

That is not to say university isn't broadening, but a lot of Newfoundlanders are becoming highly educated in the university of experience, of life in a global economy based on commodities—"smart commodities" with a technological and scientific component.

We are a small population in a large country, but we are hampered by narrow provincial views. We should take our direction from those adaptable Newfoundlanders who have been fearless through the centuries about tackling an ocean, a new country, or a vast forested field of bitumen—hearty and hardworking folk who go out into the world with big ambitions but who still carry a blazing torch for home.

That is what it takes to be Canadian in the oil sands age.

ACKNOWLEDGEMENTS

THIS BOOK IS MORE THAN just a collection of research—it is a voyage across Canada and I want to thank my fellow voyageurs. The *Globe and Mail* has been tremendously supportive, led by *Report on Business* editor John Stackhouse and deputy editor David Thomas. Thanks to them, I was able to balance my responsibilities at the *Report on Business* with the demands of a book that required wide travel and a cross-country focus. I was helped immeasurably by other *Globe and Mail* people including Alberta reporters David Ebner, Katherine O'Neill, Dawn Walton, and Norval Scott, as well as former colleagues, such as the *Calgary Herald*'s Deborah Yedlin and the *Edmonton Journal*'s Gary Lamphier. Welcome support came from Dave Pyette, Greg Keenan, Richard Blackwell, and Brent Jang and Grant Robertson, who kindly read the manuscript and made valuable comments and contributions.

I am tremendously indebted to the University of Alberta's business school led by Dean Mike Percy, and to Monica Wegner, Lloyd Steier, Royston Greenwood, Doug Olsen, Barry Scholnick, Jennifer Jennings, and Joseph Doucet, among many others. I am thankful that the Alberta Business Family Institute offered me the role of writer-in-residence for two months in Edmonton. Special thanks to entrepreneur-in-residence Gary Coskey and to Stephen Dyck, the institute's former executive director, now at Lethbridge College. I was aided immensely by people close to the institute including Marc de la Bruyère, and Bunny and John Ferguson. And thanks to Professor Emeritus Rolf Mirus, a wise friend, and to Aunt Lela Redner and Catherine and Marshall Stachniak, whom I am proud to call family. In Fort McMurray, Barry and Helen Duncan gave me a great welcome.

The people who truly deserve a co-author tag are my Calgary friends Joanne Wiens and Howard Robertson, who made their comfortable house my home away from home. Thanks very much. Ken and Rene Taylor are always guiding lights, as are Dave Scobie and Maureen Moore. Todd Hirsch is a great sounding board, and Dick Haskayne has been a terrific role model. Doug Black and his colleagues at the law firm Fraser Milner Casgrain were critical in opening doors and providing insights. It was a special treat to reconnect with Simone Marler after thirty-five years. In effect, the student has become the teacher—and a good friend, as well.

In the midst of writing this book, I learned of the death of my friend, *Globe and Mail* reporter Val Ross. As writers, we can all draw inspiration from her passion, strength, and intelligence.

It is a pleasure, as always, working with my agent, Dean Cooke, and with editor Jonathan Schmidt, as well as Jordan Fenn, publisher at Key Porter.

I have, of course, the best family a writer could have—interested, supportive, loving. Mom, my ninety-one-year-old catalyst, gets me fired up; Gayle and Grant provide a welcome sanctuary; and Jayne is always willing to listen. So too are Lib, Steve, Scott, and Doris. Martha and Katie are the lights of my life, as is, increasingly, Thomas. Elaine, you are simply my strength, my pillar—and Molly, my fiercely opinionated collaborator for four books now. Thank you.

INDEX